823.

D1579162

OXFORD WORLD'S C

AUTHORS IN CON

General Editor: PATRICIA INGHAM, University of Oxford
Historical Adviser: BOYD HILTON, University of Cambridge

THOMAS HARDY

AUTHORS IN CONTEXT examines the work of major writers in relation to their own time and to the present day. The series provides detailed coverage of the values and debates that colour the writing of particular authors and considers their novels, plays, and poetry against this background. Set in their social, cultural, and political contexts, classic books take on a new meaning for modern readers. And since readers, like writers, have their own contexts, the series considers how critical interpretations have altered over time, and how films, sequels, and other popular adaptations relate to the new age in which they are produced.

PATRICIA INGHAM is Senior Research Fellow and Reader in English at St Anne's College, Oxford. She has edited texts by Hardy, Dickens, Gaskell, and Gissing, as well as writing widely on the Victorian novel. Her work includes *Thomas Hardy: A Feminist Reading* (1989), *Dickens, Women and Language* (1992), *The Language of Gender and Class: Transformation in the Victorian Novel* (1996), *Invisible Writing and the Victorian Novel* (2001), and *The Brontës: A Critical Reader* (2002).

OXFORD WORLD'S CLASSICS

For over 100 years Oxford World's Classics have brought readers closer to the world's great literature. Now with over 700 titles—from the 4,000-year-old myths of Mesopotamia to the twentieth century's greatest novels—the series makes available lesser-known as well as celebrated writing.

The pocket-sized hardbacks of the early years contained introductions by Virginia Woolf, T. S. Eliot, Graham Greene, and other literary figures which enriched the experience of reading. Today the series is recognized for its fine scholarship and reliability in texts that span world literature, drama and poetry, religion, philosophy and politics. Each edition includes perceptive commentary and essential background information to meet the changing needs of readers.

OXFORD WORLD'S CLASSICS

═

PATRICIA INGHAM

Thomas Hardy

═

OXFORD
UNIVERSITY PRESS

OXFORD
UNIVERSITY PRESS

Great Clarendon Street, Oxford OX2 6DP

Oxford University Press is a department of the University of Oxford.
It furthers the University's objective of excellence in research, scholarship,
and education by publishing worldwide in

Oxford New York

Auckland Bangkok Buenos Aires Cape Town Chennai
Dar es Salaam Delhi Hong Kong Istanbul Karachi Kolkata
Kuala Lumpur Madrid Melbourne Mexico City Mumbai Nairobi
São Paulo Shanghai Singapore Taipei Tokyo Toronto

Oxford is a registered trade mark of Oxford University Press
in the UK and in certain other countries

Published in the United States
by Oxford University Press Inc., New York

© Patricia Ingham 2003

The moral rights of the author have been asserted

Database right Oxford University Press (maker)

First published as an Oxford World's Classics paperback 2003

British Library Cataloguing in Publication Data

Data available

Library of Congress Cataloging-in-Publication Data

Ingham, Patricia.
Thomas Hardy / Patricia Ingham.
p. cm.—(Oxford world's classics. Authors in context)
Includes bibliographical references (p.) and index.
1. Hardy, Thomas, 1840–1928—Fictional works. 2. Hardy, Thomas, 1840–1928—
Criticism and interpretation—History. 3. Literature and society—England—History—
19th century. 4. Wessex (England)—In literature. I. Title. II. Oxford world's classics
(Oxford University Press). Authors in context.

PR4757.F5 I54 2003 823'.8—dc21 2002030311

ISBN 0–19–283980–2

1 3 5 7 9 10 8 6 4 2

Typeset in Ehrhardt
by RefineCatch Limited, Bungay, Suffolk
Printed in Great Britain by
Clays Ltd, Bungay, Suffolk

For Josh, Jo, and Sebastian

ACKNOWLEDGEMENTS

I am much indebted to Jenny Harrington for her help in preparing this book and to Judith Luna for her invaluable advice and suggestions. I am also very grateful to Michael Millgate and James Gibson for their generous permission to quote from primary sources they have edited. In addition I wish to thank Rosemary Kelly, Bronwyn Rivers, Phil Wickham (British Film Institute), the staff of St Anne's College Library, and the News International Research Fund.

CONTENTS

LIST OF ILLUSTRATIONS

A CHRONOLOGY OF THOMAS HARDY

	Life	*Historical and Cultural Background*
1835		Telegraph comes into use.
1837		William IV dies and is succeeded by Victoria.
1838		Anti-Corn Law League set up.
1839		Chartist riots.
1840	2 June: Thomas Hardy born, Higher Bockhampton, Dorset, eldest child of a builder, Thomas Hardy, and Jemima Hand, who have been married for less than six months. Younger siblings: Mary (b. 1841), Henry (b. 1851), Katharine (Kate) (b. 1856).	Victoria marries the German prince, Albert. Penny postage instituted. Charles Dickens, *The Old Curiosity Shop* serialized. Charles Darwin, *The Voyage of HMS Beagle*
1842		Underground labour banned for women and children. Robert Browning, *Dramatic Lyrics* Alfred Tennyson, *Poems*
1843		Dickens, *A Christmas Carol* John Ruskin, *Modern Painters*
1844		Factory Act limiting working hours for women and children. Robert Chambers, *Vestiges of the Natural History of Creation* (popularizing an evolutionary view)
1845		John Henry Newman joins the Roman Catholic Church. Benjamin Disraeli, *Sybil* F. Engels, *Condition of the Working Classes in England in 1844*
1846		'Railway Mania' year: 272 Railway Acts passed. Repeal of the Corn Laws which have protected farm prices. Irish potato famine (1845–9) kills over a million people.
1847		Ten Hour Factory Act (limiting working hours). Charlotte Brontë, *Jane Eyre* Emily Brontë, *Wuthering Heights*

Life	*Historical and Cultural Background*
1848–56 Schooling in Dorset.	
1848	Chartist Petition to Parliament and end of Chartism. Year of revolutions in Europe. Public Health Act (inspired by Edwin Chadwick's Report into the Sanitary Conditions of the Working Classes). Pre-Raphaelite Brotherhood founded. Dickens, *Dombey and Son* Elizabeth Gaskell, *Mary Barton* Anne Brontë, *The Tenant of Wildfell Hall* William Makepeace Thackeray, *Vanity Fair* Marx and Engels, *The Communist Manifesto*
1850	Public Libraries Act. Dickens, *David Copperfield* Tennyson, *In Memoriam*
1851	The Great Exhibition at the Crystal Palace in Hyde Park, supported by Prince Albert, a great success. Ruskin, *The Stones of Venice*
1852	Thackeray, *Henry Esmond*
1853	Vaccination against smallpox becomes compulsory. Dickens, *Bleak House* Charlotte Brontë, *Villette* Gaskell, *Cranford* Matthew Arnold, *Poems*
1854	Outbreak of the Crimean War: Britain and France defend European interests in the Middle East against Russia; Florence Nightingale goes out to Scutari in the Crimea. Dickens, *Hard Times*
1855	Gaskell, *North and South* Anthony Trollope, *The Warden* (first of the Barchester novels)
1856 Hardy watches the hanging of Martha Browne for the murder of her husband (thought to be remembered in the death of Tess Durbeyfield on the gallows).	Crimean War ends; Victoria Cross for bravery instituted. Elizabeth Barrett Browning, *Aurora Leigh* (lengthy and melodramatic verse narrative of a woman writer's life)

Life	*Historical and Cultural Background*
1856–62 Articled to Dorchester architect John Hicks; later his assistant; late 1850s, important friendship with Horace Moule (eight years older, middle-class, and Cambridge educated) who becomes his intellectual mentor and encourages his self-education in the classics.	
1857	Matrimonial Causes Act makes divorce possible without an Act of Parliament, but on unequal terms for men and women. Dickens, *Little Dorrit* Trollope, *Barchester Towers* Gustave Flaubert, *Madame Bovary*
1858	Indian Mutiny crushed. George Eliot, *Scenes of Clerical Life*
1859	Darwin, *The Origin of Species* Samuel Smiles, *Self-Help* J. S. Mill, *Liberty* Dickens, *A Tale of Two Cities* Eliot, *Adam Bede* Tennyson, *Idylls of the King*
1860	Cobden Act extends free trade. Eliot, *The Mill on the Floss* Wilkie Collins, *The Woman in White*
1861	Death of Prince Albert: Victoria goes into seclusion. Outbreak of American Civil War. Dickens, *Great Expectations* Eliot, *Silas Marner* Francis Palgrave, *Golden Treasury* (much quoted by Hardy) Isabella Beeton, *Book of Household Management* (sells over 60,000 copies in one year)
1862 Employed as a draughtsman by London architect, Arthur Blomfield. Self-education continues, including earlier English writers.	Mary Elizabeth Braddon, *Lady Audley's Secret* (the best known of the lurid sensational novels of the 1860s)
1863	Work begins on first London underground (steam) railway. Football Association founded as professional sport. The Metropolitan Line is developed. Thackeray dies. Eliot, *Romola* Mill, *Utilitarianism* in book form

	Life	Historical and Cultural Background
1864		Albert Memorial is constructed. Newman, *Apologia Pro Vita Sua* Trollope, *Can You Forgive Her?* (the first of the political series, the Palliser novels)
1865		Founding by William Booth of what becomes the Salvation Army. End of American Civil War. Dickens, *Our Mutual Friend*
1866		After the defeat of the Reform Bill to extend the vote: rioting in Hyde Park. Eliot, *Felix Holt, the Radical* Gaskell, *Wives and Daughters*, left unfinished at her death
1867	Returns to Dorset as a jobbing architect. He works for Hicks on church restoration.	Second Reform Act increases voters to two million; Mill tries to include women in the Bill but fails. Paris Exhibition. Trollope, *The Last Chronicle of Barset* (last of the Barchester novels) Marx, *Das Kapital*
1868	Completes his first novel *The Poor Man and the Lady* but it is rejected for publication (see 1878).	Founding of the Trades Union Congress. Collins, *The Moonstone* Browning, *The Ring and the Book*
1869	Works for the architect Crickmay in Weymouth, again on church restoration.	Suez Canal opened. Founding of Girton College. Arnold, *Culture and Anarchy* Mill, *The Subjection of Women*
1870	After many youthful infatuations thought to be referred to in early poems, he meets Emma Lavinia Gifford, his future wife, on a professional visit to St Juliot in north Cornwall.	Married Women's Property Act gives wives the right to keep their earnings. Elementary Education Act enabling local authorities to set up schools. Dickens dies, leaving *The Mystery of Edwin Drood* unfinished. D. G. Rossetti, *Poems*
1871	*Desperate Remedies* published in volume form by Tinsley Brothers.	Legalizing of trade unions. First Impressionist Exhibition in Paris. Religious tests abolished at Oxford, Cambridge, and Durham universities. Eliot, *Middlemarch* Darwin, *The Descent of Man*
1872	*Under the Greenwood Tree* published in volume form by Tinsley Brothers.	

	Life	Historical and Cultural Background
1873	*A Pair of Blue Eyes* (based on his meeting with Emma) and previously serialized in *Tinsleys' Magazine*. Horace Mould commits suicide in Cambridge.	Mill, *Autobiography* Walter Pater, *Studies in the History of the Renaissance* (encouraging 'Art for Art's sake' and an impetus towards the later Aesthetic Movement)
1874	*Far from the Madding Crowd* (previously serialized in the *Cornhill Magazine*). Hardy marries Emma and sets up house in Surbiton, London. (They have no children, to Hardy's regret, and she never gets on with his family.)	Factory Act.
1875	Emma and Hardy return to Swanage in Dorset.	Artisans' Dwellings Act (providing housing for the 'respectable poor' or 'artisans'). Efficient system of compulsory vaccination of children against smallpox introduced. Trollope, *The Way We Live Now* (fierce satire on contemporary society and its greed)
1876	*The Hand of Ethelberta* (previously serialized in the *Cornhill Magazine*) published in volume form.	Disraeli creates Victoria Empress of India. Alexander Graham Bell patents the telephone. Invention of the phonograph. Eliot, *Daniel Deronda* Henry James, *Roderick Hudson*
1878	*The Return of the Native* (previously serialized in *Belgravia*) published in volume form. The Hardys move back to London (Tooting). Serialized version of part of the unpublished first novel appears in *Harper's Weekly* in New York as *An Indiscretion in the Life of an Heiress* (never included in his collected works).	London University grants degrees to women for the first time. G. H. Lewes dies.
1879		Beginning of a long though intermittent economic depression in Britain, lasting into the 1890s. William Morris's lecture, *The Art of the People*, explaining ideas which led later to the Arts and Crafts Movement in the latter part of the century. Henrik Ibsen, *A Doll's House* James, *Daisy Miller*

	Life	*Historical and Cultural Background*
1880	*The Trumpet-Major* (previously serialized in *Good Words*) published in volume form. Hardy is ill for many months.	Gladstone becomes Prime Minister for the second time. George Eliot and Gustave Flaubert die. Education Act makes elementary education compulsory. Charles Parnell demands home rule for Ireland. George Gissing, *Workers in the Dawn* Tennyson, *Ballads and Other Poems* Trollope, *The Duke's Children* (last of the Palliser novels)
1881	*A Laodicean* (previously serialized in *Harper's New Monthly Magazine*) published in volume form. The Hardys return to Dorset, living at first in Wimborne.	Death of Carlyle. 'Otto' safety bicycle patented: Hardy and Emma become keen cyclists. By the 1890s many have succumbed to 'bicycle mania'. Ibsen, *Ghosts* (involving syphilis but later seen by Queen Victoria) James, *Portrait of a Lady*
1882	*Two on a Tower* (previously serialized in the *Atlantic Monthly*) published in volume form.	
1882–90		Parliament repeatedly vetoes votes for women.
1883		Andrew Mearns, *The Bitter Cry of Outcast London* (exposé of poverty)
1884	Hardy becomes a Justice of the Peace and serves as a magistrate in Dorchester.	Third Reform Bill. Founding of the Fabian Society.
1885	The Hardys move for the last time: to a house, Max Gate, outside Dorchester, designed by Hardy and built by his brother.	Death of General Gordon at Khartoum. Criminal Law Amendment Act (raises age of consent to 16).
1886	*The Mayor of Casterbridge* (previously serialized in the *Graphic*) published in volume form.	Repeal of the Contagious Diseases Act. Irish Home Rule Act.
1887	*The Woodlanders* (previously serialized in *Macmillan's Magazine*) published in volume form. Hardy begins to visit London for 'the Season'. Visit to Italy.	Victoria's Golden Jubilee.
1888	*Wessex Tales*. Visit to Paris.	Matthew Arnold dies.

	Life	*Historical and Cultural Background*
1889		London dock strike. Robert Browning dies. William Booth, *Life and Labour of the People in London* (exhaustive documentary account) starts publication. G. B. Shaw, *Fabian Essays on Socialism* Ibsen, *A Doll's House* staged in London. Gissing, *The Nether World*
1890		Decline of the circulating libraries and the death of the three-volume novel. William Morris founds the Kelmscott Press. Housing of the Working Classes Act. Oscar Wilde, *The Picture of Dorian Gray* Ibsen, *Hedda Gabler*
1891	*Tess of the d'Urbervilles* (previously serialized in censored form in the *Graphic*) published in volume form. It simultaneously enhances his reputation as a novelist and causes a scandal because of its advanced views on sexual conduct. *A Group of Noble Dames* (tales) also published.	
1892	Hardy's father, Thomas, dies. Serialized version of *The Well-Beloved*, entitled *The Pursuit of the Well-Beloved*, published in the *Illustrated London News*. Hardy's estrangement from Emma increases.	Death of Alfred Tennyson. Wilde, *Lady Windermere's Fan* Rudyard Kipling, *Barrack-Room Ballads*
1892–3	*Our Exploits at West Poley*, a long tale for boys, published in an American periodical, *The Household*. Serial version of *The Pursuit of the Well-Beloved*—virtually a different novel from the later book version.	
1893	Meets Florence Henniker, one of several society women with whom he had intense friendships. Collaborates with her on *The Spectre of the Real* (published 1894).	Keir Hardie sets up the Independent Labour Party. Wilde, *A Woman of No Importance*

	Life	Historical and Cultural Background
1894	*Life's Little Ironies* (tales)	Kipling, *The Jungle Book*
1895	*Jude the Obscure* appears in volume form: a savage attack on marriage which worsens relations with Emma. Serialized previously in *Harper's New Monthly Magazine* in bowdlerized form. It receives both eulogistic and vitriolic reviews. The latter are a factor in his ceasing to write novels.	Oscar Wilde jailed for homosexual offences; serves three years. The first Bristol electric tramway. Wilde, *The Importance of Being Earnest* H. G. Wells, *The Time-Machine*
1895–6	First collected edition: the Wessex Novels (16 volumes). This includes the first book edition of *Jude the Obscure*.	
1896		Locomotive on the Highways Act (car speed maximum 14 m.p.h.). Death of William Morris. Wells, *The Island of Dr Moreau*
1897	*The Well-Beloved*, a newly rewritten version of the 1892 serial, added to the Wessex Novels as volume XVII. From now on he only publishes the poetry he has been writing since the 1860s.	Queen Victoria's Diamond Jubilee. Existing suffrage organizations unite as National Union of Women's Suffrage Societies. Havelock Ellis, *Sexual Inversion*
1898	*Wessex Poems and Other Verses*. Hardy and Emma continue to live at Max Gate but are now estranged and 'kept separate'.	Germany begins the building of a large battle fleet. Britain responds by doing the same. Wilde released from prison. Wilde, *The Ballad of Reading Gaol*
1899–1902		Boer War in South Africa over the Transvaal gold mines; Britain crushes the Boers.
1900		Labour Representation Committee set up to get Labour candidates into Parliament. Wilde and Ruskin die.
1901	*Poems of the Past and the Present* (post-dated 1902)	Victoria dies and is succeeded by Edward VII.
1902	Macmillan becomes his publisher.	James, *The Wings of the Dove*
1903		First manned flight by Wright brothers in the USA. Motor Car Act raises speed limit to 20 m.p.h. James, *The Ambassadors*

	Life	*Historical and Cultural Background*
1904	Hardy's mother Jemima, the single most important influence in his life, dies. Part 1 of *The Dynasts* (epic drama in verse on Napoleon) published.	Anglo-French Entente. James, *The Golden Bowl*
1905	At about this time Hardy meets Florence Emily Dugdale, his future second wife, then aged 26. She is soon a friend of Hardy and Emma, and his part-time secretary.	Increased trade-union activity. E. M. Forster, *Where Angels Fear to Tread*
1906	Part 2 of *The Dynasts*.	Thirty Labour MPs are elected in General Election.
1907		Anglo-Russian Entente. Act allowing marriage with deceased wife's sister. First London cinema. Forster, *The Longest Journey*
1908	Part 3 of *The Dynasts* completes the work.	Non-contributory state pension is set up. Forster, *A Room with a View*
1909	*Time's Laughingstocks and Other Verses*.	Housing and Town Planning Act (to help provide working-class housing). Labour Exchanges Act (seeking employment previously difficult).
1910	Is awarded the Order of Merit, having previously refused a knighthood. Also receives the Freedom of Dorchester.	Edward VII dies and is succeeded by George V.
1911		National Insurance Act. D. H. Lawrence, *The White Peacock*
1912	27 November: Emma dies, still estranged. Her death triggers the writing of Hardy's finest love lyrics, *Poems of 1912–1913*, about their early time together in Cornwall which he now revisits.	William Morris produces first cheap Morris Oxford car. George V attends first Royal Command Variety Performance.
1912–13	Publication of a major collected edition of novels and verse by Hardy: the Wessex Edition (24 volumes).	
1913	*A Changed Man and Other Tales*.	A suffragette throws herself under the King's horse at the Derby. Lawrence, *Sons and Lovers*

	Life	Historical and Cultural Background
1914	10 February: Hardy marries Florence Dugdale (who was hurt by the poems written about Emma after her death). *Satires of Circumstance*; *The Dynasts: Prologue and Epilogue*	Start of First World War. A million copies of books now available in free public libraries. James Joyce, *Dubliners*
1914–15		Joyce, *A Portrait of the Artist as a Young Man*
1915	Mary, Hardy's sister, dies. His distant relative, Frank George, is killed at Gallipoli.	Virginia Woolf, *The Voyage Out* Lawrence, *The Rainbow*
1916	*Selected Poems*	Self-proclamation of an independent Irish Republic.
1917	*Moments of Vision and Miscellaneous Verses*	T. S. Eliot, *Prufrock and Other Observations*
1918		First World War ends. Vote extended to men over 21 and some women over 30. Those Irish who want independence set up their own parliament, the Dáil, and the Irish 'troubles' begin. British troops ruthlessly repress the rebels. Education Act raises the school-leaving age to 14 and extends education for some to 16.
1919		Russian Revolution helps stir up working-class militancy. First satisfactory contraceptive for women is devised.
1919–20	Mellstock Edition of novels and verse (37 volumes).	
1920		Increased social awareness is indicated by extension of National Insurance against unemployment. Lawrence, *Women in Love*
1921		Ireland splits into new republic and the North, which remains part of the United Kingdom.
1922	*Late Lyrics and Earlier with Many Other Verses*	BBC is set up. Joyce, *Ulysses* Woolf, *Jacob's Room* T. S. Eliot, *The Waste Land*
1923	*The Famous Tragedy of the Queen of Cornwall* (drama). Florence Henniker dies. The Prince of Wales, the future Edward VIII (later the Duke of Windsor), visits Max Gate.	

	Life	*Historical and Cultural Background*
1924	Dramatized version of *Tess* performed at Dorchester. Hardy is infatuated with the local woman, Gertrude Bugler, who plays Tess.	First Labour Government formed by Ramsay MacDonald. Forster, *A Passage to India*
1925	*Human Shows, Far Phantasies, Songs and Trifles*	Woolf, *Mrs Dalloway* and *The Common Reader* (essays)
1926		May: General Strike, lasting 9 days. James Ramsay MacDonald forms a coalition government which he leads until 1935 but is expelled from the Labour Party who refuse to support it.
1927		Invention of talking pictures. Woolf, *To the Lighthouse*
1928	11 January: Hardy dies. His heart is buried in Emma's grave at Stinsford, his ashes in Westminster Abbey. *Winter Words in Various Moods and Metres* published posthumously. Hardy's brother, Henry, dies.	Vote is extended to women over 21. Lawrence, *Lady Chatterley's Lover* Woolf, *Orlando*
1928–30	Hardy's autobiography is completed by his second wife and published on his instructions under her name.	
1937	Florence, Hardy's second wife, dies.	
1940	Hardy's last sibling, Kate, dies.	

ABBREVIATIONS

Biography   Michael Millgate, *Thomas Hardy, A Biography* (Oxford and Melbourne: Oxford University Press, 1982)

Interviews   *Thomas Hardy, Interviews and Recollections*, ed. James Gibson (Basingstoke and London: Macmillan, 1999)

Letters   *The Collected Letters of Thomas Hardy*, vols. 1–6 (1840–1925), ed. Richard Little Purdy and Michael Millgate (Oxford: Clarendon Press, 1978–87); vol. 7 (1926–7), ed. Michael Millgate (Oxford: Clarendon Press, 1988)

Life   *The Life and Work of Thomas Hardy, by Thomas Hardy*, ed. Michael Millgate (London and Basingstoke: Macmillan, 1984) (Hardy's own account)

OED   *Oxford English Dictionary*

Poems   *The Complete Poetical Works of Thomas Hardy*, ed. Samuel Hynes, 5 vols. (Oxford: Clarendon Press, 1982–95)

Wives' Letters   *The Letters of Emma and Florence Hardy*, ed. Michael Millgate (Oxford: Clarendon Press, 1988)

CHAPTER 1

THE LIFE OF THOMAS HARDY

THE third Thomas Hardy, the novelist, was born on 2 June 1840, some five and a half months after their marriage, to Jemima (née Hand) and the second Thomas Hardy. Jemima and her husband had three more children later: Mary (1841–1915), Henry (1851–1928), and Katharine (1856–1940). The four siblings remained close throughout their lives. Their father, the second Thomas Hardy, was a small-scale mason or builder who employed two men in 1851, six men in 1861, and eight men and a boy in 1871. The business had been set up by the novelist's grandfather, the first Thomas Hardy. It was run from a cottage in Stinsford (later Higher Bockhampton) in Dorset which was held on a lifehold tenancy on the lives of the first Thomas and his two sons, James and Thomas. The cottage, which stood alone, had a thatched roof and mud walls.

Neither Hardy's grandfather nor his father was particularly ambitious and they seem to have been less than eager entrepreneurs. His mother Jemima, however, who was to influence him throughout her life, was a strong and forceful woman, ambitious for her eldest son. After her marriage she moved into the family cottage with her widowed mother-in-law. There she gave birth to Thomas, the poet and novelist, who, like some traditional hero, was born in dramatic circumstances: 'At his birth he was thrown aside as dead till rescued by her [the monthly nurse] as she exclaimed to the surgeon, "Dead! Stop a minute: he's alive enough, sure!"' (*Life*, p. 501).

By contrast with his beginning, his funeral was a national event. It took place in 1928 in Westminster Abbey and the names of his pall-bearers are the measure of how far he had travelled in obvious ways from his origins. They included the Prime Minister Stanley Baldwin and the Leader of the Opposition Ramsay MacDonald, as well as the heads of the two Oxford and Cambridge colleges where he was an honorary fellow. The rest were major literary figures of the day: Sir James Barrie, John Galsworthy, Sir Edmund Gosse, A. E. Housman, Rudyard Kipling, and George Bernard Shaw. Others attending included Arnold Bennett, John Masefield, Virginia Woolf, and Walter de la Mare.

But this long journey from Stinsford to the Abbey was not a movement away from his origins. From the wealth of biographical material it can be seen that certain deep-rooted concerns and pre-occupations show unbroken lines persisting throughout his life. The material captures him from many different angles since it includes seven volumes of his letters; letters of his first and second wives; the 'biography' (1928–30) which he ghosted and which was published after his death under his second wife's name; reports of interviewers; and reminiscences of those who met him at Max Gate, the house he built for himself in Dorset (not to mention those who merely claimed to have met him and offered anecdotes).

The most obvious of the concerns and preoccupations in Hardy's life were Dorset, the area in which he grew up and to which he returned in 1881, social class and its conseqences, the role and status of women, and the distressing fading of religious belief. The persist-ence in his life and works of these subjects did not take the form of unchanging ideas and attitudes. On the contrary, they varied and developed like the branches of a tree, as experiences, events, and the prevailing climate of ideas changed. Some beliefs developed, some atrophied but these topics formed the basic structure of his mental landscape. Unusually also, he grew less not more dogmatic as he grew older. His uncertainty, like his curiosity, never ceased.

Dorset and its Significance

Hardy's familiarity with the Dorset countryside was acquired in his childhood when such a landscape circumscribed his visual horizons. His only major excursion outside it took place when at the age of 9 his mother took him 'for [her] protection' to stay with her pregnant sister Martha in Hatfield, Hertfordshire. This involved a trip to London by rail and then to Hatfield by coach. The pair spent one night in London near the meat market, 'the pandemonium of Smithfield, with its mud, curses, and cries of ill-treated animals', as Hardy wrote (*Life*, p. 22). Hardy's life-long horror at the cruel treatment of animals was a persistent concern throughout his life, as the pig-killing episode in *Jude the Obscure* (1895) shows. Apart from this trip, Hardy journeyed only on foot to and from his schools. The first of these was possibly a dame school in Lower Bockhampton and in 1848 a local National (Anglican) school. Then he went at the age of 10 in 1850 to the (Nonconformist British) school three miles away in Dorchester and later, from 1853 to 1856, a more advanced school there called the Academy where he learnt, in addition to basic subjects, some Latin, French, and mathematics. So for six years he walked daily to and from Dorchester through the countryside, using the powers of observation which he himself recognized in the poem 'Afterwards'. In it he writes his own preferred epigraph after describing minute details of a twilight landscape: 'He was a man who used to notice such things' (*Poems*, ii. 308).

His observation of detail can be noted in and described by his account of the two characters of whom he says in *The Woodlanders* (1887):

The casual glimpses which the ordinary population bestowed upon that wondrous world of sap and leaves called the Hintock woods had been with these two, Giles and Marty, a clear gaze. They had been possessed of its finer mysteries as of commonplace knowledge; and had been able to read its hieroglyphs as ordinary writing; to them the sights and sounds of night, winter, wind, storm, amid those dense boughs ... were simple occurrences whose origin, continuance, and laws they foreknew ... they had, with the run of years, mentally collected those remoter signs and symbols which seen in few were of runic obscurity, but altogether made an alphabet. (chapter 43)

The alphabet they have learnt to decode relates in this passage solely to natural phenomena and is done by touch, hearing, and sight:

From the light lashing of the twigs upon their faces when brushing through them in the dark either could pronounce upon the species of the tree whence they stretched; from the quality of the wind's murmur through a bough either could in like manner name its sort afar off. They knew by a glance at a trunk if its heart were sound, or tainted with incipient decay.

As is already evident here, his observation was sensitive not only to detail but to change, alteration, decay, or flourishing, both in that detail and at large. To such a watcher the scene viewed is not just or mainly a pretty picture. It is the face of his clock—as Hardy says also in *The Woodlanders*: 'The countryman who is obliged to judge the time of day from changes in external nature sees a thousand successive tints and traits in the landscape which are never discerned by him who hears the regular chime of a clock, because they are never in request' (chapter 15). Because Hardy observed in this way, the narrow physical horizons of his childhood did not confine him but opened his mind to wider issues. He saw unceasing change and he saw the layers of human life and activities which were written upon familiar scenes. The outsider Fitzpiers is bored in Little Hintock in the winter because he lacks the knowledge given by

old association—an almost exhaustive biographical or historical acquaint-ance with every object, animate and inanimate, within the observer's horizon. He must know all about those invisible ones of the days gone by whose feet have traversed the fields which look so grey from his windows; recall whose creaking plough has turned those sods from time to time; whose hands planted the trees that form a crest to the opposite hill; whose horses and hounds have torn through that underwood; what birds affect that particular break. (chapter 17)

Entwined with these human events are the stories and songs that record such dramas or happy moments of celebration. These Hardy learnt first from Jemima and his paternal grandmother Mary (née Head). He continued to collect and make use of folk-tales, supersti-tions, country customs, and country songs by recording them in his biographical writings and using them in his novels. His music-making in various churches and elsewhere, where he played the fiddle with his father, also provided settings in which he could hear and learn more folk songs and superstitions.

But he found even more than this folklore and village history inscribed across an already changing environment. Other 'hiero-glyphs' were imprinted on it beside those revealed by the sight, sound, and touch of its plants and animals, and by folk memories. Much of this further layer of meaning he discovered during the time of his first career which he took up on leaving school in 1856. Thanks to his father's building contracts he was articled to a Dorchester architect, John Hicks, to learn architectural drawing and surveying. At this time he was befriended by the son of the Rector of Fordington who became his friend and intellectual mentor. Horatio 'Horace' Moule was a Cambridge graduate, cultivated and intelli-gent but unstable. He and Hardy remained close until Moule cut his throat in his rooms at a Cambridge college in 1873. It was during this

The Beginning: Hardy's birthplace, drawn by himself.

Life as a celebrity: Florence and Thomas Hardy visited by the Prince of Wales in 1923.

early period with Moule that Hardy nourished hopes of becoming an undergraduate in Cambridge until he abandoned the project. With Moule's help and advice he began to read avidly in Latin and Greek as well as in English and to move on to some science and philosophy. Among the books that Moule advised Hardy to read was Gideon Algernon Mantell's *The Wonders of Geology* (1838) which he acquired from Moule in 1869 and kept all his life. In surveying a landscape now, he came to recognize as more basic than the trees, plants, and animals the geological formations from which they grew and which formed the environment for their development. He saw the geological formation of every scene.

While working for Hicks, Hardy became involved in a minor capacity in the main work of the practice, the so-called 'restoration' of Gothic churches. This was in reality a process combining repair with modernization. With increasing knowledge Hardy came in time to regret it as something akin to vandalism. Later, in the early twentieth century he and his brother Henry travelled assiduously round the cathedrals of Lichfield, Worcester, Hereford, Canterbury, Lincoln, Ely, and others 'in pursuance of a plan of seeing or reseeing all the English cathedrals' (*Life*, p. 382). Typically in an essay on 'Dorset in London' Hardy reads St Paul's as part of Dorset:

To be sure, it has been standing here in London for more than two hundred years, but it stood, or rather lay, in Dorset probably two hundred thousand years before it got here. How thoroughly metropolitan it is; its facade thrills to the street noises all day long, and has done so for three or four human lifetimes. But through what a stretch of time did it thrill all day and all night in Portland to the tides of the West Bay, particularly when they slammed against the island during south-west gales.[1]

St Paul's is made of Portland stone and so it carries its place of origin and its history within it, ready to be recognized by expert eyes.

Hardy's knowledge of historical building was enhanced, as his architectural notebooks testify, when in 1862 he moved to London and found employment with another architect, Arthur Blomfield, to help 'restore and design churches and rectory houses'. There he enjoyed his first taste of city life, visiting galleries and theatres as well as reading voraciously. After a return to Dorset in 1867 because of poor health, he worked first for Hicks and then similarly as a jobbing architect for G. R. Crickmay. His temporary employer famously sent him to 'Lyonesse' as his poems call it, otherwise St Juliot in Cornwall. There he met the Rector's sister-in-law Emma Lavinia Gifford, who was to become his first wife. And so between 1856 and 1872 (when he abandoned architecture to concentrate on a career as a writer), he later recalled, he helped destroy 'Much beautiful ancient Gothic, and particularly also Jacobean and Georgian work' (*Life*, p. 35). Man-made artifacts in the shapes of buildings of all kinds from cottages to mansions and churches he now realized were encoded history. As Hardy told the writer Frank Hedgecock, when viewing 'an extensive panorama' near Max Gate, 'the scene interested him most as a record of history. On it generations long dead had left their mark' (*Interviews*, p. 92).

Nor did this apply only to relatively recent history such as the Napoleonic Wars which Hardy dealt with in *The Trumpet-Major* (1880) and *The Dynasts* (1904–8). As Hardy continued his self-education it came to include Roman and prehistoric remains which he learnt to recognize and interpret. He always does so in the same way: by seeing them as records of the lives of those who once inhabited them. This was brought home to him by the discoveries made when the foundations of his house, Max Gate, were being dug. In a lecture given to a meeting of the Dorset Natural History and Antiquarian Field Club in 1884 he describes 'Some Romano-British Relics Found at Max Gate, Dorchester'. These included 'three human skeletons' in separate oval graves, 'the tight-fitting situation being strongly suggestive of the chicken in the eggshell'.[2] The bronze and iron fibula or clasp which evidently fastened a headband became a feature of the Max Gate drawing-room. Hardy concludes that it would be worthwhile to try to reconstruct on paper 'the living Durnovaria of fourteen or fifteen hundred years ago—as it actually appeared to the eyes of the then Dorchester men and women'. He is intensely curious to know

how did the roofs group themselves, what were the gardens like, if any, what social character had the streets, what were the customary noises, what sort of exterior was exhibited by these hybrid Romano-British people . . . ? Were the passengers up and down the ways few in number, or did they ever form a busy throng such as we now see on a market day?[3]

The same Dorset club instigated the excavation of the Maumbury Ring, an amphitheatre at Dorchester, and Hardy wrote to *The Times* on 9 October 1908 about it. He offers his account as that of a 'mere observer who possesses a smattering of local history, and remembers local traditions that have been recounted by people now dead and gone'.[4] He interprets the Ring as a record of 'the civil wars of Charles I', the visit of Sir Christopher Wren when he passed it on his way to choose Portland stone for St Paul's. Then, characteristically, he remembers the local girl hanged there in 1705–6 for poisoning her husband; the more recent burning of effigies of the Pope and Cardinal Wiseman which he saw as a child. Small wonder the journalist Evelyn Sharp said of him later 'Hardy's tendency to relate gruesome and horrible incidents he had experienced or heard of . . . struck me as slightly morbid: it seemed as though we could not avoid the macabre in any conversation to which he contributed' (*Interviews*, p. 76). In making Dorset the basis of his fictional Wessex, it must be recognized that for him, as well as being the environment of insects, birds, and animals, it is also a place which forms the environment for past and present human beings who shared and share reciprocal relationship with it. They both form it and are formed by it in ways not always understood. It is living evidence for the view that nothing is static or certain.

Social Class

What the contrast between Hardy's birth and his splendid Abbey funeral crystallizes is a dichotomy never far from Hardy's attention both in his life and in his novels: the complexities of social class and of cross-class relationships captured in the title of his unpublished novel *The Poor Man and the Lady*. This was rejected by Macmillan in 1868 because, despite the fact that one reader had thought the rural scenes very promising, Alexander Macmillan, the publisher, found it offensive about the class to which he himself belonged. Though he agreed that the contempt shown in the novel by the upper class towards the working class had some truth, it exaggerated. He added that 'nothing could justify such a wholesale blackening of a class but large & intimate knowledge of it'. Hardy did not have such a knowledge and meant '*mischief*' according to Macmillan (*Biography*, p. 110). The work was only published in a partial and mutilated form under the ironic title *An Indiscretion in the Life of an Heiress* in 1878 and has not been included in Hardy's collected works. His own upward mobility began when he left behind the building work that occupied his father (and later his brother Henry) to train for a profession as an architectural assistant and then a jobbing architect. In the mid-nineteenth century social class was an omnipresent fact, visible in where people lived, what they wore and ate, how and where they were educated, what occupation they followed, and how much money they earned. University education was almost entirely the preserve of those who were educated by public schools in the Latin and Greek which enabled them to meet the requirements of the older universities.

Hardy was born to an unambitious father, just a cut above the village labourers, some of whom he employed. Hardy in later life was always anxious to stress this division between the two sections of the working class when, usually against his wishes, accounts of his origins were given to the public. Certainly he was never very willing to discuss his social origins or to bring his family into the limelight. This may have also been because of the affection he always felt for them and the consequent desire to protect them in their Dorset homes and habits. In various essays Hardy several times gave a precise account of the class to which his socially unambitious father belonged. Characteristically he described it as a detached observer might:

Down to the middle of the last century, country villagers were divided into two distinct castes, one being the artisans, traders, 'liviers' (owners of freeholds), and the manor-house upper servants; the other the 'work-folk' i.e. farm labourers (these were never called by the latter name by themselves and other country people till about 70 years ago). The two castes rarely intermarried, and did not go to each other's house-gatherings save exceptionally. (*Biography*, p. 26)

Thomas the second may have been satisfied to remain in this caste but his wife was certainly not similarly unambitious for her elder son. She had been toughened rather than crushed by a childhood with a father who was a violent drunkard and by being sent in her early teens to work as a servant. Her experiences left her determined that Thomas the third should rise from the class into which he was born. Reportedly a keen reader, she saw education as important in the process. From an early age she provided Thomas with books, some of which are identifiable. Her open-mindedness is indicated by the inclusion amongst them, along with Samuel Johnson's moralizing *Rasselas*, of Dryden's translation of Virgil and a translation of the eighteenth-century French novel by Jacques-Henri Bernardin de Saint-Pierre, *Paul and Virginia*, which draws on Rousseau's ideas about nature as a moral force. When Jemima's role as mentor passed to Horace Moule during Hardy's architectural days, he too provided the books and encouragement for his younger friend to go further in his Latin reading and to learn Greek, since at this stage Hardy was still hoping one day to become an undergraduate at Cambridge. This was the beginning of a lifetime of self-education continued into old age. Hardy's supposed 'biography' is punctuated by lists of books he read avidly at different periods. Before the age of 27 he had tried the Greek New Testament, Homer, Virgil, *Essays and Reviews*, J. H. Newman's *Apologia Pro Vita Sua*, Horace, Byron, and much else. His visits to galleries left him with a store of visual images on which he drew to fix a descriptive detail in his novels. Typically his second published novel, *Under the Greenwood Tree* (1872) carried the stilted subtitle 'A Rural Painting of the Dutch School'.

In 1866 Hardy underwent a crisis of choice in regard to his course in life when, after obtaining through Horace Moule information about the requirements for matriculating at Cambridge, he abandoned his hopes of reading for a degree there and of entering the Church. This was apparently because he recognized that his laborious self-preparation in the classics was not extensive enough. By giving up the prospect of a university education, he seemed also to have failed in his mother's project of moving up the social ladder (or greasy pole). Ironically the step upwards came about indirectly as a result of his passionate love for Emma Gifford. Her father (who became an alcoholic) was a solicitor by profession and her uncle, Canon Edwin Hamilton Gifford, was later Archdeacon of London. The latter's brother-in-law, Francis Henry Jeune, was a judge who became Lord St Helier. According to a letter from Hardy's second wife, Emma's father referred to his son-in-law as a 'low born churl who has presumed to marry into *my* family' (*Wives' Letters*, p. 78). In fact the nature of the 'step up' socially was ambiguous. The Giffords did not see it as affecting and enhancing Hardy's social class, as they made plain. Nor is it clear that Emma did, either. The marriage, which took place in London in September 1874, was not attended by any of Hardy's family. Canon Gifford performed the ceremony and another Gifford, her brother Walter, was a witness. The only other person present was the daughter of Hardy's landlady who served as the second witness.

By this time Hardy was legitimately able to describe himself in the register as 'author' since in 1872 he had given up architecture—with Emma's strong approval. Though socially a move upwards, becoming a full-time writer was financially precarious. The decision was taken only after considerable thought. Still, by the time of the wedding, although he had failed to find a publisher for *The Poor Man and the Lady*, Hardy had published *Desperate Remedies* (1871), *Under the Greenwood Tree* (1872), and *A Pair of Blue Eyes* (1873), and he felt able to marry. *Desperate Remedies* had made a small loss and *Under the Greenwood Tree*, which was more successful, a small profit. But for the serial rights of *A Pair of Blue Eyes* he received £200, a moderately large sum at that date. By this time he was thought of as a rural novelist. The adoption of a middle-class profession, however, did not automatically secure acceptance as a social equal by those who had known Hardy as a social inferior. Millgate points out the patronizing tone of a letter from Horace Moule's brother, Charles, writing to him after his decision: 'I trust I address you rightly on the envelope. I conjectured that you wd prefer the absence of the "Esqre" at Upper Bockhampton' (*Biography*, p. 149). This refers to the distinction between addressing someone as the middle-class 'Esquire' and addressing them as the less deferential 'Mr'. The implication of Moule's remark is that the locals at Bockhampton who already knew Hardy might consider 'Esqre' a pretentious form for him. This interpretation is borne out by a scene in *A Pair of Blue Eyes*. In it the local labourer William Worm claims that he is as independent as anyone else 'even if they do write 'squire after their names'. The snobbish rector Swancourt, commenting on this, asserts 'that word "esquire" is gone to the dogs—used on the letters of every jackanapes who has a black coat' (chapter 4). Like his brother, Horace Moule had also been somewhat lofty when he told Hardy in 1873 'You understand the *woman* infinitely better than the lady' (*Biography*, p. 150).

By the time Hardy had published three more novels, *Far from the Madding Crowd* (1874), *The Hand of Ethelberta* (1875), and *The Return of the Native* (1878), he apparently began to feel himself a literary man of some standing. In 1878 he and Emma (who wanted to take a place on the social scene) moved to London. As he put it in the self-ghosted *Life*: 'the practical side of his vocation of novelist demanded that he should have his head-quarters in or near London' (*Life*, p. 121). His election to a well-known literary club, the Savile, soon after this move to Tooting clearly constituted the possible beginning of 'acceptance'. As the *Life* puts it, 'he was elected a member of the Savile Club, and by degrees fell into line as a London man again' (*Life*, p. 125). A 'London man' meant a London society man rather than a mere inhabitant of the city. It is at this stage in the *Life* that Hardy began to record meetings with the middle-class journalists, writers, publishers, and others whose circle he joined. Publishers included George Smith (of Smith, Elder), Charles Kegan Paul, and Alexander Macmillan. Amongst the writers were Matthew Arnold, Robert Browning, Alfred Lord Tennyson, and Henry James, as well as the scientist Thomas Huxley. Such men were at this time lionized by some members of the establishment and, through this means, a number of aristocratic and upper-class men and women also became part of Hardy's particular social and intellectual circuit.

It was after the publication of *The Trumpet-Major* (1880), when Hardy was confined to bed by a serious illness which meant that he had laboriously to dictate *A Laodicean* to Emma, that his London life began to pall. The *Life* records the effect of Hardy's bedridden life: 'Skin gets fair: corns take their leave . . .: watch dim, boots mildewed; hat and clothes old-fashioned' (*Life*, p. 152). He himself explains the move to Dorset: for 'reasons of health and for mental inspiration, Hardy finding, or thinking he found, that residence in or near a city tended to force mechanical and ordinary productions from his pen, concerning ordinary society-life and habits' (*Life*, p. 154). From 1881 the Hardys lived permanently in Dorset and 'did' the London season for three or four months a year. Their trips abroad, apart from the honeymoon they had spent in France in 1874, were limited to fashionable holiday trips to France, Italy, Holland, Belgium, Switzerland, and Germany.

The return to Dorset seems to have served its purpose of revitalizing Hardy's creativity. In the next fifteen years he produced his major novels *The Mayor of Casterbridge* (1886), *The Woodlanders* (1887), *Tess of the d'Urbervilles* (1891), and *Jude the Obscure* (1895). Though the last two were highly controversial because of their treatment of sexuality and religion, they were also hugely successful— perhaps in part because of the controversy. Hardy as usual suffered greatly as a result of the hostile and vindictive reviews of the two latter novels, describing him in one instance as a decadent whose views on sexual morality were subversive. These reviews were a factor in his turning in 1895 to the poetry which he had always written, making that the staple of his writing for the rest of his life. It was a repeated statement of his that he had always intended (and felt himself) to be a poet.

Hardy's standing in the literary world had by now risen phenomenally. Consequently he was sought after and lionized in London by the literary world and the establishment generally. He records some of the social whirl with obvious satisfaction. For instance in 1887 he reports: 'At dinner at (Juliet) Lady Pollock's, Sir F. told Emma that he had danced in the same quadrille with a gentleman who had danced with Marie Antoinette' (*Life*, p. 209). And later in the same year: 'The remainder of this London season in the brilliant Jubilee-year was passed by the Hardys gaily enough. At some houses the scene was made very radiant by the presence of so many Indian princes in their jewelled robes' (*Life*, p. 210). Not that Hardy was entirely uncritical of the aristocracy, at least as to matters of speech-making. He describes the Duke of Cambridge (grandson of George III and commander-in-chief of the army) making a speech at the Royal Academy uncertain as to whether he had finished or not so that he 'tagged and tagged on a bit more, and a bit more, till the sentences were like acrobats hanging down from a trapeze' (*Life*, p. 207).

By contrast with his standing on the London literary scene, Hardy was not popular in the vicinity of his home in Dorset. After he moved in 1885 to the house that he built for himself at Max Gate outside Dorchester, the local 'work folk' seem to have distrusted him. One visitor to Max Gate reports the comment of a Dorchester bookseller who refused to stock what one reviewer had referred to as 'Jude the Obscene': 'Perhaps we have not the same opinion of Mr Hardy in Dorchester as you have elsewhere' (*Interviews*, p. 53). Hermann Lea, a photographer who knew Hardy well, tells of similar local reactions, such as that of one woman he questioned: 'Why the man could not try to do some useful work in the world beats me. Why could not he have done some building like his father, instead of writing a lot of rubbish that no one wants to read' (*Interviews*, p. 55). Hardy also encountered some resentment from local landowners because of his and Emma's common hostility to blood sports which he attacked in the pheasant-killing episode in *Tess*. Yet he and his family were emotionally as well as physically rooted in Dorset.

This dichotomy was something that he never completely came to terms with. Sometimes he adopted a tone of fairly lofty detachment, as in a piece in the *Pall Mall Gazette* in January 1892: 'All that I know about our Dorset labourers I gathered . . . from living in the country as a child and from thoroughly knowing their dialect. You cannot get at the labourer otherwise. Dialect is the only pass-key to anything like intimacy' (pp. 1–2). As he had made clear in the comment cited earlier, Hardy's natural usage for those he refers to here was 'work folk'. His use of the term 'labourers' and the implication that he was an observer bent on 'getting at' such people is not quite an accurate account of his early life. He was in fact obsessively interested in language, including dialect words: in later life he carefully annotated his own copy of the *Oxford English Dictionary* with 'missing' Dorset words. He developed a strong interest in vocabulary generally, collecting and recording words that interested him and including many of them in his poetry.

His attitude to dialect reflects the fact that, like many brought up in a dialect-speaking community, he felt it to be a particularly expressive style of language and at the same time a marker of social inferiority. Hence the contradictions in his statements about the Dorset dialect made at different times. The whole family is likely to have used local dialect pronunciation to a marked degree in Hardy's youth. A relative reports of Jemima, Hardy's mother, saying of his wife Emma in 1862 'in a broad Dorset accent' that she was 'A thing of a 'ooman . . . She were wrong for I' (*Biography*, p. 415). Informants who had known Hardy and his siblings in the early twentieth century reported that signs of the Dorset dialect survived in their speech. H. L. Voss who acted as chauffeur when Hardy hired a car asserts that Kate and Henry had 'noticeable Dorset accents'.[5] A long-standing acquaintance remarked in 1920 that whereas thirty years before Hardy had had 'a decided accent of some kind', he now had a 'gentle and smooth voice' (*Biography*, p. 531). And in the same year another acquaintance, W. M. Parker, was still able to detect 'just a faint suggestion of rough rustic flavour'.[6]

Yet significantly Hardy wished to conceal the change in his speech habits. When in 1911 he read in the critic Frank Hedgcock's essay on his work, *Essai de Critique: Thomas Hardy, penseur et artiste*, that in his youth he must have spoken the local dialect, he wrote angrily in the margins of his copy (now in the Dorset County Museum): 'He knew the dialect, but did not speak it . . . it was not spoken in his mother's house, but only when necessary to the cottagers, & by his father to his workmen'.[7] His continuing ambivalence about dialect into the twentieth century is illustrated by the fact that a few years before this comment was made he expressed a different view. In 1908 he wrote in his Preface to the poems of William Barnes, the Dorset poet, that the glosses he provides are 'a sorry substitute for the full significance the original words bear to those who read them without translation, and know their delicate ability to express the doings, joys and jests, troubles, sorrows, needs and sicknesses of life in the rural world as elsewhere.'[8]

The *Life* covering the 1880s and 1890s mirrors the split in Hardy's life: it is a bizarre mixture of accounts of society events juxtaposed against notes of rustic superstitions and sensational stories. Remarks like 'Lodging at the Jeunes. Lord Rowton, who is great on lodging-houses, says I am her "dosser"', appear close to a summary of a curious story of a girl who had an illegitimate child by the local doctor: since the doctor had a squint, 'to identify him still more fully as the father she hung a bobbin from the baby's cap between his eyes, and so trained him to squint likewise' (*Life*, p. 241). Even this con-trast between his two lives was sometimes productive as can be seen by a remark made on his return to Dorchester from London in 1888 where the change prompts the thought of 'the determination to enjoy. We see it in all nature, from the leaf on the tree to the titled lady at the ball' (*Life*, p. 222). Millgate makes an illuminating dis-tinction in relation to Hardy's reaction to social class at this time: he says that Hardy, finding himself

in a world that was by no means anti-intellectual, and the respectful welcome he there received gave him a sense not so much of 'arrival'—since he never thought of himself as anything other than an occasional visitor—as of recognition. That he was there at all was an acknowledge-ment of his status as a successful author, and the active interest of men and women of rank, importance, intelligence, and beauty provided a flattering reassurance to set off against the cheerful incomprehension of most of his own family, the envious disbelief of many of his neighbours, and the multiplying disappointments of his marriage. (*Biography*, p. 266)

In spite of his pleasure in well-connected and intelligent friends, Hardy was not a sycophant. At the height of his fame he constantly struck visitors as unpretentious in habits, manner, and speech— sometimes to their disappointment. He turned down the offer of a knighthood to which so many other writers like Gosse and Barrie succumbed. Though always painfully vulnerable to adverse criticism of his work, he disliked sycophancy. The enduring difficulty he had so far as social class was concerned seems to have been the tension between a mental landscape and a close family which together held ineradicably in place the social identity of his childhood and his contrasting status as a giant of literature fêted by the establishment.

The Women in Hardy's Life

By the late 1880s, as Hardy's marriage gradually broke down, Emma's insistence on her own social superiority was causing difficulties. Some commentators attribute this preoccupation to her increasing unhappiness. Others see it as a cause rather than a symptom of the breakdown of the marriage. According to one family friend, Emma was always conscious of her own higher social class, claiming that she had 'the fixed idea that she was the superior of husband in birth, education, talents and manners'. Gissing said of a meeting in 1895, 'Most unfortunately he has a very foolish wife—a woman of higher birth than his own, who looks down upon him, and is utterly discontented' (*Interviews*, p. 50). Another visitor relates how a conversation with Hardy was cut short by Emma's entering the room and insisting on taking him away to show her water-colours. He adds, 'And I, being weak, and courteous to the nieces of archdeacons, was wafted away' (*Interviews*, p. 53). Another told how 'The marriage was thought a misalliance for her, when he was poor and undistinguished, and she continues to resent it' (*Interviews*, p. 106). Such episodes became more frequently noticed as time went on.

The first marriage had been the culmination of many encounters with women which swept him off his feet and which evidence his intense interest in them. The women in his life began with the family into which he was born, which included not only his strong-minded mother Jemima (née Hand) but his widowed paternal grandmother Mary (née Head) whose home she shared. His closest sibling was his sister Mary, born a year after him in 1841. They remained very close emotionally and in their interests until her death in 1915. His brother Henry and other sister Kate were both more than ten years younger than Thomas and Mary, and somewhat less close in consequence. Though Thomas the second and third were on affectionate terms and had a shared interest in the church music they performed, the father was not a dominant influence on his son. Jemima was the matriarch, the most obvious source of the largely feminine influence surrounding Hardy as he grew up. Not only did he live amongst women and girls but he became the pet of a local middle-class woman Julia Martin. He describes himself at the age of 8 or 9 as 'more attached than he cared to own' to Mrs Martin (*Life*, p. 24).

This was not the only sign of his susceptibility. The *Life* records many early infatuations. At the age of 14 he 'fell madly in love with a pretty girl who passed him on horseback near the South Walk, Dorchester' and smiled at him (p. 29). He 'lost his heart for a few days to a young girl just after he had been reading Ainsworth's *Windsor Castle*' at about the same time. These were followed by 'another young girl, a game-keeper's pretty daughter' who attracted him because she had 'beautiful bay-red hair'; and a well-to-do farmer's daughter named Louisa. Somewhat ironically he adds in the *Life* 'There were more probably' (p. 30). What is surprising about this is not the number of girls he fell for but the fact that decades later when concocting the 'biography' with his second wife he remembered them so precisely and thought the details worth recording. Characteristically there is a sudden note in his account of his life in 1887 which abruptly lists 'Youthful recollections of four village beauties':

1. Elizabeth B——, and her red hair.
2. Emily D——, and her mere prettiness.
3. Rachel H——, and her rich colour, and vanity, and frailty, and clever artificial dimple-making.
4. Alice P—— and her mass of flaxen curls. (*Life*, pp. 214–15)

As a young adult he became more seriously involved with the women who attracted him. He appears to have been more or less engaged from 1863 to 1867 while in London to a servant-girl, Eliza Nicholls. Shortly after this there is evidence of a strong attachment to his 'cousin', Tryphena Sparks, though the assertion that she bore him an illegitimate son, Randy, is not sustainable. Like his sister Mary, she was a lively and intelligent woman who became a teacher. When she died in 1890 he wrote a poem 'Thoughts of Phena: at News of Her Death' describing his sense of loss.

Not a line of her writing have I,
　　Not a thread of her hair,
No mark of her late time as dame in her dwelling, whereby
　　I may picture her there;
And in vain do I urge my unsight
　　To conceive my lost prize
At her close, whom I knew when her dreams were upbrimming with light,
　　And with laughter her eyes.

(*Poems*, i. 81)

Such poetry draws attention to the fact that the infatuations he experienced often triggered poems about the girls or women who were their object. Elizabeth B——, for instance, was the starting point for his poem 'To Lizbie Browne' (*Poems*, i. 165).

In his fiction also, from the beginning, women played an unconventionally prominent role—as the explicit title of his (first) unpublished novel *The Poor Man and the Lady* shows. Reflecting on this fact later, Hardy told Edmund Gosse:

The first book of all had no story at all. There was just the Woman interest. It is amusing to me that I thought I knew so much about women. I was so confident about it, knew exactly what they felt and what they wanted. That was what struck Meredith with the Woman interest in the book. But he said it would never do, so I tore it all up.

Strangely, however, he does not seem to think that in his youth he got it wrong: 'But about Women; I wonder how I came to write like that. Now I know them better, I should write just the same. I think I must be right—the women always hate it so' (*Interviews*, p. 108). As this reveals, his interest went much further than physical attraction. It is true to say that, with the exception of *The Dynasts*, all his narrative work focuses on the 'Women interest' and the wider issues it involved.

The interest in and susceptibility to women that marked his childhood and early adult life found new material to react to in London. He records in the *Life* the society beauties who drew him just as he had noted the 'village beauties'. In fact the *Life* gives the impression that it is only their beauty that attracts him. For it is routine with him there to give vignettes of their appearance:

Lady Marge W—— looked pretty in gauzy muslin . . .

Lady Coleridge could honestly claim to be a beauty. Responsive and open in manner. Really fine eyes.

Miss Amélie Rives was the pretty woman of the party—a fair, pink, golden-haired creature, but not quite ethereal enough, suggesting a flesh-surface too palpably.

Presently Ellen Terry arrived—diaphanous—a sort of balsam or sea-anemone, without shadow. (*Life*, pp. 208, 229, 230, 244)

In practice his more serious relationships with upper-class women were all with those whose beauty was animated by their intelligence, cultivated tastes, and social poise. They also had literary ambitions which, to an extent, they fulfilled. They offered amongst other things the intellectual companionship which Emma could not now provide. All of them were married women: Rosamund Tomson, Agatha Thorneycroft, Agnes Grove, and most importantly Florence Henniker. Rosamund Tomson, wife of an artist Graham Tomson, had already published a volume of poems (under her husband's name) when Hardy met her in 1889. Towards the end of the year he wrote her several mildly flirtatious letters: urging her to visit Dorset, refusing to visit her himself in Sussex, adding 'but then my con-science does not prick me in saying my negative as yours ought to prick you in saying yours; for, you see—I never raised anybody's hopes' (*Letters*, i. 200). This episode lasted only for a few months. By then he had already met Agatha, wife of a sculptor, Hamo Thorney-croft. Her appearance made a deep impression on him: 'Of the people I have met this summer, the lady whose mouth recalls more fully than any other beauty's the Elizabethan metaphor "Her lips are roses full of snow" . . . is Mrs H. T——' (*Life*, p. 230). This reminder of the obsessive descriptions of Tess's pouting red mouth into which Alec d'Urberville famously forces a strawberry is not chance. Hardy later told Gosse (who reported it to Hamo Thorney-croft, who repeated it to Agatha) that he had been 'cheered up by seeing the most beautiful woman in England or rather her whom *I* think the most beautiful woman in England, her on whom I thought when I wrote Tess of the d'Urbervilles'.[9] This friendship lasted throughout his life as Agatha did not die till 1958.

But the most significant impact on Hardy during this period was made by Florence Henniker (1855–1923). So serious were Hardy's feelings for her that biographers have been forced to consider whether in this instance Hardy had real hopes of a physical relationship. This was probably the case, though he apparently remained physically faithful to Emma throughout her life. Millgate believes that by this time Hardy was explicitly looking for someone to fall in love with and that he fastened on Florence without encouragement from her. She was the daughter of Lord Houghton and the wife of a soldier, Arthur Henry Henniker-Major, and had also published three novels when they met in 1893. The meeting took place with Thomas (and Emma) Hardy at the Viceregal Lodge in Dublin where Florence's brother was Lord Lieutenant of Ireland. Hardy made use of Florence's literary ambitions to begin a correspondence that made them close friends. He evidently longed for more than this. His letters to friends are formal in style but those to Florence show an increasing warmth. The early letters of June 1893 when she was 37 and Hardy was 53 are on literary matters: books she wants, his comments on her writing, performances of Ibsen. Originally he signs himself 'Ever/ Always yours sincerely Thomas Hardy'. By 20 June he sends her 'the sermon I promised about *Tess*' and moves to a more informal signature: 'Ever sincerely yrs. T. H.'. More literary gossip follows and by August he is 'Your ever sincere friend Tom H.' By October she has sent him 'beautiful large photographs' of herself. Finally he is permanently 'Tom H.' and she becomes 'My dear little friend' (*Letters*, ii). They even collaborated on a short story, 'The Spectre of the Real'—mainly her work—which was published in 1894. Again the one-sided romance triggered poetry: according to his second wife, 'A Broken Appointment' and 'A Thunderstorm in Town' both referred to Florence Henniker. The first of these tells of a tryst not kept and reproaches a woman for not being compassionate enough:

> You love not me
> And love alone can lend you loyalty;
> —I know and knew it. But, unto the store
> Of human deeds divine in all but name,
> Was it not worth a little hour or more
> To add yet this: Once you, a woman, came
> To soothe a time-torn man; even though it be
> You love not me?

(*Poems*, i. 172)

The second poem describes a couple sheltering in a hansom cab from the rain which ceases a minute before he would have kissed her (*Poems*, ii. 18).

There is no real evidence to show that the poems describe actual moments at which Hardy felt the relationship might move to a physical level, however much he may have wanted this, since Florence evidently did not. Similarly, though it is likely that Florence influenced his conception of Sue Bridehead in *Jude* which he was writing in 1894, it is unwise to read fiction as straight biography any more than to read poems as direct personal statements of fact. The relationship continued until Florence's death in 1923, though with much-reduced intensity on Hardy's side after about 1895 when he became briefly obsessed with the lively younger woman (later Lady) Agnes Grove (1863–1926), wife of (Sir) Walter Grove. She too had literary ambitions and wrote a book on contemporary manners as well as other social commentaries. He advised her on a paper on 'What Children should be told on Physiology' (*Letters*, ii. 115).

Hardy did not keep these friendships secret. Emma knew of the correspondence and of the meetings with these women and it is clear that she resented them. The result of all this came at the end of 1894, while Hardy was at work on *Jude*, and alterations and additions were made to Max Gate. When, after this, Hardy moved his study to a new room at the back of the house, Emma took over two attic rooms immediately above. She described this separate haven to an American correspondent, Rebekah Owen, in 1899: 'I–sleep in an *Attic* or *two*! . . . My boudoir is my sweet refuge & solace—not a sound scarcely penetrates hither [*sic*]' (*Biography*, p. 391). In a letter to a recently married friend, Elspeth Graham, she speaks of the wisdom of married couples keeping apart:

Keeping separate a good deal is a wise plan in crises—and being both free—& *expecting little* neither gratitude nor attentions, love, nor *justice*, not *anything* you may set your heart on. Love interest—adoration, & all that kind of thing is usually a *failure—complete*—some one comes by & upsets your pail of milk in the end. If he belongs to the public in any way, years of devotion count for nothing. Influence can seldom be retained as years go by, & *hundreds* of wives go through a phase of disillusion—it is really a pity to have any ideals in the first place. (*Wives' Letters*, p. 15)

The estrangement that caused this physical separation had many causes. Among them were Emma's frustration at her own failure to achieve literary success, her inability to match Hardy intellectually, his reserve, his agnosticism, his obvious admiration for other women and theirs for him, and his views on marriage as expressed in *Jude*. As any wife might, she assumed that her husband's generalizations in *Jude* referred to their own marriage. Her natural jealousy at this made matters worse and they were compounded by her estrangement from Hardy's own family while he remained permanently rooted in their heart. It is impossible and unhelpful to attribute 'blame' to either Thomas or Emma. No doubt both had a share in the collapse of the marriage. Emma's feelings and resentments were recorded at the time by her in notebooks which were destroyed after her death, though not before Hardy had suffered the pain of reading them. Many of her letters were also destroyed but a few remain. One of these, to Hardy's sister Mary in 1896, reveals the depths of Emma's anger and misery. She accuses Mary of having said that she is unkind to her husband and claims:

Your brother has been outrageously unkind to me—which is *entirely your* fault: ever since I have been his wife you have done all you can to make division between us; also, you have set your family against me, though neither you nor they can truly say that I have ever been anything but, just, considerate, & kind towards you all, notwithstanding frequent low insults.

As you are in the habit of saying of people whom you dislike that they are 'mad' you should, & may well, fear, least the same be said of you; . . . I defy you ever to say such a thing of me or for you, or any one, to say that I have done anything that can be called unreasonable, or wrong or mad, or *even unkind*! And it is a wicked, spiteful & most malicious habit of yours.

The letter ends with a coda of abuse: 'You are a witch-like creature & quite equal to any amount of evil-wishing & speaking. I can imagine you & your mother & sister on your native heath raising a storm on a Walpurgis night' (*Wives' Letters*, pp. 7–8). Hardy's father, Thomas the second, died in 1892 and his mother, Jemima, in 1904 but Emma remained hostile to the rest of the Hardy family for as long as she lived. Her misery had been made worse by the works which Hardy published in the 1890s. They included in the first volume of his poetry, *Wessex Poems* (1898), poems about the women he had been infatuated with. While these fuelled her jealousy, his novels *Tess* and

Jude the Obscure also shocked her profoundly by what she saw as their sexual immorality and irreligion.

Despite his obsessively romantic attitude to women, Hardy did not see them merely as sexual objects. He held advanced views on the role of women in society. These opinions were such that they shocked even those arguing for allowing women to vote. In 1908 Millicent Fawcett, the women's suffrage leader, asked him to contribute to a pamphlet written by eminent men in support of the cause. Hardy wrote in reply:

I have for a long time been in favour of woman-suffrage. I fear I shall spoil the effect of this information (if it has any) in my next sentence by giving you my reasons. I am in favour of it becuase I think the tendency of the woman's vote will be to break up the present pernicious conventions in respect of manners, customs, religion, illegitimacy, the stereotyped household (that it must be the unit of society), the father of a woman's child (that it is anybody's business but the woman's own, except in cases of disease or insanity). (*Letters*, iii. 238)

He believes that men who have hesitated to speak out on such matters while women were helplessly dependent will speak out to further these changes once women are equal citizens with the vote.

Though Emma was a (pacific) supporter of women's suffrage, she was always strictly conventional in moral and religious matters. This meant that his views on the evils of marriage which Hardy elaborated in *Jude* and elsewhere, alienated her. He referred specifically to the difficulty of divorce in an article in *Nash's Magazine*, 'Laws the Cause of Misery', and asserted his belief that 'a marriage should be dissolvable at the wish of either party, if that party prove it to be a cruelty to him or her'. He described the current marriage laws as 'the gratuitous cause of at least half the misery of the community'.[10] By the time he was awarded the Order of Merit in 1910 she commented bitterly that he had refused the knighthood which would have given her the title of 'Lady Hardy' because he only wanted honours for himself.

It came, however, as a violent shock to Hardy when, shortly after the piece in *Nash's Magazine*, Emma who had suffered what he took to be only minor symptoms for her age, was found by a maid dying in her attic on 27 November 1912. In a state of grief and guilt he then found and read (before destroying) Emma's unhappy record of her life with him. In doing this he could no longer cut himself off from the wretched existence she had led which made such a brutal contrast to their early days in Cornwall. He had partly been enabled to alienate himself in this way by taking refuge in the intimacy he had formed with Florence Emily Dugdale (1879–1937) from 1905 onwards. How he met her is unclear: possibly through Florence Henniker, possibly as a result of a fan-letter from her to him. She too, like Mary and his cousin Tryphena, had trained as an elementary school teacher. She had also published children's stories and some journalism. Though when they met she was 26 or so to his 64 or 65, he was able (as with Agatha Thorneycroft, Agnes Grove, and Florence Henniker) to forge a bond from their shared literary interests and her admiration for him. Gradually she made herself useful, even invaluable, as typist and companion not only to him but to Emma. Clearly, in view of what followed, Hardy fell in love with her, though the relationship was probably not consummated before Emma's death. Immediately after the death Florence, to whom he was already writing as 'My dearest F.' (*Letters*, iv. 136), moved into Max Gate with Kate, his sister, as chaperone. By the next summer (1913) he had proposed to her. But already the remorse and guilt he felt about Emma had been inscribed in the message on his wreath at Emma's funeral when she was buried at Stinsford: he described himself as 'lonely' and signed himself 'with the old affection'.

What happened next ironically supports Emma's claim that he only understood the women he created in fiction. In March 1913 accompanied by his brother, Henry, he returned to St Juliot in Cornwall where in 1870, forty-two years earlier, he had met and fallen in love with Emma. He found it very painful and as usual his strong emotion about a woman triggered the writing of poetry. This consisted of the 'Poems of 1912–13': some twenty-one poems recalling brilliantly his early days with his first wife whose loss he now mourned:

> You were she who abode
> By those red-veined rocks far West,
> You were the swan-necked one who rode
> Along the beetling Beeny Crest,
> And, reining nigh me,
> Would muse and eye me,
> While Life unrolled us its very best.

Why, then, latterly did we not speak,
Did we not think of those days long dead,
And ere your vanishing strive to seek
That time's renewal? We might have said,
'In this bright spring weather
    We'll visit together
Those places that once we visited.'

(*Poems*, ii. 47–8)

The past was a country which always moved Hardy to creativity intellectually and imaginatively and these outstanding poems are no exception. He published the poems in 1914 in *Satires of Circumstance*. By this time he had already married Florence Dugdale who, not surprisingly, was deeply pained by the poems which recalled so powerfully his early time with Emma and gave it enduring magic and value. No wonder she wrote to Lady (Alda) Hoare in December 1914: 'But I must confess to you—& I would confess this to noone else—the book pains me horribly, & yet I read it with a terrible fascination. It seems to me that I am an utter failure if my husband can publish such a *sad, sad* book.' (*Wives' Letters*, p. 104). As the tone suggests hers was a sad, sad personality and Hardy's second wife does seem to have been of a melancholy disposition. She even found Max Gate, where they continued to live, lonely and depressing despite the many welcome (and unwelcome) visitors. The welcome included T. E. Lawrence (Lawrence of Arabia), Siegfried Sassoon, E. M. Forster, John Galsworthy, George Bernard Shaw, John Drinkwater, and the Prince of Wales. There were also players from Oxford who performed a Greek play and the London cast of the dramatized version of *Tess* who acted in the house. For Hardy himself, when recovered from Emma's death, the second marriage appears to have been reasonably successful—much more so than the first. Florence was on more equal terms than Emma had been and better able to understand her husband. She was also from the start ready to subordinate her needs and interests to his entirely. She was only 35 and he 73 when they married and she was therefore still of an age to have children. In a letter to Marie Stopes, the pioneer of contraception, after thanking her for advice, she mentions a discussion with Hardy: 'I find on talking to him that the idea of my having a child at his age fills him with terror ... He said he would have welcomed a child when we married first, ten years ago, but now it

Emma (facing the camera), Nellie Gosse and Hardy, 1890.

Florence and Hardy at Max Gate $c.$1920.

would kill him with anxiety to have to father one' (*Wives' Letters*, p. 203).

Florence's melancholy moved to outright distress when, like Emma before her, she became jealous—of a local Dorset woman, Gertrude Bugler. The latter had appeared in amateur perform- ances of dramatizations of Hardy's novels. When she finally took the part of Tess in a 1924 performance of the play, he saw in her the living incarnation of Tess as he had imagined her. Apparently infatuated, he became her patron and tried to further her acting career by suggesting that she should appear in the London pro- duction of *Tess*. Rumours were active and Florence, angry and jealous, went privately to see Mrs Bugler to ask her to withdraw from the project in order to protect Hardy's reputation. This Gertrude Bugler agreed to do and he never knew how she had been manipulated.

Religion and its Loss

From the mid-1880s, however, and throughout his second marriage Hardy remained amazingly productive and was writing his self- ghosted 'biography' when he died. When he abandoned novel- writing for poetry he felt that he had found his true vocation from which writing prose had distracted him for a temporary period. This belief found justification in the poetic volumes that he produced: *Poems of the Past and the Present* (1901), *Time's Laughingstocks* (1909), *Satires of Circumstance* (1914), *Moments of Vision* (1917), *Late Lyrics and Earlier* (1922), *The Famous Tragedy of the Queen of Cornwall* (1923), *Human Shows, Far Phantasies, Songs and Trifles* (1925), *Winter Words* (1928). But what he may have seen as his major achievement was the long verse-drama *The Dynasts*, published in three parts in 1904, 1906, and 1908. It was written to be read rather than acted, though parts of it were dramatized and performed. It drew together in a panoramic form many of his interests. It centres on Napoleon I whose aggressive activities in Europe between 1805 and 1812 are covered in relation to their impact on ordinary English people. These events are watched over by supernatural personifica- tions: the Spirit of the Years, the Spirit of the Pities, the Spirit of Rumour, the Spirits Sinister and Ironic, all with their accompanying choruses. *The Dynasts*, which had some success, though much less than his novels and poems, addressed the question of the nature and cause of human history. The Cause is provisionally labelled the Immanent Will. The work represents in part an attempt by Hardy to come to terms with a loss of faith in a Christian God. This is the fourth strand which threads through his whole life and one with which he is particularly concerned in the last phase of his life. During the period there are many recorded comments which reveal fluctuating views.

Hardy's loss of faith was not a sudden event. He himself claimed that as a child to be a clergyman had been his dream. It appears that it was a susceptibility to the ritual and music of the High Church form of worship that drew him rather than matters of doctrine. When articled to the architect Hicks between 1856 and 1860 his interest in institutional religion was still strong enough for him to become involved in ardent discussion with a fellow pupil Henry Bastow on the comparative merits of infant and adult baptism. Even when he moved to London in 1862 he was still at first a regular worshipper at St Mary's church, Kilburn, and occasionally attended church until about 1864 when his attendance, like his reading of scripture, declined. By this time he had read works like Mantell's *The Wonders of Geology* and Charles Darwin's *The Origin of Species* (1859) which were likely to shake belief in the accuracy of the biblical account of creation. The abandonment of his university and clerical ambitions in 1866 marked a further stage in his estrangement from Christian orthodoxy which slowly developed as his reading increased. By 1885 he had declared himself in favour of disestablishing the Anglican church and separating it from the state, 'leaving to voluntary bodies the organization of whatever societies they may think best for teaching their various forms of doctrinal religion' (*Letters*, i. 136–7). As has been said, while he was shedding 'doctrinal religion', Emma was unwaveringly clinging to it, as well as discounting evolutionary theories. Even for Hardy the emotional and social pull remained for the rest of his life. As late as 1922 he told an acquaintance: 'The liturgy of the Church of England is a noble thing. So are Tate and Brady's Psalms. These are the things that people need and should have.' At the same time he said 'I believe in going to church. It is a moral drill, and people must have something. If there is no church in a country village, there is nothing' (*Interviews*, p. 178).

As to his own beliefs in the early twentieth century, one thing is clear: he had lost any trust in the idea of ultimate justice offered by Christianity. He speaks in 1899 of Robert Browning having the 'smug Christian optimism worthy of a dissenting grocer' (*Letters*, ii. 216). The injustice of life was the rock on which his belief foundered, leaving acceptable only 'the religion of emotional morality and altruism that was taught by Jesus Christ'. But he sees even this as not specific to Christianity: 'other moral religions within whose sphere the name of Christ has never been heard, teach the same thing' (*Life*, pp. 358–9). Although tormented by the problem represented by human misery and the apparently blind injustice of existence, he repeatedly denied that he saw the Ultimate Cause as a being who 'rejoices in the mischief he has wrought' (*Life*, p. 256) or as an 'imbecile jester' (*Life*, p. 438).

The point he makes is that his hostile references to religion were not fixed or permanent beliefs on his part but 'fanciful alternatives to several others'. He offers a sharp rebuke to Alfred Noyes, a critic who had taken this erroneous view of his work, in a letter of 1920:

In my fancies, or poems of the imagination, I have of course called this Power all sorts of names—never supposing they would be taken for more than fancies, ... as mere impressions of the moment, exclamations, in fact. But it has always been my misfortune to presuppose a too intelligent reading public, and no doubt people will go on thinking that I really believe the Prime Mover to be a malignant old gentleman, a sort of King of Dahomey,—an idea which so far from my holding it, is to me irresistibly comic. (*Letters*, vi. 54)

In asserting that the prime mover is *not* like the King of Dahomey or one who wishes for human sacrifices, he spells out a view of what in his opinion it *is* (or is at least for now):

my sober opinion—so far as I have any definite one—of the Cause of Things has been defined in scores of places, and is that of a great many ordinary thinkers:- that the said Cause is neither moral nor immoral, but *un*moral:- 'loveless and hateless' I have called it; 'which neither good nor evil knows'—etc.,—etc. (you will find plenty of these definitions in 'The Dynasts' as well as in short poems, and I am surprised that you have not taken them in).

The opinions he describes in this letter to Noyes are perhaps precisely captured when he calls them 'exclamations'. They are exclamations of horror and despair at the real or fictional sight of human or animal suffering and misery. These parallel his comments on war in his poetry and in his letters. The Boer War (1899–1902), with its huge slaughter, stirred him in this way so that he wrote to Florence Henniker (whose husband was a soldier) of the attack on a Boer general and his troops: 'How horrible it all is: they say that his wife & other women are in that river-bed with his unfortunate army' (*Letters*, ii. 248). The First World War (1914–18) elicited the same response, although he came to believe that England was innocent for once. But as he is still inclined to attribute blame, he castigates organized religion. This is illustrated by a response to the request of a daily newspaper for his views on the war:

While as to general opinions & prophecies, they would be laughed at: e.g., such a highly rational one as that all the Churches in Europe should frankly admit the utter failure of theology, & put their heads together to form a new religion which should at least have some faint connection with morality. (*Letters*, v. 43)

No doubt his mood was also darkened by the death in December 1915 of his sister Mary, of whom he wrote that in childhood she was 'almost my only companion' (*Letters*, v. 135). So much so that when the war was over in 1918, he wrote 'I confess that I take a smaller interest in the human race since this outburst than I did before' (*Letters*, v. 289). Despite this pessimistic claim, there is evidence that Hardy retained a nostalgia for a benign Absolute. Hence his comment in the early 1900s 'I often wish that I had lived in the Middle Ages, when the Church was supreme and unquestioned' (*Interviews*, p. 75). William Archer, a friend, quotes remarks which bear a similar inference—though the tone is playful. They were made in answer to Archer's question as to whether he had ever seen a ghost:

Never the ghost of a ghost. Yet I should think I am cut out by nature for a ghost-seer. My nerves vibrate very readily; people say I am almost morbidly imaginative; my will to believe is perfect. If ever ghost wanted to manifest himself, I am the very man he should apply to. But no—the spirits don't seem to see it! (*Interviews*, p. 68)

He writes similarly to an acquaintance, Caleb Saleeby:

Half my time (particularly when I write verse) I believe—in the modern use of the word—not only in things that Bergson does, but in spectres, mysterious voices, intuitions, omens, dreams, haunted places &c., &c.

Then characteristically he reverses his position: 'But then, I do not believe in these in the old sense of belief any more for that' (*Letters*, v. 79).

His thinking on religious belief is thus marked by a dichotomy between a savage pessimism and a nostalgic desire to take an optimistic view. A similar conflict is visible in his attitude to the social class from which he came: a desire to laud and defend it and a desire to disown it. It is also possible to see a clash between the sympathy and understanding for the contemporary plight of women displayed in his novels and his treatment of Emma in the latter part of his life, as well as his insensitivity to Florence's feelings over the 'Poems of 1912–13'. His own contrasting lives in London and in Dorset take a similar double shape. In a final irony of circumstance, on his death on 11 January 1928, after much discussion, the ashes of his body were buried in Westminster Abbey with great pomp and his heart (which had been kept in a biscuit tin) was buried in Stinsford with Emma. The symbolism seems perfect for a writer whose major novels are marked by an ambiguity which reflects the conflicts of his age.

CHAPTER 2

THE FABRIC OF SOCIETY

THE personal life described in the last chapter spanned a period not only of major change in all aspects of society but one in which there was a startling increase in the rapidity with which change took place. In Hardy's early childhood, the railway had not yet reached the nearby town of Dorchester. By his sixties he was accustomed to being driven around the area in a hired car, though he refused to travel at more than twenty-five miles per hour.[1] By 1917, when he was 77 years old, he watched searchlights scouring the skies for German aircraft which were attacking London. When he was born, in 1840, no woman could vote in parliamentary elections though for three years the country had been ruled by a queen. The franchise was confined to men of the upper class and the better-off part of the middle classes. This meant that there were less then a million voters out of a population of over 26 million. By 1918 all men over the age of 21 and some women over 30 could vote. It was 1928 before all women over 21 received the vote.

The economy of the country also swung fairly rapidly between periods of prosperity and depression. There was a period of decline in 'the hungry forties' which were also marked by the rise of Chartist demands for, amongst other things, universal male suffrage. This situation changed after the repeal of the Corn Laws in 1846 which, by protecting the price of British corn and the interests of land-owners against foreign imports, damaged industry and was thought to keep the price of bread, the 'first food' of the working classes, high. In the 1850s and 1860s followed the so-called 'high-Victorian' period of prosperity for the middle and upper classes and of relative adequacy for their 'inferiors'. But the boom ended in about 1873 as one phase of industrial development world-wide gave place to an-other. In the earlier phase Britain had been in the forefront of advance and flourished in part as a result of helping to provide through its own industries the infrastructure such as railways and ships of those who were to become, in the later phase, their competitors. A long depression then persisted through the 1880s and into the mid-1890s.

The financial prosperity of the High Victorian period was accompanied amongst the upper and middle classes by a surge of national confidence which is exemplified by the Great Exhibition in 1851 and the national hullabaloo surrounding it. Partly at the instigation of the Prince Consort, Albert, this was organized as a competitive exhibition of the art and manufacture 'of all Nations' for the purposes of 'exhibition, of competition and of encouragement'. The suggestion of self-congratulation in the last phrase is borne out by the nature of the Exhibition and responses to it. It was grandiosely housed in the purpose-built 'Crystal Palace' in Hyde Park: a glass structure with an iron framework six times larger than St Paul's and more importantly four times larger than St Peter's in Rome, and complete with gigantic fountain and huge trees. It was a monument not only to consumerism but to self-preening nationalism. The *Illustrated London News* of 17 May 1851 asserts that French criticism of London as 'sombre' has given way before 'the gayest, most fairy-like, most beautiful and original building in the world'. Furthermore 'London is not simply the capital of a great nation, but the metropolis of the world'.[2]

Feeding this jingoism was the imperialism of the politicians and military establishment which led to two of the three wars that took place in Hardy's lifetime, the Crimean War against Russia from 1854 to 1856 and the Boer War of 1899 to 1902 against the Boer domination. Hardy, who was largely anti-imperialist and fiercely distressed by the war in South Africa, did not believe that Britain was responsible for the last war in his lifetime—the First World War.

Throughout all these kaleidoscopic changes Hardy remained emotionally rooted in rural Dorset. He was drawn back there irresistibly in 1881 as he felt his creative powers atrophying in London and settled in Dorset for the last forty-seven years of his life. What determined the nature and quality of life in his rural society, however, was the wider society described above of which the West Country was a part and to which Hardy moved as a young man. It was in that matrix that social and industrial changes were taking place.

Country and Town

Britain is a small island and in the nineteenth century it was already becoming overcrowded and apparently shrinking. In 1851 England, Wales, and Scotland had about 21 million inhabitants; and by 1901 there were some 38 million people occupying the same space. The shrinkage referred to was effected by the new speed of travel. The focus on industries producing textiles, steel, and machinery had led to the development of an efficient railway system (to add to the existing canal network). The rapid expansion of railway lines during the 'Railway Mania' of the 1840s transformed the speed of travel as the invention of the jet-engine did in the 1940s. By the 1840s the journey from London to Birmingham could be made in five and a half hours; that from London to Edinburgh, which took two days and two nights by horse-drawn coach, could by 1862 be made in ten and a half hours. One traveller wrote of the latter trip that he spent it 'travelling in an armchair in a little carpeted drawing-room without fatigue and almost without motion . . . Our successors can have no such gain on our present travelling even if they are shot like a cannon ball through a pneumatic tube'.[3] By the 1860s when Hardy moved to London, long-distance trains averaged about forty miles per hour and speeds continued to increase. In terms of time for getting from one place to another, distances became shorter. Nor was such travel confined to the rich, for there were three classes of accommodation in rail carriages and by 1875 the third class was used by three-quarters of all who travelled by train. In 1863 (before the death of Dickens) London had acquired its first underground (steam) railway, the Metropolitan Line. The coming of railways also effected the standardization of timekeeping throughout the country.

Hardy does not seem to have seen railways as symbolic—with one exception. In *A Laodicean* the threat from a passing train to the hero and heroine while they are admiring the construction of a tunnel built by the woman's father creates a sexual frisson between them:

They were crossing the railway to ascend by the opposite path, Somerset keeping his eye on the interior of the tunnel for safety, when suddenly there arose a noise and shriek from the contrary direction behind the trees. Both knew in a moment what it meant, and each seized the other as they rushed off the permanent way . . . [The train] rushed past them, causing

Paula's dress, hair, and ribbons to flutter violently . . . Neither spoke, and they went up several steps holding each other by the hand, till, becoming conscious of the fact, she withdrew hers; whereupon Somerset stopped and looked earnestly at her; but her eyes were averted . . . (chapter 12)

The building of railways made great changes to the landscape through which they were driven. Dickens had earlier seen them as agents of devastation such as he describes in *Dombey and Son* (1848). From another viewpoint the railways were a miracle of engineering and human determination comparable with the Pyramids. Huge viaducts were built with little machinery, as were cuttings and embankments, made necessary by the terrain that had to be negotiated over rivers or valleys or through hills. Certainly the main London termini like St Pancras, Euston, and Paddington were created with the appearance of huge temples to man's invincible conquest of nature. The similarity was noticed by a writer in the *Quarterly Review* in 1872, though with some aesthetic distaste on the grounds of the inappropriateness of such size and decoration to a mere railway station. Referring to the 'Midland Railway Terminus' he asserts tartly:

here the 'public taste' has been exactly suited, and every kind of architectural decoration has been made thoroughly common and unclean; the building, inside and out, is covered with ornament, and there is polished marble enough to furnish a Cathedral; the very parapet of the cab road is panelled and perforated, at a cost that would have supplied foot-warmers to all trains for years to come.[4]

Other forms of communication between different parts of the country also came into use in the early part of Hardy's adult life as he embarked on his career as a novelist. Already the railways had enhanced the postal service to a high level of efficiency, with next-day delivery a normal expectation that was regularly fulfilled. In addition, in the 1870s the telephone came into use and the electric telegraph which had been developed in the 1840s (an obtrusive plot mechanism in Hardy's *A Laodicean*, 1881) had been taken over by the GPO. Further, personal freedom of travel became available in the 1880s with the development of the pneumatic tyre which facilitated the use of the bicycle. It caused huge excitement and meant a new freedom for women as well as men. Certainly it fired Hardy with an interest he seems never to have shown in railways. He and Emma were a familiar sight to neighbours on their bicycles towards the end of the century.

While these hectic changes were taking place nationwide, the countryside to some extent withered or at least shrank. In England and Wales in 1801 approximately 65 per cent of the population lived and worked in the countryside and the rest in towns and cities. By the end of the century the figures were reversed and only approximately 23 per cent of people lived in the country and 77 per cent in urban areas. The reasons for this mass movement were economic: unemployment, poverty, and homelessness. Many popular novelists in the mid-century focused on the horrors of urban working-class life at home and in factories. These are familiar from 'condition-of-England' novels such as Frances Trollope's *Michael Armstrong, the Factory Boy* (1840); Elizabeth Gaskell's *Mary Barton* (1848) and her *North and South* (1855); and Charles Dickens's *Hard Times* (1854). The conditions these narratives describe were also known at the time from the reports of government commissions and other bodies into matters like housing, factory conditions, sanitation, and prostitution in major cities. Some of these resulted in attempts at improvement by Parliament through the Factory Acts (such as those of 1844, 1847, 1850, 1864, and 1878 attempting to regulate hours and conditions) and Public Health Acts (such as those of 1848 and 1875).

The nature of working-class life in the country is summed up by a social historian, John Burnett:

The general state of the rural labourer between 1850 and 1914 was one of chronic poverty and want, acute at the beginning of the period, slightly alleviated towards the end of it. His real position was summed up accurately enough by Sidney Godolphin Osborne when he remarked, 'The constant wonder is that the labourer can live at all', and even more succinctly by Canon Girdlestone's comment that labourers 'did not live in the proper sense of the word, they merely didn't die'.[5]

In rural areas virtually the only work was on the land (apart from a few other trades like saddlers and blacksmiths) and it was seasonal, particularly if the farming was arable. So periods of hardship had become established as part of the cycle. In addition the workers were at the mercy of annual variations in the weather which produced good or bad harvests. Sometimes, as in 1879, summers were too wet and sometimes, as in 1894, there was too little rain. In both cases bad harvests resulted. Such conditions are crucial in the downfall of Henchard in *The Mayor of Casterbridge*: 'The farmer's income was ruled by the wheat-crop within his own horizon, and the wheat-crop by the weather. Thus in person he became a sort of flesh-barometer, with feelers always directed to the sky and wind around him' (chapter 26). The agricultural depression of 1873–96, mentioned earlier, was bad enough to bring about the setting up of commissions in 1882 and 1897 to enquire into the causes. Nor did agricultural prosperity for landowners always benefit their workers. By the mid-century farmers had begun to review their methods of working. This led to the introduction of better drainage, better seeds, new breeds of cattle, and machinery which improved their profits. But these benefits did not trickle down to those whom they employed. Ironically, agricultural workers in areas like Lancashire and Yorkshire fared better than those remote from towns because competition from factories (which paid better) forced a slight increase in agricultural wages.

Dorset, like the West Country, was a blackspot in Hardy's time and had the lowest agricultural wages in England. These averaged seven shillings and sixpence a week in 1850, which was two shillings and sixpence less than the cost of keeping a man in the workhouse, entry into which was after 1834 the main method of obtaining public welfare assistance. A slight rise in Dorset wages after 1872 only came about because agricultural trade unions developed and migration to towns made labour scarcer. In the period after 1872, the region's farmers shifted from arable farming to more livestock and dairy production. So better wages for some were accompanied by unemployment and migration or the workhouse for others. Further, women, who were paid less than men, could conveniently be employed in dairy work. At the same time the problems of housing increased because the older system of tenancies attaching to two or three lives gave way to annual leases, as Hardy noticed more than once.

A measure of the level of rural poverty is provided by an overview of the expenditure of a particular labourer in Somerset in the relatively prosperous period for the West Country of the early 1870s. The man had a wife and four children and earned £31. 16s. 6d. in a year. Out of this the largest amount, £11. 14s., about one-third, was spent on bread; £5. 4s, about one-sixth, went on rent. Three pounds, about one-tenth, was spent on renting ground and buying seed potatoes for the growing of a crop, the second major food item.

Other items of diet—treacle, butter, and tea etc.—cost £2. The rest was spent on necessaries such as coal, soap, candles, butter, repairs, and a penny a week for each child's education in the local school. It is noticeable that the diet of the family contained no meat and even in areas where any meat was eaten, the usual type was bacon, the cheapest. If a small amount could be afforded it would go to the man of the house as 'bread-winner', a term which takes on a particular resonance in the light of this particular family's diet.

A similar general picture emerges from a contemporary account of conditions in North Devon:

The labourer has no privileges whatever. He rents his potato-ground at a high rate. Though fuel is said to be given to him he really pays its full value by grubbing up for it in old hedges in after-hours. In wet weather or in sickness his wages entirely cease so that he seldom makes a full week. The cottages, as a rule, are not fit to house pigs in. The labourer breakfasts on tea-kettle broth, hot water poured on bread and flavoured with onions; dines on bread and hard cheese at 2d. a pound, with cider very washy and sour, and sups on potatoes or cabbage greased with a tiny bit of fat bacon. He seldom more than sees or smells butcher's meat. He is long lived, but in the prime of life 'crippled up', i.e. disabled by rheumatism, the result of wet clothes with no fire to dry them by for use next morning, poor living and sour cider.[6]

This picture is substantiated by the precise example of the diet of a particular Dorset farm worker and his family in the 1860s. The following was a typical day: '*Breakfast*—water broth, bread, butter, tea with milk. *Dinner*—husband has bread and cheese; family take tea besides. *Supper*—hot fried bacon and cabbage, or bread and cheese'.[7] This was the life of the poorest class of worker on the land when Hardy was training in Dorchester and London as an architect's assistant.

Social Class

THE SHIFT TO A CLASS SYSTEM

As is already evident, manifestations of social position and perceptions of one's own and that of others were all-pervasive in Victorian society. By the time of Hardy's birth a class system was securely in place so that the dominant discourse—though not the only one— was an account of society as three classes or groups with various subsections: upper, middle, and lower or working class. This took precedence over the earlier language of *rank* which for centuries had offered an interpretation of society more suited to an agrarian society. Metaphorically *rank* was encoded as a divinely ordered dance or a 'Great Chain of Being'. The traditional significance of these metaphors was that society was a mathematically elegant arrangement devised by God for the benefit of all concerned, whether high or low. The picture seemed to offer security and permanence, with benevolence always trickling down from rank to rank and service passing equally efficiently up and down.

This interpretation of society as ranked was based on a grading largely dependent on inherited status at birth, ownership or non-ownership of land, as well as profession or occupation. Its basic unit was the individual, not the group, and it provided each with a personal identity, a role to play, a status, and a set of social mores including, at least theoretically, mutual respect between the ranks. In practice, though, in contradicting the interpretation of *rank* as expressive of the harmony of a neatly graduated system, an association existed between the idea of the 'lower orders' and inferiority. They had always been potentially a *rabble* or a *mob*, not just 'plebeian' but 'coarse', 'ill-bred', or worse. This implied superiors who were élite in all senses, with the necessary intelligence and experience to control the rest who represented the lesser species of mankind. It was and persists as an *us/them* model alongside the class model. The rank system had a certain plausibility in an agrarian society where there was personal contact between the landlord, the tenant farmer, and the farm labourer or other village workers. The practice survived in rural areas well into the nineteenth century of referring to workers and apprentices who lived on the farm for at least a year, not as 'labourers' but as 'servants'—a term implying a relationship with the family.

The description of society as class-based is not of course merely a matter of terminology. The new language of class at first competed with and then dominated but never entirely ousted that of rank/order/station as industrialism developed in the latter part of the eighteenth century. The location of the workplace was changed as cotton and other goods were produced in factories by large groups of workers for a single employer. The term *class* had previously been used in a neutral or empty sense of 'sort' or 'kind'. It was referring often to the classification of natural species. By the 1780s it had also come to have a social application for the general gradings of people as *lower*, *middling*, or *higher*. A factor in attaching class terminology to three groups in this way was the writings of classical political economists beginning in the latter half of the eighteenth century: Adam Smith's *An Inquiry into the Origin and Nature of the Wealth of Nations* (1776) and David Ricardo's *The Principles of Political Economy and Taxation* (1817), as well as J. S. Mill's *Principles of Political Economy* (1848) which set up trade unionism as one of the most significant issues of the day. These writers were trying to describe mechanistically and in terms of economics the nature and relationships of the elements comprising industrial society: land, stock/capital, and labour. The elements corresponded roughly but obviously in human terms to three groups of people: landowners, entrepreneurs, and labourers. Smith, Ricardo, and others were concerned to describe precisely, at an abstract level, how the three components of the economy interacted. It seems their assumption was that they would provide a description that was accurate in economic terms; and they were not concerned with the social status of the groups involved. But what was argued over as an economic value lent itself easily to an equation with social value or status. Thus the broadly three-class system seemed to have the support of economic theory, though still overlapping with the perception of rank. It was also clearly a more accurate picture of the relations between employers and workers than a supposedly ranked system.

Such a framework, and the language in which it was couched, was unsuited to the remaining agrarian workers. They still in a sense represented a ranked society, based on individual not group relationships, in which the worker had direct contact with his employer. Many workers on the land moved, as has been said, to the new industrial society but presumably with feelings of disorientation. Hardy's upbringing in a still fairly remote Dorset village means that he spent his early life in a more obviously ranked society. Like others he moved from country to town and in his case the shift to a different kind of social organization was complicated by a move across a class border.

INDICATORS OF CLASS

Which class one belonged to determined most aspects of life, as did the subclasses; for the three general groupings were too broad to provide a satisfactory account of individual status and identity for each of those included. Physical arrangements often spelt out social status: three differently priced classes of accommodation on trains; saloon bars for the lower middle class and public (or working-class) bars in public houses; the types of housing available; the absence of state schools. Even seating arrangements in churches, with rented well-placed pews for the better-off, indicated class status: the 1851 census of England and Wales commented on poor church attendance by the working classes:

One chief cause of the dislike which the labouring population entertain for religious services is thought to be the maintenance of those distinctions by which they are separated as a class from the class above them. Working men, it is contended, cannot enter our religious structures without having pressed upon their notice some memento of inferiority. The existence of pews and the position of the free seats are, it is said, alone sufficient to deter them from our churches.[8]

The census goes on to point out that where sects such as Methodists have given up rented pews, more working-class people attend services.

These comments suggest a fairly widespread recognition and dislike of marks of 'inferiority' by those subjected to them. More serious markers were the absence of a right to vote even after the 1832 Reform Act had extended the franchise to include a substantial proportion of middle-class men. Gradations within the working and middle classes became important as a form of self-assertion at a time when a large number of people were assumed by those in a superior class to compose a homogeneous group with the same characteristics. By the middle of the century the descriptive phrases 'lower middle class' and then 'upper middle class' came into use. Clearly, one determining factor in fixing class status was the money available to procure a particular lifestyle in terms of housing, education, food, clothing, and the rest. *A Manual of Domestic Economy* (1857) by J. H. Walsh, originally addressed to families spending from £100 to £1,000 a year, gave in its 1873 edition an estimate of the income which produced the four gradations into which it divided the middle class. These were: salaries of £150 for the lower middle class and then upper grades at £350, £750, and £1,500 per annum. Those at the bottom of the scale were likely to be some clerks, small shopkeepers, and trained elementary school teachers, all aspirants to respectability.

At the upper end of the social scale were the aristocracy and the rich, whether newly so or with inherited money. Here markers of inclusion were significant for those who made money in manufacturing or commerce or through some artistic talent. Hardy's aspirations in this direction have already been indicated. Those who were accepted could follow a social course dictated by 'Society's' rituals. These were based on a summer 'Season' at the London house (or in Hardy's case with friends or in lodgings), involving receptions, visits to the theatre, or the Royal Academy exhibitions. The Season was followed by a return to the country in the autumn and visits to others' country house parties. Marriageable girls were put on the market by being presented at Court and attending a coming-out ball. These are some of the activities in which Hardy involved himself and where he met the women who successively captivated him. In this layer of society, by the 1860s, elaborate dinner parties such as he attended had become important symbols of prestige, both in respect of the elaboration of food and the rituals of its service and consumption. The Queen apparently ate only a boiled egg for breakfast but her status was made clear by the fact that she ate it from a gold egg-cup with a gold spoon. The rest of the royal family had five courses for breakfast and the future Edward VII sustained himself for the day by choosing from (typically) eggs, bacon, trout, cutlets, chops or steak, woodcock, snipe, or chicken. Royal luncheons required ten or twelve courses, as did dinner. Lower down the social scale, Isabella Beeton's *The Book of Household Management* (1861) gives directions for a 'Ball Supper' menu of six courses or a plain family dinner for the professional family of four substantial courses. In the 1860s and 1870s ritual required guests to be punctually late by exactly a quarter of an hour.

Food, clothes, and entertainment suited to a higher class could be bought if money became available. What was not so readily acquired in crossing from one class to another was the 'correct' way of speaking. In a class-obsessed society speech was the great giveaway amongst aspirants to gentility, including men who wished to be accepted as gentlemen. Amongst the many handbooks of advice on domestic habits such as food, manners, household arrangements, and forms of address to different people from dukes downwards were works such as *Vulgarities of Speech Corrected* (1826) or John Walker's *Critical Pronouncing Dictionary and Expositor of the English Language* which, already published in 1791, was extremely popular well into the nineteenth century. James Murray, who became General Editor of the *Oxford English Dictionary*, described Walker's volume as 'supreme in the domain of pronunciation': supreme, that is, in describing how to get rid of a local accent and acquire the kind which since the early eighteenth century had been prescribed as the correct pronunciation of a gentleman or lady. Though all varieties of a language represent a complete and efficient system of communication, this particular variety of London English had been, since the sixteenth century, regarded as a marker of superior status which did not reveal the speaker's place of origin. It was 'educated' or 'correct' though, like other varieties, it changed markedly between 1550 and 1800 and more slowly thereafter. The status of this variety of language is reflected in Hardy's own changing speech as well as in literary conventions of the day. Throughout the century there prevailed a tendency in novels to treat such correct speech as more than a marker of gentility. Or rather, as more than a marker of gentility viewed only as a matter of surfaces. To speak 'correctly' was necessary for a gentleman but being a gentleman supposedly involved considerations of moral as well as social worth. Consequently a convention developed of habitually making any central character in a novel who was held up as an example of sound morality speak 'a language fit for heroes'. A prime example is the eponymous hero of Dickens's *Oliver Twist* (1838) who, though born and brought up in a workhouse, speaks like all the middle-class characters in the text because, as the Preface explains, he represents 'the principle of Good surviving through every adverse circumstance, and triumphing at last'.

References to socially unacceptable lapses in speech abound in novels throughout the period. In Elizabeth Gaskell's *North and South* the middle-class heroine Margaret Hale is reproved by her mother for picking up working-class terms in a northern factory town: 'Margaret, don't get to use these horrid Milton words. "Slack of work": it is a provincialism. What will your Aunt Shaw say if she hears you use it on her return?' (volume ii, chapter 4). As late as the 1880s and 1890s George Gissing, the son of a small shopkeeper in Yorkshire who, like Hardy, moved to London to a life as a writer, makes such comments. Gissing, too, is preoccupied with social (and linguistic) borderlines. Cusse, in *Born in Exile*, is a doubtful case: 'There was no flagrant offence in the man. He spoke with passable accent . . . but one could not dissociate him from the counter' (chapter 3). Such comments are frequent in this novel. Peak is vitriolic in his comments which indicate his own social insecurity:

Now, I by no means hate all orders of uneducated people . . . But the London vulgar I abominate, root and branch. The mere sound of their voices nauseates me; their vilely grotesque accent and pronunciation— bah! I could write a paper to show that they are essentially the basest of English mortals. (part 2, chapter 2)

Widdowson in Gissing's *The Odd Women* (1893) has inherited enough money to live in a middle-class style but is only on the very verge of social acceptability: 'His utterance fell short of perfect refinement but seemed that of an educated man' (chapter 4). It is in this context that Hardy's change in speech habits and his wish to conceal it needs to be set. Such alteration was virtually predictable at the time in someone moving to a middle-class occupation and lifestyle. Demonstrably, most external aspects of everyday life were constrained by perceptions of class.

THEORIES ABOUT THE CLASS SYSTEM

The inequity of the social system in terms of the physical privations of a majority of the population was plain enough to require a rationale which showed such conditions to be necessary and to be compatible with a Christian society's view of itself. Broadly the assumptions that made this possible were: that 'betterment' was available to such of the working class as were worthy of it; and that the middle and upper classes had the wisdom and experience to do what was best for everyone. Briefly, these theories could be summed up as a belief in social mobility and in paternalism.

The first of these explanations of inequality is represented in Samuel Smiles's best-selling *Self-Help* (1859) which might today be subtitled 'It could be you!' This work elaborates the view that society is a gymnasium full of ladders up which the virtuously self-reliant and diligent, as opposed to the viciously dependent and idle, could climb to prosperity and respectability. Its opening asserts: 'The spirit of self-help is the root of all genuine growth in the individual . . . it constitutes the true source of national vigour and strength. Help from without is often enfeebling in its effects.'9 This convenient argument, not unfamiliar at the close of the twentieth century, shifted the onus for inequality from the prosperous while inciting the poor to struggle harder. Only will-power and some talent was needed to achieve monetary and social success. Smiles supports this theory with examples of those who have risen through their own efforts. In his first chapter he runs through various trades—day labourers, weavers, tailors, blacksmiths, and others—to find examples of artistic, commercial, or military success. Sheer perseverance is seen as the key even to Isaac Newton's achievements.

Smiles was of course crystallizing existing opinions. He gave them what proved to be a memorable form, and *Self-Help* was translated into many languages. Logically, the ideas expressed were partly contradicted by another prevalent view of the working classes as dangerous. This had been fostered by the civil unrest of groups such as Luddites who destroyed machinery, Chartists who demonstrated for voting rights, and trade unionists who were often thought of—as in Dickens's *Hard Times* (1854)—as political agitators responsible for strikes. The reports of government commissions and others on the physical conditions of the working classes and on such matters as prostitution, as well as sociological reports such as Henry Mayhew's *London Labour and the London Poor* (1851), enforced this view of the lower classes as a threat.

The reports had, amongst other things, provided detailed accounts of conditions of life which made it easier to regard these groups as 'lower' in a judgemental sense. They could be shown as associated commonly with crime, drunkenness, violence, prostitution, or even sometimes with incest. By the mid-century the question had been explicitly articulated as to whether the 'amelioration of the working classes has limits beyond which it cannot pass'.10 This was the phrasing of the economist Alfred Marshall in a paper delivered at Cambridge in 1873. His attempt to answer it makes it clear that in this context 'amelioration' refers to more than the improvement of physical conditions. Marshall believed that the working classes could, given adequate education and suitable occupations, progress 'till the official distinction between working man and gentleman has passed away'. Nonetheless, he feels that the work of the former tends 'to keep his character rude and coarse'. It has lowering influences on 'those vast masses of men who, after long hours of hard and unintellectual toil, are wont to return to their narrow homes with bodies exhausted and with minds dull and sluggish'. He makes a link between 'physical fatigue in its extremest forms' and 'physical unrest and physical cravings that hound a man on to his undoing'. Toil dulls the brain, leaving it open only to 'the coarser pleasures—drink, ignoble jests and noise'.[11] By the 1880s an increasingly pessimistic view was taken with respect to the working classes as surveys revealed what poverty was like in major cities.

Marshall's insistence on education as a mechanism for 'amelioration' is reasonable since it seems a necessary requirement for improving the lot of the poor. So does the demand for extension of the vote as a means of empowering them. True, the Reform Act of 1832 had, in general terms, enfranchised more of the middle class, but by the 1860s there were vigorous demands for further enfranchisement. The question for politicians was how far to go. Statistics proved central to their parliamentary debates. There were detailed calculations by individual MPs as to how their own majorities might be affected. At the same time there was a widespread belief, as John Bright put it, that there existed among the working classes 'a residuum . . . in every constituency of almost hopeless poverty and dependence' (*The Times*, May 1867). These dregs were supposed to constitute a threat to prosperity, property owners, and the stability of society generally. So extreme were the views on them expressed in the House of Commons, that Gladstone rebuked his fellow MPs:

But I do object to the whole mode of dealing with this question of statistics, as adopted by Honourable Members . . . They seem as if they were engaged in ascertaining the numbers of an invading army; but the persons to whom their remarks apply are our fellow-subjects, our fellow-Christians, our own flesh and blood.[12]

Despite Gladstone's protest, the representation of the working class as composed of a respectable artisan group and an irredeemable residuum was confirmed as orthodoxy by the franchise debates, contrary views notwithstanding. Much future social reform was aimed specifically at the hardworking, thrifty, and virtuous 'artisan'. Hence the creation of 'artisans' dwellings', sometimes by charitable associations. The vote was only cautiously extended by the Reform Act of

1867, mainly to skilled workers: urban householders with one year's residence, and lodgers paying a rent of £10 per annum. In the counties it went to copyholders and leaseholders with property of an annual value of £5 and to the £12 ratepayer. Such connections with property were at once an indication of some substance and presumed thrift as well as an assurance that the new voters would be favourably inclined to the protection of property and property owners. By 1869 (when some single women had been given the right to vote in municipal elections), Matthew Arnold could allude without argument to the diligent working class as 'one in spirit with the industrial middle class'.[13]

EDUCATION

As for education—some disagreed with the view that it might lessen the dangerous proclivities of the working classes. They feared it might make them more dissident, not less. Up to 1870 the state had not taken the responsibility of providing elementary schooling nationwide. It had only given grants to voluntary denominational schools such as Hardy attended. His Dorchester school was run by the Nonconformist British and Foreign Schools Society; those of the established church by the National Society. Before the passing of the 1870 Education Act, elementary school places were available for only one child in two in London and one in three, four, or even five elsewhere. The new Act was an enabling measure to allow local authorities power to levy a rate and set up school boards to establish schools. Such boards *could* compel attendance from the age of 5. Further Acts in 1876, 1880, and 1899 extended the range of compulsory education. An Act of 1891 made elementary schooling free; and another in 1899 raised the leaving age to 12. A system of national inspection was developed which allowed for a scheme of 'payment by results' which fostered the learning by rote of basic information in the 'three Rs'. There was hostility amongst some towards allowing school boards to use their local levies to provide secondary education. A complaint by a London ratepayer in 1899 led to a court ruling that such use of rates to fund secondary schools was illegal. H. G. Wells's comments in his *Experiment in Autobiography* that the 1870 Act was 'not an Act for a common universal education, it was an Act to educate the lower classes for employment on class lines, and with specially trained inferior teachers who had no university quality'.[14] The Act laid the basis, however, for common universal education. What is now called secondary education was largely the preserve of middle- and upper-class boys in public and grammar schools. By the mid-century there were 400 of these, all charging fees. In 1869 the Endowed Schools Act streamlined endowments and charity funds to help subsidize these schools and provide affordable education for the middle classes. An expansion of such education followed. But not until 1908 was there an increase in the availability of secondary schools in the state sector for those moving on from state primary schools.

The category of teachers of which Wells wrote so harshly was a group familiar to Hardy. Both his sisters attended Salisbury Training College: Mary from 1860 to 1862, Kate from 1877 to 1879. Each then taught in elementary schools for over thirty years. His cousin, Tryphena Sparks, whom he knew so well, took a training course at Stockwell Normal College of the British and Foreign Bible Society from 1870 to 1872. She then became headmistress of a girls' elementary school in Plymouth. Only half the teachers in primary schools had undergone such a training (which placed these women in the lower middle class). Hardy uses his knowledge of such training colleges in *Jude the Obscure* (1895).

In the same novel he also deals with the subject of access to education at the older universities for working-class boys. By 1890 university provision generally had been extended by the founding of provincial university colleges such as Owens College, Manchester (1851), which in 1880 temporarily became federated with similar colleges at Leeds and Liverpool as Victoria University. There were also university colleges in London. But Oxford and Cambridge (to which Hardy had aspired) still remained almost impregnable except to middle-class boys educated in public schools. From the 1850s an intense debate had raged over the older universities. The central issue was, roughly, a struggle between, on the one hand, the upper and upper-middle classes who wished to preserve them in their existing form, and, on the other hand, men of business who wished to open them more widely by providing a greater range of curricula. As one historian says of Oxford and Cambridge:

Many of their students had no particular academic ambitions; they were sent up by their fathers to enjoy the type of education considered suitable for their class . . . The role of the [older] universities was, in a sense, social rather than intellectual. They were devoted to producing gentlemen rather than scholars.

Some, like Fitzjames Stephens, urged a change. He wrote in 1879 to Lord Lytton:

This is not the age for public life; it is emphatically the age for special knowledge and study, the age for engineers, men of science, lawyers and the like.[15]

The question of including marginalized groups (women and poor men) had already been bypassed. There was more difficulty of access for poor men in the 1890s than in the earlier part of the century. This was because the high cost of life at Oxbridge colleges was now less likely to be met by even the occasional scholarship. These had previously been restricted to the poor but were now open to competition from any quarter. This combined with a requirement up to 1864 for a first degree in Classics and Scripture before one could be taken in any other subject, and after 1864 to take a first examination at any rate in Latin or Greek. These subjects were routinely taught in public schools but not elsewhere and therefore added an intellectual hurdle to the financial one. As a result in 1897–8, for instance, only eight sons of working men and twenty-eight sons of tradesmen entered Oxford. They constituted only 1 per cent and 3.5 per cent of the total intake.

The reforms to the electoral and educational systems represented the argument which complemented Smiles's 'self-help'. This was the idea that the proper attitude to the working classes was paternalistic. Paternalism could take many forms. It was the usual remedy for social ills offered variously in condition-of-England novels, where personal reconciliation of worker and employer is usually mediated by the heroines. J. S. Mill sums it up scornfully in his *Principles of Political Economy* (1848): 'The rich should be *in loco parentis* to the poor, guiding and restraining them like children. Of spontaneous action on their part there should be no need. They should be called on for nothing but to do their day's work, and to be moral and religious'.[16] At its best this attitude could lead to social reforms in housing, sanitation, schools, or factory hours and conditions. But it was adaptable enough to be used to discourage individuals from getting above themselves. Those who bent it in this way, for instance, included people hostile to any opening of universities to working men. Such people accused university extensionists of offering an 'inducement which tempts so many away from their more appropriate occupations';[17] or of turning 'a good workman or clerk into a bad schoolmaster'.[18] The idea of treating inferiors with a patronizing paternalism as a mark of gentlemanliness persisted up to the end of the century and beyond.

Women's Place in Society

The nature and role of women was one of the hottest topics of discussion throughout the nineteenth century to a degree only partly matched at the end of the twentieth. More than almost any other subject it was one with which Hardy engaged. As is evident from the account of education above, at the beginning of the century girls were virtually invisible. In this they were like the working class generally. If middle-class they too, like working men, were felt to be a proper object for paternalistic treatment by men. Famously, along with peers, lunatics, and working-class men, women were denied the vote. The spread of paternalism was an example of a shift in society towards a nuclear family as the basic unit (replacing a larger kinship model) brought about by economic, social, and political change.

The essential inferiority of women to men was an orthodoxy challenged by an articulate and persistent minority that increased in effectiveness as the century wore on. Women's lesser status was sometimes supposed to rest on a restricted evolutionary development. As late as 1887 this extreme view is expressed for instance by George Romanes, a scientist and friend of Charles Darwin. He describes 'Mental Differences between Men and Women', claiming that the latter were less rational, more intuitive, and more at the mercy of their emotions. He attributes these differences and their consequences to a physical development stunted in relation to the brain to compensate for the development of necessary sexual attractiveness and procreative capacity. So women in general are supposed to have a 'marked inferiority of intellectual power', creativity and judgement. To make up for these deficiencies they possess a greater 'refinement of the senses' and a rapidity of perception which he illustrates. His illustration takes the form of an anecdote of a woman who, 'seeing another lady "pass at full speed in a carriage, could analyse her toilette from her bonnet to her shoes, and be able to describe not only the fashion and quality of the stuffs, but also to say if the lace were real or only machine made"'. There seems to be no irony in this account and he concludes

The man has always been regarded as the rightful lord of the woman, to whom she is by nature subject, as both mentally and physically the weaker vessel; and when in individual cases these relations happen to be inverted, the accident becomes a favourite theme for humorists—thus showing that in the general estimation such a state of matters is regarded as incongruous.[19]

Romanes then proceeds to show that the inferior characteristics of women are to be viewed (presumably by them) as assets, thus turning negatives into positives such as aesthetic sensitivity, sympathy, modesty, self-denial, purity, and an aptitude for religion. But he is careful to point out that all these spring from weakness while men's characteristics result from strength. These differences make the case for the necessity of men (fathers, brothers, or husbands) taking the role of women's instructors and guides as well as fighting competitively in the world outside the home. On this view, women at home, like workers in the factory, are seen as children in need of care and control by those with stronger intellects and better judgement.

WOMEN'S EDUCATION

By the mid-century this account of women was challenged by some middle-class women and a smaller number of men, such as J. S. Mill, who argued for better education for women. The reformers were given ammunition by demographic facts. The belief had prevailed that women's sphere was domestic and that the education they needed was one that prepared them for marriage. But with the increase in the proportion of women to men in the population, there arose the problem of 'surplus' women: women for whom no husband was available to support them. This is discussed in well known articles such as W. W. Greg's 'Why are Women Redundant?' (1862). Greg uses this article to argue against letting women into the professions, though he does not object to working-class women replacing more costly machines in menial jobs which it would be 'wasteful and foolish (*economically considered*) to set a man to do'.[20] But the need for many women to be able to support themselves financially if unmarried made a cogent argument for better education.

The campaign for this focused on middle-class girls. The pioneers for women's education founded a number of fee-paying secondary schools for such pupils which offered a rigorous curriculum along with the physical exercise necessary to prevent a deterioration in the health of potential mothers through excessive brainwork. These schools were the North London Collegiate School (1850), Cheltenham Ladies' College (1854), and Camden School (1870). Fees at the last were from four guineas to fifteen guineas and were cheaper by far than at the other two earlier foundations. In 1865 the then headmistress of Cheltenham listed the subjects routinely taught there: French, German, English Literature and Language, Mathematics, Geography, History, Natural Science, Astronomy (as well as drawing, music, and dancing). By this time (from 1864) girls had been allowed to take the same Cambridge local examinations as boys for an experimental period. This arrangement was made permanent in 1867. After 1845 a few women were able to attend classes at King's College, London. Then colleges were established specifically for women. In 1848 Queen's College, London, had been founded, followed in 1849 by Bedford College, London. Then in 1868 came Girton Hall (later College), Cambridge, and in 1871 Newnham Hall (later College), Cambridge, though women still could not take degrees there. At Oxford in 1879 some provision was made for lectures and examinations for women, and halls of residence were opened called Lady Margaret Hall (1878), Somerville Hall (1879), St Hugh's Hall (1886), and St Hilda's (1893).

The opportunities offered by these institutions and arrangements were still open only to a very small number of the relatively wealthy, although they formed a bridgehead in new territory. But none of Hardy's middle-class heroines (such as Cytherea, Elfride, Bathsheba, Eustacia, Ethelberta, Grace Melbury) is able to take advantage of such education. While the education debate concentrated attention on middle-class 'ladies', working-class 'women' received only occasional mention. Emily Shirreff, for instance, a founder of the Women's Education Union to foster the education of girls, wrote in 1873 that 'the poorer class . . . are provided for' by the state.[21] The next year Isabella M. S. Tod noted:

In considering the right of women to enter lucrative employments, it is only necessary to show that these are not inconsistent with the high status which theoretically is assigned to women. Practically it is a matter of notoriety that in the lower ranks of life the women work as hard as the men, and at tasks often as noxious and trying, the only difference being that those who are paid at all are paid worse in proportion to their work. Amongst the poorer middle classes the case is much the same, only that paying work is not always as readily found by these women as by those who accept the wages of unskilled labour.[22]

The impression seems to have been common amongst those arguing for the improvement of education for middle-class girls that, in any case, too much education was not good for girls of the lower classes. Jessie Boucherett wrote in 1862:

The working classes seem at first glance to have the strongest claim, but we are told on high authority that they are already so well provided with National Schools that there is a strong probability of their becoming more intelligent than the class immediately above them, and the Commissioners themselves and the general public seem to be of opinion that they have lately received a higher education than is likely to be of use to them in their humble station.[23]

Boucherett had started the Society for Promoting the Employment of Women, and was active in the cause of women's education, but still wrote coldly in 1862: 'Among women of the labouring classes a good education is of comparatively little importance, for health and strength are of more service to a labourer's daughter than knowledge or intelligence.' Wealthier girls are another matter: 'in the middle ranks, a woman cannot become a domestic servant: she would feel that to do so was a degradation; and even if she did not, she would not possess the requisite physical powers from want of early training'.[24]

In practice working-class girls had only the same limited access as their brothers to an adequate elementary school, even after the 1870 Education Act. There they were taught up to predetermined 'standards' under the payment-by-results system. This system classified children into 'standards' according to their age. Under this infamous arrangement a strict and detailed syllabus laid down by the code of the Education Department had to be adhered to. There were seven 'standards' that had to be successively achieved by the children in schools to secure funding. Each child was tested annually by one of Her Majesty's Inspectorate—a frightening experience for teacher and pupils, as in *Jude*. In the early 'standards' (as classes came to be called), children were examined annually on material prescribed in arithmetic and writing, much of which they had learnt by rote. In higher standards more memorizing was needed as other subjects such as grammar, geography, music, and recitation were added to the syllabus. Tess Durbeyfield is said to have 'passed the sixth standard in the National school under a London-trained mistress'. In other words she had had a modestly satisfactory education at an elementary level.

WOMEN'S EMPLOYMENT

Partly for tactical reasons, the argument for women's education was often based on the need for surplus women to work, but opportunities were severely limited. In the 1851 census a substantial number—36 per cent—of British women were employed. But only 7 per cent were middle class. Of this 7 per cent about half were independent and owned businesses or farms, as Bathsheba Everdene does in *Far from the Madding Crowd* (1874). The rest were mainly governesses, though some were writers or artists. It was relatively acceptable for a woman to be a writer, especially as this did not seem to fall into the undesirable category of work that might keep a man out of a job. Even Romanes writes that, although the male–female disparity is most conspicuous in original work, at least in terms of writing women can be said to have approached men. Elfride Swancourt in *A Pair of Blue Eyes* (1873) is an instance in Hardy's novels of a woman who has published work. Manifestly, real examples like Jane Austen, Charlotte and Emily Brontë, Elizabeth Gaskell, George Eliot, not to mention innumerable minor writers like Frances Trollope, Margaret Oliphant, Mary Elizabeth Braddon, and many others, made it difficult to claim that women could not write sellable fiction or journalism. They were likely, as both Charlotte Brontë and Gaskell knew, to be assessed critically by very different standards from those applied to men. Although they published under a male pseudonym, there was intense activity to discover their gender. Once they were revealed to be female, they were routinely judged against what it was thought appropriate for genteel women to feel or think. There was also considerable hostility not only to middle-class women possibly taking work from men but to the idea of their accepting paid work at all.

The majority of women in employment were working-class and at least half of these were domestic servants. In towns others were factory workers or engaged in some kind of needlework, or acted as nurses, a discredited occupation until the latter part of the century. A writer in *Fraser's Magazine* for May 1848 on 'Hospital Nurses as They Are and as They Ought to Be' asserted: 'There are some [nurses] whose honesty and temperance may be trusted, but they make up for the restraint in one direction by a greater licence in another'.[25] In the country women mainly worked on farms or as dressmakers in neighbouring towns and villages or as barmaids such as Arabella Donn in *Jude the Obscure*. Farm work for women in Dorset changed over the course of the century: by the 1860s, as farm sizes increased and the number of workers needed decreased, it was men who took most of the work. By the 1860s women were largely confined to dairy work and by 1900 even this was often done by men. So by the 1890s farm work for women was scarce, a situation reflected by the need for Tess to work at Flintcomb-Ash.

WOMEN AND PROSTITUTION

By the 1880s the earning capacity of female agricultural workers was declining and there was a 'progressive domination of the economy by men' in some areas.[26] Some women resorted to badly paid domestic service, the demand for which increased as the century progressed. Another resource for ill-paid or impoverished women was prostitution, which flourished in urban centres and seaport towns. Prostitutes were throughout the period mainly 'the unskilled daughters of the unskilled classes'.[27] Sometimes they were prostitutes on a part-time basis. By 1850 prostitution was known as 'the Great Social Evil' through the details provided by government and sociological reports. What represented to the women a purely financial resource was readily viewed as proof of the moral laxity and tendency to promiscuity of the class to which they belonged.

The topic became a matter of public debate among social and moral reformers, politicians, and military and civic leaders. Some wished to 'save' and 'rescue' the women but a dominant view concerned itself with the spread of venereal disease, particularly amongst the army and navy. Attitudes varied but some believed that prostitution was a necessary evil, given the uncheckable nature of male sexuality. Consequently in 1864, 1866, and 1869 the Contagious Diseases Acts were passed which allowed a woman putatively identified as a prostitute to be subjected to medical examination, and if necessary to be detained in hospital for three months. The Acts were first suspended, and later repealed in 1886. A common view persisted, however, that prostitution was 'another form of disruptive sexual behaviour' amongst the working classes. According to a report in 1843 on prostitution in Liverpool, it was 'no different from common-law marriage, concubinage, and other "illicit intercourse of the sexes" which generally characterized the lower classes'.[28]

Though figures show that most prostitutes did not take to their trade because they were seduced as innocent girls, that was a prevalent stereotype. It facilitated the equation of the seduced girl with 'fallen' women generally. Hence the weight of condemnation attached to those who experienced seduction, a topic addressed in *Tess*. In law the child of a girl such as Tess who had been seduced was *filius nullius*—the child of nobody—and had no right of inheritance from his father. It is as 'nobody's child' that Henchard thinks of Elizabeth-Jane when he discovers that she is not his daughter but Newson's illegitimate child (*The Mayor of Casterbridge*, chapter 43). Tess's child is 'of kin to nobody, and has no ancestor from whom any inheritable blood can be derived':

The social reality, at which the law only hints, was that the stigma of illegitimacy cast a very real shadow over the lives of many illegitimate children. The very presence of the illegitimate was a reminder of an immorality within society which must be discouraged. Some orphanages were closed to him—although others did sterling work on his behalf—on the ground that the bastard might inherit his parents' weakness and contaminate others.[29]

In his early work *Desperate Remedies* (1871), Hardy seems to adopt the conventional view of the 'bastard'. The villainous, bigamous, and murderous Aeneas Manston turns out to be the illegitimate son of Miss Aldclyffe and he appears to be a prime instance of someone born outside marriage who has inherited his mother's taint. A far more compassionate view is taken of the stigma attaching to Tess's illegitimate baby son, Sorrow.

WOMEN AND MARRIAGE

The importance of maintaining a distinction between legitimate and illegitimate children is the key to understanding the divorce law in this period. Up to 1857 a divorce could only be obtained by an individual Act of Parliament for the petitioner. Except in extraordinary circumstances, which only rarely came to light, the petitioner was a husband who sued on grounds of his wife's adultery. The reason for this special parliamentary provision which became established in the early eighteenth century was to allow a nobleman to divorce an adulterous wife and avoid the possibility of accepting an heir who was in fact not legitimate or of his blood. Such a divorce was extremely costly: it was not likely to cost less than £800 in the nineteenth century and, if contested, might run to many thousands of pounds. From 1840 to 1856 only twenty-four such Acts granting divorces were passed.

Until the 1880s this inequity was not the only one to which women were subjected. An improved position on divorce that resulted from the Matrimonial Causes Act of 1857 still disadvantaged wives. From that date a divorce no longer required an Act of Parliament but was dealt with in a civil court. The grounds for dissolving a marriage were now dealt with separately for each partner. In fact they crystallized the prevailing sexual 'double standard'. Such a standard did not regard a man's adultery as the same kind of offence against the marriage as a wife's. A man could divorce his wife for even a single act of adultery; a wife needed to prove not only adultery by her husband but also some aggravating factor such as incest, bigamy, sodomy, bestiality, or extreme cruelty. Adultery was tolerable in a man but not in a woman. This attitude was widely current and it was sometimes taken as a matter of course that what for a young man was merely a sowing of wild oats was in a woman an irrevocable fall into degradation. So it is that Angel Clare admits to youthful fornication which confession to his new wife will erase. He takes, however, a very different view of her affair with Alec: it is a barrier to the consummation of their marriage and turns her into a new and deceitful person. Divorces rose from 148 in 1857–67 to 582 in the 1890s. It is divorce on these new terms that allows the husbands Jude and Phillotson in *Jude* to divorce Arabella and Sue Bridehead. But when in *The Woodlanders*

Grace Melbury wishes to divorce her unfaithful husband Edred Fitzpiers, she cannot do so.

Both before and after the Act of 1857 a wife's position in law and her role in society depended on a principle enunciated by Sir William Blackstone in the eighteenth century:

By marriage the husband and wife are one person in law: that is, the very being or legal existence of the woman is suspended during marriage, or at least is incorporated or consolidated into that of the husband: under whose wing, protection, and cover, she performs everything: and is therefore called in our law-french a feme-covert.[30]

The expression of a husband's absolute power over his wife is captured by the scene in *The Mayor of Casterbridge* where Henchard publicly sells his wife for five guineas. The practice continued through the eighteenth century and into the nineteenth among poor people. Legal writers record: 'The practice appears to have resulted from the unavailability of divorce to the people: either prior to the introduction of judicial divorce in 1857, or because of the cost thereafter.'[31]

The practical implications of the state of women as described by Blackstone were extensive. It meant that, as non-persons in law, wives could not bring a legal action on their own behalf. Nor could they own property unless a trust had been specially created before the marriage—a resource available only to the very rich. If no trust were set up, then any property or money that a woman owned at the time of the marriage, or acquired or earned after it, belonged to her husband. This was not changed until the Married Women's Property Act of 1870 brought about a partial improvement. The 1870 Act allowed a wife to keep money earned during the marriage. In 1882 a similar Act allowed a married woman to hold or acquire property and money and to dispose of it by will as though unmarried. This is the background which possibly explains why the Laodicean (or lukewarm) Pamela Power, a wealthy heiress, resists marriage in *A Laodicean*. Perhaps more painful was the fact that after a Custody Act of 1839 a mother might only claim custody of her children up to the age of 7, if she were the innocent party. Not until 1873 could she claim them up to the age of 16.

A minor feature of Victorian matrimonial law concerned degrees of kinship within which marriage was prohibited. This was a barrier to a widower's right to marry his deceased wife's sister, a question much debated in the 1880s and later. It was a prohibition that many ignored. In the first half of the century as many as nine-tenths of those marriages contracted within prohibited degrees were with a deceased wife's sister. The injunction came about because of an ambivalence as to whether to treat a man and his sister-in-law as brother and sister. The law treated them as though they were siblings whose marriage would be incestuous. On the other hand, convention decreed that since they were not brother and sister, it was unaccept-able for them to live together in the same house unmarried after the wife's death. And this was at a time when wives often died in child-birth and when it was quite usual for an unmarried woman to be living with her married sister and sharing the care of any children. The flouting of the law, particularly by the middle classes, led to the repeal of this law, but not until 1907. So when Tess suggests to her sister Liza-Lu that she should marry Tess's husband Angel Clare after her death, she is suggesting something which would be illegal. Women's role in society and relationships between the sexes were a vital concern for Hardy, particularly in his late and best-known novels.

The Loss of Religion

THE INSTITUTIONAL CHURCH

The background to Hardy's thinking is an absence: the one cre-ated by the loss of his early religious faith which was strong enough in the 1850s and 1860s to inspire a wish to become a clergyman and to discuss keenly the question of whether there should be infant or adult baptism. The subject of belief in God was a major concern to many people and their fierce interest was fed by a wide range of sources, particularly amongst the intelli-gentsia. Religious attitudes took many different forms. In relation to religious belief the Victorian period was not so much one of transition as of turmoil. To understand the upheavals it is neces-sary first to understand the role which the established Anglican Church played in social as well as religious life. If social class was the warp of the fabric of society, the Church was the woof that interlocked and supported it.

The institution itself controlled entry into Parliament, Oxford and Cambridge universities, and consequently into many professions. Until 1829 Roman Catholics, for instance, could not become Members of Parliament, hold government or local office, or high office in the armed services. Dissenters could not hold government office until 1828 and Catholics could not become MPs until 1829. In this way, through an insistence on the right religious affiliation, the Church acted as the gatekeeper for several lucrative professions. Further, the government of the day appointed the archbishops of Canterbury and York as well as all the other bishops. This meant that Church leaders were locked into an establishment founded on rigid class distinction. More significantly still, 10,500 of all the approximately 12,000 'livings' in the Anglican Church were in the gift of individual landowners or the public schools and Oxford and Cambridge colleges; only 1,500 were in the gift of the bishops. These 'livings' were posts as parish priests with regular incomes attached, sometimes of high value. It was common practice for colleges to appoint promising or favoured 'fellows' to well-paid livings and for landowners to appoint their younger sons who would not inherit the family property.

This is a usual occurrence in Anthony Trollope's Barsetshire novels which deal with the lives of a group of Anglican clergy and their machinations. A typical instance is mentioned in Trollope's *Framley Parsonage* (1861). The living of Framley, worth £900 a year is at the disposal of the dowager Lady Lufton. Her only son, Lord Lufton, is already well provided for by the family estate; his university friend, Mark Robarts, is not so lucky. Lady Lufton decides to give him the living: 'Had Lady Lufton had a second son, that second son would probably have had the living, and no one would have thought it wrong—certainly not if that second son had been such a one as Mark Robarts' (chapter 1). Robarts, like herself, tends towards a High Church position; she wants her son to be friendly with 'his' clergyman who might influence him for good; and she wants someone who will be more 'subject to her influence', as an older man might not be. Yet these are the reflections of a woman who, according to the narrator, 'thought much on religious matters' (chapter 1).

Owners of livings who were less 'scrupulous' about religion would not even regard a vocation for clerical life as a necessity for selection.

The chosen younger son, friend, or client would become a minor country gentleman, living a life not very different from his neighbours'. Some activities, such as playing cards, as Mr Farebrother does in *Middlemarch* (1872), were frowned on. So too was hunting, though 'hunting parsons' were not unknown. Mark Robarts succumbs to this particular temptation since, when Lord Lufton asks him what harm it would be, he feels 'It would be absurd to say that his time would be better employed at home in clerical matters, for it was notorious that he had not clerical pursuits for the employment of half his time' (chapter 12). Mark indeed is led into worse temptation and debt. He is forgiven and rehabilitated, however, by Lady Lufton and his long-suffering wife without bringing God into the matter.

Clergymen in Hardy's novels are usually worldly and snobbish but these facts are presented routinely rather than as a focus of attack. These men conform to the pattern described above. Maybold, the vicar in *Under the Greenwood Tree* (1872) is snobbishly ashamed of his infatuation with Fancy Day, the pretty daughter of a mere local carrier or 'tranter'. Elfride Swancourt's father in *A Pair of Blue Eyes* (1873) is described as a man with 'a mind whose pleasures were taken amid genealogies, good dinners and patrician reminiscences' (chapter 9). In *Tess* (1891) Angel Clare's two brothers, Felix and Cuthbert, share Swancourt's attitude to working-class people.

From Elizabethan times onwards the Anglican Church had attempted to consolidate its position as a temperate middle way between Catholicism and dissent. Its institutional practice was based on the Bible and on the Book of Common Prayer which laid down the order of services for different events and times. The latter contained the services and biblical readings for all the major events of the congregation's lives: baptism, marriage, burial. There was also provision for such matters as Confirmation and 'churching' (cleansing after childbirth). Prayers were given to frame requests for rain, fair weather, good harvests, and the needs of parliament. And there were petitions for protection against dearth, famine, sickness, or plague. The Church marked the seasons as much as the weather did; and in the cycle of life collective prayers were the figures on the clock of existence. For those accustomed from childhood to attending services and Sunday school, the Bible and the Book of Common

Prayer provided an iconography on which writers could confidently draw.

Frequently repeated stories and texts stuck in the memory; and the stories themselves were often depicted visually. Pictures such as that of Samson and Delilah on the wall of the inn in *Jude* offered visual representations of ideas. The significance of Samson and Delilah to Jude Fawley and his temptress Arabella Donn, who sit drinking below the picture, would have been readily decodable. So would quotations from the two sacred texts such as the epigraph to the novel, the half quotation 'The letter killeth'. Its meaning requires the complete 'but the spirit giveth life' and that also would be readily supplied. But perhaps it would be better to speak of three sacred texts. John Bunyan's *The Pilgrim's Progress* (1678–84), the great allegory of a Christian's difficult progress through life, had by the nineteenth century almost achieved that character. It was almost as widely known as the Bible and many had preferred it as acceptable 'Sunday reading' in childhood, rather than the alternative of long, boring sermons. A clergyman, writing in 1849 on the village libraries connected to the parish church, tells how 'Many of the books . . . lie upon the shelves unread, and the consequence is, we require duplicates over and over again of such works as Bunyan's *Pilgrim's Progress*'.[32] This book was also part of Hardy's earliest literary heritage.

By the time of Hardy's birth, changes had already developed in the Church of England. The Church's role in making rigid distinctions between the social classes with the resulting tendency to treat the 'lower orders' as a different species—fish that felt no pain—had alienated many, or at least made them indifferent to institutional Anglicanism. A less class-conscious and more immediately appealing form of Christianity had arisen which many working-class people responded to. This was the Methodist movement founded by John and Charles Wesley in the eighteenth century. The avowed aim of John Wesley was to reform dispositions and lives, not opinions, and to encourage the abandonment of vice. Unlike the Anglican Church, Methodism had not assumed a captive audience. Conversion of an experiential kind was the beginning of becoming a Methodist. The process of converting individuals was organized around the work of lay preachers. Direct appeal to the emotions as well as reason was thought to be necessary. By 1850 the movement had an estimated membership of about 2 million, and continued to grow, gradually taking in the better-off as well as the working classes. But significantly chapels either had no rented pews, or very few.

After Methodists had broken away from the Anglican Church another section developed a more conservative option for dissatisfied Christians in the shape of Tractarianism. This group began in 1833 in Oxford, which gave it the alternative name, the Oxford Movement. Its chief proponents were John Keble, Edward Pusey, and John Henry Newman. The movement was fiercely intellectual and élitist, concerning itself with elaborate logical arguments for seeing the Church as authoritative because it was the direct descendant of the Church founded by Christ's apostles. The name Tractarianism derived from the ninety tracts or articles in which mainly Newman spelt out their arguments. The Tracts were thought to be the slippery slope to Rome, which for some was almost equivalent to damnation. Certainly Rome *was* the destination of many Tractarians including Newman, who finally became a Roman Catholic cardinal.

This institutional turmoil went along with an overall decrease in church attendance, particularly among the working classes. The official Census of 1851 collected statistics on church attendance by including the number of those attending a place of worship on the day known as Census Sunday. The results shocked 'respectable' Victorians, though by today's standards the numbers would be regarded as impressive. It emerged that of those not too young, too old or physically disabled to attend, on average only one in two had done so. Worse still, the figure fell to one in three in industrial towns and cities. Since the majority of the nation were working class it was evidently they who had voted with their feet. Friedrich Engels, writing of *The Condition of the Working Class in England* (1845), using what he had seen while living in Manchester, asserted 'But among the masses there prevails almost universally a total indifference to religion' and 'The mere cry: "He's a parson!", is often enough to drive one of the clergy from the platform of a public meeting'.[33] The reason for the middle-class shock over the state of church attendance in industrial towns was that religious conformism was seen as a safeguard against working-class disorder, dissention, and disruption which had already surfaced in strikes, riots, machine-breakings, and Chartists demonstrations. This decline in working-class religion is fully recognized by Hardy.

THE IMPACT OF SCIENCE ON RELIGION

The revitalizing of the Anglican Church by the Methodist and Oxford movements was a thin surface over a volcano that was about to erupt. The eruption was to change radically what people thought and believed, or at the least to create profound disturbance. The metaphor of the volcano has a literal aptness because it was discoveries about the natural world which uprooted traditional understanding of the physical basis of experience.

Space and time had seemed to be the normal co-ordinates of existence against which the individual orientated herself with every utterance. Merely saying 'I went to London' indicated that she had been there and now was again at some distance from the city; and that the visit took place earlier than the time of utterance. Space was only a problem when speed in reaching some place was urgent; time was a problem when there was too little of it to complete an action or when there was nothing to fill it. Space and time seemed to a large extent controllable. With the advent of an efficient and speedy railway system space even seemed to be becoming more controllable, not less. But already in the eighteenth century the understanding of space had been startlingly transformed. The astronomer William Herschel had, amongst other things, discovered that *nebulae* were clusters of stars unimaginably far from the earth. Space was suddenly stretched beyond the imagination and evidently yet more was to be discovered.

The chilling picture that Herschel presented was made more disturbing by discoveries of geologists, particularly Charles Lyell. He crystallized them in his *Principles of Geology* (1830–3). For centuries the Bible was read literally as history by most Christians. The very development of Protestant Christianity had involved giving lay people direct access to God's word without the interpretations of interfering clergy. It was for that very reason that the Bible had been first translated into English (and of a colloquial sort) in the fifteenth century. The length of time since the world was created in the way described in Genesis was calculated to be 6,000 years, a long but comprehensible period of time. A universal flood was also taken to be an actual meteorological event. But geologists, instead of confirming the tidy account of God creating species one by one and designing the world for humanity's benefit, drew a shocking picture which suggested divine neglect.

Though many scientists were able to accommodate these discoveries to religious belief, doubts were raised among others. Geology was a hot topic in the early nineteenth century, not just a museum subject. The excitement in the twentieth century over rocks from the moon comes nowhere near it. Interest in the subject developed from a mixture of 'cosmological theorizing, mineral surveying, natural history collecting, biblical exegesis [interpretation] and continental mining conditions'. Many people 'from physicians and aristocrats to engineers and farmers' practised or dabbled in geology.[34] Lyell worked, by much careful investigation of the existing state of geological formations of many kinds, to discover the sequence of their development and the events which caused them. With the publication of *Principles* it became clear that the idea of 6,000 years of creation had to be replaced by a period of millions and millions of years—too many in fact to number precisely. As Lyell concludes:

In vain do we aspire to assign limits to the works of creation in *space*, whether we examine the starry heavens, or that world of minute animalcules which is revealed to us by the microscope. We are prepared therefore to find that in *time* also, the confines of the universe lie beyond the reach of mortal ken.[35]

Discarded with the old time span of 6,000 years of creation was the notion of explaining major changes in whole continents and huge landscapes by a series of rapid catastrophic events such as floods. Instead geologists demonstrated that these changes had occurred by processes that needed 'an indefinite lapse of ages'.[36] Among those who listened to such ideas when Lyell propounded them at Oxford were many Victorian notables including Dr Thomas Arnold, John Ruskin, and John Henry Newman. Among writers who engaged with the debate in their works were Thomas Carlyle, Benjamin Disraeli, Charles Kingsley, Robert Browning, Alfred Tennyson, George Gissing, and Hardy himself. Though some of Lyell's arguments were subsequently modified, the central conclusion stated about the length of time the earth had existed was undeniable. Many religious believers remained firm and optimistic about the new revelations. But in 1860 a book of essays unexcitingly entitled *Essays and Reviews* marked a crisis point in the debate. They were written by seven Anglican clergymen who became known as 'The Seven Against Christ'. The essays argued that Christians had to accept the findings of geologists and biologists and could not simply ignore them. One of the authors, Benjamin Jowett, asserted that the events described in the Bible needed to be confirmed by other historical evidence. In brief, the Bible should be treated like any other historical text. By implication this ruled out the idea that the literal accuracy of the current version was guaranteed by its divine inspiration.

The inclusion of biology along with geology in *Essays and Reviews* refers to the work done on the theory of evolution by Jean Baptiste de Monet, Chevalier de Lamarck, and his successors, Charles Darwin and Alfred Russel Wallace. Wallace reached similar conclusions to Darwin's at about the time of the publication of *The Origin of Species* (1859). Both argued inductively from huge amounts of data amassed in world-wide travel. They examined the distribution or location of living organisms, their composition, and their predecessors which were observable as fossils. Drawing on Lyell's account of changes in the geological environment, they came up with an explanation for the development of different species. This explanation denied the tradition of separate creation of all individual species. Instead, Darwin saw them as developed from a few earlier species:

As many more individuals of each species are born than can possibly survive; and as, consequently, there is a frequently recurring struggle for existence, it follows that any being, if it vary however slightly in any manner profitable to itself, under the complex and sometimes varying conditions of life, will have a better chance of surviving, and thus be *naturally selected*.[37]

This apparently straightforward account clashes, of course, with the ritualistic Genesis description of God's six days' work of creation. Darwin later added references to the Creator but for many intellectuals, though not the mass of the population, his theories meant that God was now redundant. Like Lyell's work before it, Darwin's carried conviction through its scrupulous argument from huge amounts of meticulously recorded data relating to animals and plants.

At the end of *The Origin of Species* Darwin takes a benign view of his own evolutionary picture:

There is a grandeur in this view of life, with its several powers, having been originally breathed into a few forms or into one; whilst this planet has gone cycling on according to the fixed law of gravity, from so simple a beginning endless forms most beautiful and most wonderful have been, and are being, evolved.[38]

Only at a later stage in the second edition did Darwin insert defensively (after 'breathed') the phrase 'by the Creator'.

Earlier in *Origin* he wrote approvingly of natural selection itself without reference to the Creator: 'How fleeting are the wishes and efforts of man! how short his time! and consequently how poor will his products be, compared with those accumulated by Nature during whole geological periods.'[39] These remarks indicate a second displacement that follows from Darwin's accounts: God has been rendered redundant and now humanity has been transformed from the hero and the point of the rest of creation to a random production of an inexorable law operating on whatever material it finds. Aptly, Herschel described Darwin's 'natural selection' as 'the law of higgledy-piggledy'.[40] Not that Darwin discusses the evolution of humanity in *The Origin of Species*. There man is for him 'a determining absence'.[41]

AGNOSTICISM

The loss of religious faith in the Victorian period had various causes in addition to the findings of scientists. A sophisticated examination of biblical texts had shown the revisions and changes to which the New as well as the Old Testament had been subjected during transmission and translation. Literal acceptance of their current form was shown to be impossible. At the same time some questioned what they saw as the 'ethical' implications of the Christian account of the Fall into sin of Adam and Eve tainting all humanity until Christ 'paid the price' of their 'redemption' by suffering crucifixion. To such people, who included Francis Newman, John Ruskin, and George Eliot, these doctrines suggested a commercially minded and cruel God. But even for the minority already feeling this repugnance, scientific discoveries provided a more concrete rationale for disbelief. Ruskin, for example, wrote in a letter 'If only the geologists would let me alone ... I could do very well, but those dreadful Hammers! I hear the clink of them at the end of every cadence of the Bible verses'.[42]

For doubters like this, no precise name existed. But in 1869 Thomas Huxley coined the term *agnostic*. It was from the Greek word meaning 'unknown, unknowing, or unknowable'. Huxley took the word from the New Testament account of the altar to the 'unknown God' which St Paul found the Athenians had built as a kind of insurance policy alongside those to other gods (Acts 17: 23). When Huxley coined the term to apply to himself, he gave it a precise meaning: one who holds that the existence of anything beyond and behind material phenomena is unknown or unknowable. It is not for him the strict equivalent of 'doubt'. At first for Huxley belief in a transcendent being meant believing the incredible but he later adopted his 'agnostic' position. Others were ready to attach the label to themselves, including Hardy's friend, Leslie Stephen. For some the use of the term to describe their own position was an attempt to distinguish themselves from 'atheists' who were widely regarded as depraved infidels. Consequently also agnostics such as Stephen were careful to conform to Victorian notions of respectability in relation to morals and manners. Stephen, for instance, when editing *Far from the Madding Crowd* for serial publication in the *Cornhill* magazine famously issued an instruction in relation to Fanny Robin's illegitimate child—'Omit the baby'.

The term spread to include religious doubters of various sorts including those who, like Hardy, had lost a firm religious faith. Many were far from passive in their position which involved at times an active questioning. In considering Victorian 'agnostics' it is necessary, as with Hardy, to characterize individuals rather than to assume that, because they shelter under the same umbrella, they are identical in the state of their religious views or that all were equally pessimistic.

CHAPTER 3

THE LITERARY CONTEXT

Hardy and Other Writers: Poets

HARDY acquired literary language as others acquire a second tongue: by conscious effort. The literary context of all his work is the layer upon layer of eclectic reading, already described, that he laid down throughout his life. He was always a voracious reader and no doubt the learning by rote which formed a large part of his formal education left him with a capacity to memorize what he read. The deepest stratum of such reading, consisting of the Bible, the Book of Common Prayer, and *The Pilgrim's Progress*, first supplied him with a language in which to think reflectively, as well as subjects on which he was to reflect for the rest of his life.

For subsequent layers of reading there is plenty of evidence: at 16 he began to be interested in French and the Latin classics; at 20 he would be 'reading the *Iliad*, the *Aeneid*, or the Greek Testament from six to eight in the morning' followed in the next two years by *Agamemnon* and *Oedipus*; in his mid-twenties he read 'some Horace; also Childe Harold and Lalla Rookh' and 'a fairly large tract of English poetry' as well as Swift and Defoe (*Life*, pp. 50–1). This avid devouring of literature took place while he was working as a trainee architect. During this period of the later 1860s he kept a notebook now described as *Thomas Hardy's Studies, Specimens &c. Notebook*. This copybook gives evidence of 'vocabulary-building exercises consisting of the quotation and selective underlining of brief snippets, rarely of more than three or four words in length'. The sources for quotations are '*The Golden Treasury* and . . . such solidly "canonical authors" as Shakespeare, Spenser, Milton, Burns, Wordsworth, Scott, Coleridge, Byron, and Shelley" as well as contemporaries such as Algernon Swinburne, Jean Ingelow, and Alfred Tennyson. Several other notebooks and commonplace books survive covering the period from the mid-1860s to 1927 into which Hardy and, for a time, Emma copied or pasted thousands of quotations and articles which struck him as worth preserving.

From the publication of *Desperate Remedies* onwards, reading and note-taking provided the linguistic fabric of his work. These materials were used as allusions or epigraphs or were echoed verbally in the novels. His narratives are interwoven with innumerable allusions which are striking for their frequency even in an age given to the practice. More significantly, as even his first published novel reveals, Hardy was doing more than consciously acquiring items of vocabulary or lexis. Throughout his life he made a deliberate study of vocabulary and in the early notebook shows a taste for poeticisms such as '*unweeting*', '*while-ere*' and '*neighbour nigh*'.[2] In addition to the acquisition of words, he was absorbing ideas, or rather recognizing questions that were to haunt him later.

It is evidently true that, as he claimed in the *Life*, during his time as an architect in the 1860s he chiefly read and wrote poetry, though he did not then publish any. When, many years after this, in the 1890s he abandoned novel-writing and turned entirely to poetry, he accounts for it revealingly:

The change, after all, was not so great as it seemed. It was not as if he had been a writer of novels proper, and as more specifically understood, that is, stories of modern artificial life and manners showing a certain smartness of treatment. He had mostly aimed, and mostly succeeded, to keep his narratives close to natural life, and as near to poetry in their subject as the conditions would allow, and had often regretted that those conditions would not let him keep them nearer still. (*Life*, pp. 309–10)

It is possible to read this as a typical Hardy subterfuge to conceal the part that distress over the criticism of *Tess* and *Jude* had played in his decision to give up writing novels. But as usual with him it is possible to discern some truth in what he says, if looked at from the right oblique angle. Certainly his last novel, *The Well-Beloved* (1897), a redrafting of an earlier serial, *The Pursuit of the Well-Beloved* (1892), is not exactly a 'novel proper'. Rather it is a work of a kind of magic realism in the story of a man, Pearson/Pierston, who at intervals of twenty years falls in love with three generations of women: grandmother, mother, and daughter. Its closeness to poetic fantasy (much admired by Marcel Proust) is enhanced by its interwoven verses. In the 1897 form it follows an epigraph from

Shelley's 'The Revolt of Islam', 'One shape of many names'. The three sections concerning the three different women have their own successive epigraphs also. That for the first romance is from Richard Crashaw:

> Now, if Time knows
> That Her, whose radiant brows
> Weave them a garland of my vows;
>
> Her that dares be
> What these lines wish to see:
> I seek no further, it is She.

The corresponding epigraph for the daughter of the hero Pierston's first love is from Thomas Wyatt:

> Since Love will needs that I shall love,
> Of very force I must agree:
> And since no chance may it remove,
> In wealth and in adversity
> I shall alway myself apply
> To serve and suffer patiently.

And for the granddaughter of Pierston's first love, the epigraph is Shakespearian:

> In me thou seest the glowing of such fire,
> That on the ashes of his youth doth lie
> As the death-bed whereon it must expire,
> Consumed with that which it was nourished by.

The juxtaposition of these three expressions of mainly painful love against a tale in which the lover eventually only allows himself to be seen by moonlight in order to conceal his wrinkled face says more than yards of comment from the narrator could. All three quotations, and in particular the third, raise the unanswered question of whether the pain is entirely self-inflicted or not. The text of the novel is inserted like new stanzas into the web of verse formed by the epigraphs and by the many echoes of English and classical texts that it contains. Such strange intertextuality or use of other texts anticipates that of modernists like T. S. Eliot. The form of *The Well-Beloved* certainly supports Hardy's own statement that some of his late novels aspired to the condition of poetry.

It is also true that Hardy was writing at a time when poetry was regarded as the highest form of literature, far higher than novels. As a mid-century work addressed to women put it: 'In a poem, the wildest language of passion, though it may appeal to the feelings, is generally called forth in circumstances remote from the experience of the reader.'[3] In this rather hazy way, aesthetics and morality were confused: dubious feelings were allowable in the fantasy world of poetry but not when associated with the 'real' world of naturalistic novels. One positive result of this was that poets were theoretically allowed more freedom of expression than was thought proper for a novelist. Poetry is a kind of Arabian Nights world where weird things are allowed to happen. This did not always lead to approval of poems such as those of Swinburne that treat sado-masochism, but at least they got into print. In addition, Hardy believed that poetry gave greater freedom because it did not require consistency from one poem to another and he revelled in opportunities for self-contradiction. He thought consistency was 'objectless' and in his late novels he aspired to create something equivalent to poems but which captured transient experiences in a single text in an almost exclamatory way. This perhaps explains why he regarded Shelley's 'O world! O life! O time!' as the most beautiful of English lyrics. It is this view of poetry which explains the relationship between his novels and his verses. It is the poetry which captures the certainties his narratives cannot adhere to.

The frequency of allusion to canonical works of poetry in Hardy's novels has another significance. The fact that 'great' literary texts inhabit his makes a clear assertion about his status as a writer: their presence equates him with the canon of writers thought to constitute a 'great tradition'. The confidence in his own ability that this implies makes a striking contrast to his persistent insecurity over his social as opposed to his literary standing. Significantly he comments on receiving the Order of Merit in 1910 for services to literature (when he had earlier—in 1908—refused a mere knighthood) such as many writers accepted. But he evidently felt that an honour restricted to only twenty-four people, usually of great distinction in their own fields, was an appropriate form of recognition for his talent. There is, however, considerable social unease in his account of the ceremony: 'The King received him pleasantly: "but afterwards I felt that I had failed in the accustomed formalities"' (*Life*, p. 378).

Hardy and Other Writers: Scientists and Philosophers

Hardy was acquainted socially with several novelists—George Meredith, Henry James, George Gissing, Robert Louis Stevenson, and others. But quotations from novels do not figure prominently in his notebooks, nor in his texts. He certainly made notes, however, from the Victorian sages: men of science and philosophy. They were rated more highly than novelists who tended to be thought of as mere entertainers. As has been pointed out, the bedrock of Hardy's literary language was formed by the Bible and the Book of Common Prayer, learnt at the stage when he was still a religious believer. Soon, contrastingly juxtaposed with these, under the influence of Horace Moule, were the works of naturalists like Charles Darwin and geologists like the popularizer, Gideon Algernon Mantell. In the *Life* Hardy claims to have been among the first to welcome Darwin's *The Origin of Species* (1859). Certainly in 1858 he was given the two volumes of Mantell's *The Wonders of Geology* (1838) by Moule and he kept it all his life. Moule's father's rage at his son's purchase of this dangerous work formed the basis of a similar episode in *Tess* between Angel Clare and his father who, like Moule's, is a clergyman. Mantell's work, derived from Charles Lyell's, tackles the question of religious belief boldly by insisting on his own faith. The significance of geological and biological discoveries for belief in God, however, was an issue dealt with at prolix length by the so-called social evolutionist Herbert Spencer. Spencer drew largely on the work of Auguste Comte who argued for the abandonment of absolute causes and the development of a blueprint for society founded on 'scientific' principles, suitable for an industrial age. Spencer, like Comte, was bent on producing a new system of ethics. Both these writers, who tried to push the implications of evolutionary and geological facts as far as they could, were of great interest to Hardy. They figure largely in his notebooks, though Comte is quoted in translation. The coexistence of such writers as these along with the major poets is an indication of the interlocking of the two in the nineteenth century. The connection is sharpened by the fact that both kinds of writers shared a common medium. The distinction between literary language and other kinds is of course arbitrary. Readers today accept a historian and essayist like Carlyle as a writer of 'literature'; but in the nineteenth century all serious writers shared a common language.

The very issues raised by scientists such as Darwin and Lyell were the subjects that preoccupied poets like Tennyson and novelists like Hardy. These were: the origins of the universe; human beings and their significance in the universe; the question of the existence of God; and the nature and source of ethics. Once absorbed, Lyell's and Darwin's discoveries resulted in a questioning of Christianity and the Church which had formerly been regarded as the foundation of society. But the language used by scientists and general essayists was not a carefully dispassionate and would-be clinically unambiguous medium such as scientists now aspire to. There never is transparency in language but in major works such as *The Origin of Species* it is less transparent than was hoped for. We now expect scientific language to work by a process of cool induction from the data. The method in scientific writing of the Victorian period is inductive but the perspective is not one of cool observation. Mantell, for instance, responds emotionally to new geological knowledge:

In the shapeless pebble that we tread upon, in the rude mass of rock or clay, the uninstructed eye would in vain seek for novelty or beauty; like the adventurer in Arabian story, the inquirer finds the cavern closed to his entrance, and the rock refusing to give up the treasures entombed within its stony sepulchre, till the talisman is obtained that can dissolve the enchantment, and unfold the wondrous secrets which have so long lain hidden.[4]

In addition to its exclamatory force, this passage is highly rhetorical in its parallels between phrases or clauses and is based on an elaborate metaphor equating the magic phrase 'Open sesame!' with the magic transformation effected for the observer of rock or clay by a knowledge of geology.

This is Mantell's normal language into which he instils a note of breathless wonder even into his account of what he mundanely calls the 'Extensive Duration of Geological Periods':

The insect of an hour, contrasting its own ephemeral existence with the flowers on which it rests, would attribute an unchanging durability to the most evanescent of vegetable forms; while the flowers, the trees, and the forests would ascribe an endless duration to the soil on which they grow: and thus, uninstructed man, comparing his own brief earthly existence with the solid framework of the world he inhabits, deems the hills and mountains around him coeval with the globe itself. But, with the enlargement and cultivation of his mental powers, he takes a more just, comprehensive, and enlightened view of the wonderful scheme of creation.[5]

The literariness of such language is increased by the freedom with which Mantell quotes poets like Byron and Felicia Hemans with no sense that they are out of place.

Charles Darwin's work is of course also based on the geological accounts of Lyell and its method is also inductive, based on years of detailed study of plants and animals. The approach is strictly analytical, closely argued in a web-like form, but the language he inherited for the exposition of his ideas was 'imbued with natural theology',[6] the same medium that Tennyson and Hardy used. Necessary terms such as 'contrivance' and 'design' implied an agent to contrive or design. Such language is not a problem for Mantell because it fits his belief that the Great Contriver or Designer is God. Like Mantell, Darwin only had the option of a stylized literary language characterized by rhetorical parallels, emotive expressions and figurative comparisons; and it did not suit him so well.

Darwin's argument is that natural selection is blind or empty of intent. They are simply the result of a variation in individual members of a species which is incidentally sustained by an environment which favours the characteristics of these individuals over other members of the same species. Yet nature, or Nature as Darwin calls it, is personified (sometimes as 'she') in the same way as in poetry: 'Nature cares nothing for appearances, except in so far as they may be useful to any being. *She* can act on every internal organ, on every shade of constitutional difference, on the whole machinery of life. Man selects only for his own good; Nature only for that of the being which *she* tends.'[7] Here the account of natural selection is blurred by the personification that lends agency to what is intended to be a blind process. The final comparison with man and *his* intentions supports such a reading.

Darwin was not unaware of the difficulties such language presented for him. In a vital chapter describing the 'Struggle for Existence' which is central to his theory, he writes warningly: 'I should premise that I use the term Struggle for Existence in a large and metaphorical sense only, including dependence of one being on another, and including (which is more important) not only the life of the individual but success in leaving progeny.'[8] But such an attempt to limit metaphor and let the comparison apply only so far and no further is not viable. Having set up the equation, say, between nature and a person, the writer cannot prevent the reader from seeing both as agents. In the same way verbs like 'select' and 'struggle' as well as nouns like 'success' carry implications of agency or intent evident in the contexts in which they occur. Yet metaphors and similes abound in *The Origin of Species*. Further, Darwin's emotive exclamations of wonder at the work of nature echo poems like Hardy's favourite 'O world! O life! O time!': 'whilst this planet has gone cycling on according to the fixed law of gravity, from so simple a beginning endless forms most beautiful and most wonderful have been, and are being, evolved.'[9] Such writing as this is seamlessly joined with the language in which Hardy wrote. Like his, it has a layer of religious language with, superimposed upon it, layers of poetic language and a topping of scientific terms. In his account of the natural world and man's relation to it, Hardy is engaging with the debate initiated by such scientists using the same language: they intermingle their scientific terms with literary expressions; Hardy laces his literary medium with scientific terms.

Publication and Circulation of Fiction

As the account of developments in education has shown, the numbers of those who could read rose slowly but inexorably as the century progressed. Literacy was the main test of standards in schools. Although the requirements for moving into higher 'standards' were primitive, there was then an increasing appetite for the printed word, as now for visual images. This appetite was both fed and fostered by the upsurge of religious proselytizing in the early part of the period which led to organizations such as the Religious Tract Society (founded in 1799). These existed to produce cheap religious pamphlets as ammunition in the campaign for conversion, rather on the lines of Jehovah's Witnesses today. Such tracts were handed out in huge numbers at railway stations, and left in hotels, prisons, and workhouses. Zealous individuals like Mrs Pardiggle in Dickens's *Bleak House* (1853) delivered them personally to the homes of the 'lower orders'. Such material at least provided a form of free reading when it was scarce among the less well-off members of society. Not every recipient was appreciative. The brickmaker to whom Mrs Pardiggle delivers her tract represents the reaction of many when he rails: 'Have I read the little book wot you left? No, I an't read the little book wot you left. There an't nobody here as knows how to read it; and if there wos, it wouldn't be suitable to me. It's a book fit for a babby, and I'm not a babby. If you was to leave me a doll, I shouldn't nuss it' (chapter 8). But there were many others avid to read, as is evident from the sales particularly of cheaply produced works. Cheaper production was already made possible by improvements in printing such as the development of the steam-press and new ways of reproducing illustrations. A typical example of a cheap work was the *Penny Cyclopedia* (1833–44), published in weekly parts at a price of one penny. At its peak this sold 75,000 copies of a single part. It was one of many such popular packages of information.

But the major factor in the success of publishing *fiction* in parts was Dickens. His first published novel, *Pickwick Papers* (1836–7), was a double text of narrative and pictures, sold in monthly parts at one shilling (one-twentieth of a pound sterling). By the fifteenth part 40,000 copies were sold. *Pickwick Papers* was followed rapidly by many other narratives in parts. Towards the end of the century a more upmarket form of this kind of publication developed in the shape of serialization in periodicals for middle-class readers. These were magazines such as the *Graphic*, the *Cornhill Magazine*, *Belgravia*, and the *Illustrated London News*. All but the first two of Hardy's novels first appeared in this form: *A Pair of Blue Eyes*, *Far from the Madding Crowd*, *The Hand of Ethelberta*, *The Return of the Native*, *The Trumpet-Major*, *A Laodicean*, *Two on a Tower* (America), *The Mayor of Casterbridge*, *The Woodlanders*, *Tess of the d'Urbervilles*, *The Well-Beloved*, and *Jude the Obscure*.

Entrepreneurs soon grasped the significance of linking price and circulation in securing commercial success and a specific mechanism was developed to exploit the prevailing taste for cheaply priced fiction. In many ways this mechanism, which lasted only from the 1840s to the 1890s (but therefore for the whole of Hardy's career as a novelist) resembled those practices in operation at the end of the twentieth century. In this latter period, control of publication and circulation fell into fewer and fewer hands: those of increasingly global publishing groups who bought up smaller traditional firms. In the mid-nineteenth century the control of circulation (and through circulation of publication) was also in the hands of a few individuals like Charles Edward Mudie and William Henry Smith. In both periods these external agents (global firms or individuals) were able to affect the content as well as the physical form of works which were to achieve mass circulation. The recent formulas for such works, appropriately described as the commodity 'best-sellers', are sex-and-shopping or sex-and-violence. The requirements in the Victorian period, which will be discussed later, were different, but then as now commercial pressures were effective in influencing the subjects of novels and their treatment.

The source of pressure today is the lack of competition, which allows large companies to select their future best-sellers and market them with massive publicity—possibly in media other than print which they also own. The entrepreneurs in the nineteenth century had more modest assets but an equally efficient system in which those in control of circulation had the whip-hand over publishers and through them over authors. The crucial vehicle for circulation was, they realized, the circulating library.

Victorian readers were increasing in number and clearly had more stamina than their later counterparts. Thanks to the huge popularity of the very lengthy novels of Walter Scott, the three-volume format had become standard by the mid-century. Such works sold for thirty-one shillings and sixpence (roughly one and a half pounds sterling). This was a large sum at a time when a labouring man might earn perhaps £15 a year. In 1842 the most well-known of the circulating libraries was opened by C. E. Mudie. This library could order new works in large numbers of copies. By 1858 Mudie's had become virtually a national institution. The library offered to individual subscribers the loan of one volume at a time for just one guinea a year or four volumes at a time for just two guineas a year. Larger subscriptions could be taken out by clubs or libraries. Volumes could be either collected or forwarded. From Mudie's point of view (and that of his rival, W. H. Smith) the three-decker format was ideal. With three volumes Mudie could rapidly make available to many readers the new works that they were eager to read. As Reader A passed on to volume two, Reader B could start on volume one; to be replaced in turn by Reader C; by which time Reader A was on to volume three. 'Mudie Mania' set in, spawning visual cartoon jokes and verbal ones such as the rhyme:

As children must have Punch and Judy
So I can't do without my Mudie.[10]

Since the libraries bought large numbers of copies of new works, they were able to insist on three-deckers and to demand generous discounts. Part of the benefit to the author and publisher of such works was that if they were accepted by the library owner, a reasonably large sale was ensured and the risk of publication for an unknown author was shared. By publishing lists of his new acquisitions in middle-class periodicals like the *Athenaeum* and the *Spectator*, the 'librarian' was also able to offer secure publicity as well as a captive readership. The position of the circulating libraries was consequently so strong that, as well as insisting on three-deckers and discounts from the publishers, they could also demand an embargo on direct sale of books to the public for at least a year, except at the artificially high price of thirty-one shillings and sixpence. At the end of that period the libraries themselves sold off their own three-decker copies cheaply, leaving the publishers commercially hamstrung.

Naturally the prevalence of the three-volume format influenced the fiction written. Everyone may have one novel in them but it is not necessarily a three-decker. One obvious result of this was what came to be called stretching. Something could be done to create extra length by the physical format: wide margins and well-spaced type could add up to extra pages. But deliberate stretching beyond what the author wished could also take place: padding of episodes, extra events or characters. Many novelists disliked this and some, like Anthony Trollope and Rhoda Broughton, said so. Trollope even objected to physical stretching which, in typically commercial terms, he saw as short-changing his readership:

I have always endeavored to give good measure to the public—The pages, as you propose to publish them, are so thin and desolated, and contain such a poor rate of type meandering thro' a desert of margin, as to make me ashamed of the idea of putting my name to the book. The stories were sold to you as one volume and you cannot by any argument be presumed to have the right of making it into two without my sanction to the change.[11]

Readers frequently grew impatient, usually with the second volume of works which the author had stretched. This was often the weakest of the three. Each volume required a dramatic structure which the knotting of the plot provided for the first and the unravelling of it provided for the third. This left what was sometimes referred to as the 'sad second volume'. These were the market conditions that Hardy faced at the onset of his career as a novelist. Eight of his fourteen published novels appeared in three-decker form as volumes. These were *Desperate Remedies*, *A Pair of Blue Eyes*, *The Return of the Native*, *The Trumpet-Major*, *A Laodicean*, *Two on a Tower* (a relatively short text), *The Woodlanders*, and *Tess of the d'Urbervilles*. All of these except *Desperate Remedies* had already first appeared in serial form. Both types of publication had an impact on what Hardy wrote and how he revised it for each type. *Under the Greenwood Tree*, *Far from the Madding Crowd*, *The Hand of Ethelberta*, and *The Mayor of Casterbridge* appeared first in book form as two volumes, and *Jude* and *The Well-Beloved* each as one volume. Of these last mentioned six novels, only *Under the Greenwood Tree* was not serialized.

Censorship and Public Taste

In the early twenty-first century publishers are able to induce writers of would-be best-sellers to write to a formula with particular ingredients. The author provides the text, the publisher massive publicity and often massive sales. This is normally thought of as a response to market forces or consumer taste. In its insistence on too narrow a formula, however, it constitutes censorship. In the Victorian period it would appear that the role now taken by global players was taken by a few individual 'librarians' like Mudie and W. H. Smith. It was they who to an extent were able to enforce exclusion of certain subjects. The name 'Mudie's Select Library' was pointedly chosen to indicate that the volumes listed in his advertisements had Mudie's sanction. They were definitely 'New and Choice Books in Circulation'. The choice was Mudie's own. Since he was a Nonconformist believer of strictly puritanical views, he took a sharp line on matters of religion and sex. He always denied acting as a censor. He preferred to think of himself as responding to a market, to public taste. When attacked for censorship he sprang to defend his own right to select:

The title under which my library was established nearly twenty years ago implies this:—the public know it, and subscribe accordingly and increasingly. They are evidently willing to have a barrier of some kind between themselves and the lower floods of literature.[12]

Mudie's claim that there were commonly agreed standards of propriety requiring the exclusion of low literature from public view has a certain validity. Pornography flourished but as a subterranean culture for men. A consensus of agreement that 'shocking' treatments of sexuality should not be openly circulated is evident from the nature of fiction in middle-class periodicals, the standards of those critics who reviewed fiction, and public responses in the form of letters to the press, to librarians, and to publishers. This community of standards is underpinned by a long-standing tradition, already referred to, that novels were not only inferior to poetry aesthetically but morally as well. Novel reading was thought by many to be dissipating in its effects, an indulgence in fantasy which wasted time better spent in useful work and the development of moral fibre.

As late as 1879 Anthony Trollope still thought it necessary to defend novel reading against accusations of being self-indulgent time-wasting. In an essay 'On English Prose Fiction as a Rational Amusement' he defends novels against the charge that they propagate evil. Trollope goes further than the argument that novels are a reasonable form of entertainment. He answers the opposition on their own terms by claiming the contrary of their assertion that novels are demoralizing. He claims instead that they are actually instructive. Personal relations, he asserts—what some in the late twentieth century unwisely called 'family values'—are at the heart of Christian morality. Those values included the necessity of preserving marriages as the basic family unit, the importance of chastity in women, as well as requiring the stigmatizing of illegitimacy— on all of which topics Hardy came to hold unconventional views. Young girls and the effect of reading upon them figure largely in Trollope's essay since most family values depended on female chastity. So the effect of such reading on young girls was significant. A familiar formulation for a good novel was that it would not bring a blush to the cheek of the young daughters of the middle-class family. The context of this kind of reference was frequently the image of the paterfamilias reading aloud to his family in the evening.

Trollope, in expanding his argument that good novels are instructive in relation to central areas of existence, provides an insight into the kind of compromise the readership required:

That the novelist deals with the false and forward, as well as with the good and gracious, with lust as well as love, with the basest of characters as with the best, is of course true. How else shall he do his work as professor? Does not all our sacred teaching do the same? Are we not specially warned against murder, theft, adultery, and covetousness in the Scriptures? In treating of vice does the British novelist whom you know make vice alluring, or does he make it hideous?

This is the familiar insistence that 'The whole of human life is here' with the assurance in the last sentence that the ending of the story defines its moral quality:

That happy ending, with the normal marriage and the two children—is it the lot of the good girl, who has restrained all her longings by the operations of her conscience, or of the bold, bad, scheming woman who has been unwomanly and rapacious?[13]

The new emphasis in Trollope's argument pushes the case for openness further by allowing that the subjects he lists are actually necessary in novels; and by hinting that even good girls have longings which they need to suppress.

Trollope is not an extreme libertarian but the kind of argument he uses is that which could be used to justify the lurid sensation novels of the 1860s. These novels involved 'lust', 'longings', 'rapacity' as well as murder, adultery, and bigamy woven into an intriguing tangle. They were extremely popular, in particular those of Mary Elizabeth Braddon. In her most notorious novel, *Lady Audley's Secret* (1862), the heroine of the title abandons her child, tries to murder her first husband, believes she has done so, and attempts to poison the rich man she then marries bigamously. Her final confinement to a French asylum pays her out for all this but not until she has deliciously and horribly dominated the narrative as Becky Sharp does in *Vanity Fair*. The novel pivots on the contrast between Lady Audley's (or Lucy Graham's) extreme and seductive beauty and her dire wickedness. Such 'fast' novels had an interest beyond their readability since they formed a bridgehead in previously taboo territory. Elizabeth Gaskell had received brickbats from some as recently as 1853 for her compassionate and highly moral tale of *Ruth*. This novel concerns the life of a seduced girl and her illegitimate child. By far the larger part of the text is taken up by describing Ruth's life of painful repentance and atonement and her heroic death from a fever caught while self-lessly nursing others. In *Lady Audley's Secret* the balance is reversed and most of the text is taken up with the details of Lucy's beauty and her sins. Sensation novels, then, allowed for a limited degree of explicitness in the discussion of sexuality in relation to women. In doing so they prepared the way for later novelists, including Hardy and George Gissing, who were to deal more freely with the subject. An interesting contrast to the earlier taboo on discussion of women as sexual beings are the bland references already current as to young men's natural inclination to dissipation of this sort. Even a totally 'respectable' novel such as George Eliot's *Felix Holt, the Radical* (1866) includes such an episode. The eponymous and priggish hero who redeems Esther Lyon from her triviality and lack of earnestness is revealed to have been himself conveniently converted by 'six weeks' of debauchery of which nothing more is said. None of this suggests that the consensus Trollope relies on was unanimous. For some it was too restrictive, for others not restrictive enough, as is the case with most prevailing critical standards. Nonetheless, it was a force to be addressed by anyone writing a novel.

By the time Trollope wrote his essay in 1870, more open discussion of previously taboo areas was favoured by external events. There had long been a taste for reporting the details of murder cases, particularly if illicit passion was involved. Such reports were often hawked in the streets like ballads. Added to this in the late 1850s was a prolonged discussion of the proposed changes in the divorce law which would remove the need for an Act of Parliament in every individual case. A Royal Commission on the subject had been set up in 1850 and led to much parliamentary and public discussion. Since the Act as finally passed enshrined different grounds for divorce for men and women, it had caused controversy. Many thought, as did Caroline Norton, that allowing men but not women to obtain a divorce for adultery without any aggravating factor would '*legalise* a special indulgence to the animal passions of men'.[14] The discussion also had a class dimension since some, assuming the poor to be sexually rapacious, felt that easier access to divorce should not be available to them. The Bishop of Oxford warned that 'equal justice to the poor would be purchased at the price of the introduction of unlimited pollution'.[15] Once the Act was passed, luridly circumstantial reports of divorce cases, which became more frequent, made popular reading.

Even after this the debate on the double standard of sexual morality continued to rage. One obvious area of concern was the treatment of prostitution. After the parliamentary and other reports on prostitution in the major cities produced during the 1840s, pressure had developed to limit the damage caused by venereal disease. This discussion became serious with the campaign against the Contagious Diseases Act. The founder, Josephine Butler, summed up the central issue involved: 'It is manifest that on all sides it begins to be felt that the principle is to be decided whether male profligacy, at the expense of women, is to be condoned, excused, and darkly perpetrated, or to be sternly condemned and pertinaciously resisted'.[16]

Another event thickened the stew when in 1885 the editor of the *Pall Mall Gazette*, W. T. Stead, after a strange piece of investigative journalism, published 'The Maiden Tribute of Modern Babylon'. It retailed how, in order to bring attention to the trade in young virgins flourishing in London, Stead himself had 'bought' a girl after a midwife had guaranteed her virginity. His advertising trailer, puffing the forthcoming article, had spoken of a revelation of the horrible realities in the 'London inferno'. The piece was reprinted worldwide and created huge 'public interest' (in both senses) which justified discussion. By the late 1880s the way was open for those who wished to extend the range of serious novels and to shatter the hypocrisy of earlier writers.

Hardy's Response to the Literary Context

It is evident that the literary context with which Hardy engaged as a novelist from 1869 to 1895 was composed of many disparate elements. These included a canonical tradition which favoured poetry over fiction, though writers like Dickens and George Eliot had achieved canonical status; a written language common to literature, science, and philosophy; a mass reading public avid for fiction of all kinds, with many particularly greedy for sensation fiction; a commercial censorship requiring an overt propriety in the treatment of religion and sexuality; and a national press that could evade the taboos imposed on novels because of its role as a reporter of fact. As to the last of these—every report is in today's jargon 'a story' and many reports echo literary stereotypes such as the innocent working-class girls of Stead's report/story, doomed to the harlot's fall. The context with its sensations and controversies both social and literary was a dynamic one. Hardy, when engaging with it during the writing of his early unpublished work and his first three published novels (*Desperate Remedies*, *Under the Greenwood Tree*, and *A Pair of Blue Eyes*), fastened on elements which resonated with his deepest concerns. These, as outlined in Chapter 1 above, were: social class and social mobility; women and sexuality; and rural life.

The unpublished novel, of which no complete form survives, captures the first of these issues in its provocative title *The Poor Man and the Lady* and is a critique of the fashionable novels of the previous two decades, the 'silver fork' fiction. Thackeray, the social insider, had already satirized them in *Vanity Fair*. Hardy did so again, as his account makes clear:

The story was, in fact, a sweeping dramatic satire of the squirearchy and nobility, London society, the vulgarity of the middle class, modern Christianity, church restoration, and political and domestic morals in general, the author's views, in fact, being obviously those of a young man with 'a passion for reforming the world'—those of many a young man before and after him, the tendency of the writing being socialistic, not to say revolutionary (*Life*, pp. 62–3).

It is not surprising that this comprehensive condemnation of everything except the working classes failed to find a publisher. It did, however, generate some advice from George Meredith who had read it for a potential publisher. He recommended that Hardy should 'attempt a novel with a purely artistic purpose, giving it a more complicated "plot" than was attempted with *The Poor Man and the Lady*' (*Life*, p. 64). A 'purely artistic' novel was presumably one which did not engage in serious social criticism. Fortuitously this advice produced in Hardy's next two novels types of narrative which in modified form provided basic elements in most of his works.

Complicated plots came naturally to Hardy who was always keenly interested in improbable events which, unsurprisingly, actually happened—so this piece of Meredith's advice was not unwelcome. His next novel, *Desperate Remedies*, was a typical sensation novel full of crime, mystery, intrigue, and complicated relationships. At this stage in his career Hardy describes himself as eager 'to get into print as the author of a three-volume novel' (*Life*, p. 61) of a profitable sort that the circulating libraries would accept. The plot of *Desperate Remedies* parallels that of *Lady Audley's Secret*. For that beautiful demonic figure Hardy substitutes a man with a secret, Aeneas Manston. He too is striking in appearance with a preternaturally clear complexion:

There was not a blemish or speck of any kind to mar the smoothness of its surface or the beauty of its hue. Next, his forehead was square and broad, his brows straight and firm, his eyes penetrating and clear ... Eyes and forehead both would have expressed keenness of intellect too severely to be pleasing, had their force not been counteracted by the lines and tone of the lips. These were full and luscious to a surprising degree, possessing a woman-like softness of curve, and a ruby redness so intense, as to testify strongly to much susceptibility of heart (chapter VIII).

Manston is the illegitimate son of the rich landowner, Miss Aldclyffe, and has the same evil ruthlessness as Lady Audley. He too murders a spouse to free himself to marry again; abducts his unwilling second bride; and eventually pays the price by committing suicide. The few reviewers thought it 'remarkably coarse' and refused to believe in an '*un*married lady of position and fortune' having an illegitimate child. Such an idea was 'a miserable creation—uninteresting, unnatural, and nasty'.[17]

Significantly, there were no comments on what readers today might expect to have caused most outrage. This element is what recent reviewers recognize as the latent lesbianism (or in Victorian terms 'Sapphism') of Miss Aldclyffe. She employs Cytherea Graye, the object of her son's affection, as her maid and is herself overtly attracted physically to the girl. At one point she gets into Cytherea's bed, freeing herself 'from the last remnant of restraint'. Then 'She flung her arms round the young girl, and pressed her gently to her heart. "Now kiss me," she said' (chapter VI). Presumably this is because the scene remained 'unintelligible' to most readers at the time and paradoxically such a scene would have caused a scandalous uproar forty or fifty years *later* when it would have been intelligible to many more people.[18] Already in his first novel Hardy was treading a fine line between the sayable and the unspeakable in relation to sexual matters. The late novels on these issues are in a sense sensation novels transformed. *Tess* and *Jude* bear the same resemblance to *Lady Audley's Secret* and *Desperate Remedies* as *Hamlet* does to *The Spanish Tragedy*.

Hardy had paid Tinsley Brothers £75 towards the cost of publishing *Desperate Remedies*. He eventually received back something over £59 and so made a small loss on the project. This commercial failure showed him that he had, as he said, too crudely interpreted Meredith's suggestions about plot. His next novel shows him trying to follow the advice about writing a work 'with a purely artistic purpose'. He seems to take the advice literally to refer to artistry in the visual sense. *Under the Greenwood Tree* has the significant subtitle 'A Rural Painting of the Dutch School'. The novel itself is virtually plotless in its account of the disbanding of a village church choir and the haverings of Fancy Day between three suitors. Its visual scenes of rural life are what caught the reviewers' notice. They too chose to praise it in terms of its power as a picture. As one wrote of the subtitle: 'His present work is rather a number of studies for such a painting. The ability to paint is there, but practice only can give the power of composition.' Similarly, Horace Moule praised it as 'a series of rural pictures full of life and genuine colouring'.[19] Hardy did not ask to be thought of as a Landseer of the novel: his next work, *A Pair of Blue Eyes*, published for the first time under his own name, responded to both aspects of Meredith's advice. He quotes proudly the praise of one reviewer describing it as 'the most artistically constructed of the novels of its time' (*Life*, p. 98).

Before this third novel was published he was approached by Leslie Stephen (father of Virginia Woolf), editor of the prestigious *Cornhill Magazine*. Significantly, Stephen had read *Under the Greenwood Tree* but not *Desperate Remedies*. On the basis of the former novel he had decided that 'such writing would probably please the readers of the Cornhill Magazine as much as it has pleased me'.[20] He was so eager to get hold of what Hardy described in general terms as a pastoral tale called *Far from the Madding Crowd* concerning 'a woman-farmer, a shepherd, and a sergeant in the Dragoon Guards'[21] that he behaved rashly. He waived his usual requirement that he should see the whole manuscript of a work before accepting it and accepted the novel for serialization in the *Cornhill*.

But there turned out to be an iron hand holding a blue pencil within Stephen's velvet glove. Hardy was coerced into accepting many alterations and omissions. Sometimes Stephen simply said that some passages were not 'necessary' but in the main he wished to sanitize any sexual references. His polite ruthlessness is evident in what he wrote to Hardy as the serial progressed:

I have ventured to leave out a line or two in the last batch of proofs from an excessive prudery of wh. I am ashamed; but one is forced to be absurdly particular. May I suggest that Troy's seduction of the young woman will require to be treated in a gingerly fashion, when, as I suppose must be the case, he comes to be exposed to his wife?[22]

The bland reference to a line or two is a calculated understatement. Much more was sometimes deleted. The 'suggestion' about Troy's seduction of Fanny Robin which exposes him to Bathsheba as a philanderer is a case in point. References to Troy's past escapades were cut out either by Stephen or at his insistence by Hardy. In the manuscript Troy's character is revealed to Bathsheba when she sees a stillborn child in Fanny's coffin. But in accordance with Stephen's demands the baby is omitted, leaving its necessary presence only implicit and removing the effect of its impact on Troy's wife when Fanny's coffin is opened.

Hardy's public attitude to censorship at this early stage in his career is recorded in a letter to Stephen:

The truth is that I am willing, and indeed anxious, to give up any points which may be desirable in a story when read as a whole, for the sake of others which shall please those who read it in numbers. Perhaps I may have higher aims some day, and be a great stickler for the proper artistic balance of the completed work, but for the present circumstances lead me to wish merely to be considered a good hand at a serial. (*Letters*, i. 28)

Because he needs the money—he was newly married with a wife to support—he will yield to commercial pressures. When, however, the novel was subsequently published in two-volume form, much of what had been omitted was restored. The alterations at issue were not to material which would now be regarded as shocking: merely a reference to a pathetic dead baby is ruled out because the child is illegitimate. Again, significantly the scene of Troy's display of sword-play before the dazzled Bathsheba is now seen as the most powerful sexual allusion in the text but, like the latent Sapphism in *Desperate Remedies*, it is not the object of adverse comment on the grounds of impropriety.

Stephen was by now wary and when Hardy offered him *The Return of the Native* for serialization in the *Cornhill* he decided against it. This time he wrote bluntly that 'though he liked the opening, he feared that the relations between Eustacia, Wildeve, and Tamsin might develop into something "dangerous" for a family magazine'.[23] Stephen was right of course, since Eustacia and Wildeve are lovers when the latter marries Tamsin. Further, Eustacia turns into a Madame Bovary figure as the bored and frustrated wife of Clym Yeobright. Finally Hardy found a publisher in *Belgravia* which, despite its name, had a louche or raffish reputation, partly caused by its serialization of sensation novels by Mary Elizabeth Braddon, who cohabited with the already married editor. Even here there was possibly some minor censoring of the episode where Tamsin, believing herself married to Wildeve, lives with him for a short time as his wife. This is revised out in Hardy's handwriting, possibly at the suggestion of one or other of the magazine editors to whom he showed the first part of the serial, who would undoubtedly have told him that such an episode would not get into print.[24]

Even in a relatively 'proper' novel such as *The Trumpet-Major* there was editorial interference. Hardy met Dr Donald Macleod, the editor of *Good Words* in which *The Trumpet-Major* was serialized, in London. The only 'literary points' he remembers Macleod making were 'that he asked me to make a lover's [*sic*] meeting, which I had fixed for a Sunday afternoon, take place on a Saturday, and that swear-words should be avoided—in both which requests I readily acquiesced'.[25] In *The Mayor of Casterbridge* the relationship between Lucetta and Henchard seems to have been made less explicitly sexual and their marriage was added to the story for the serialization. Similarly, when *The Woodlanders* (1887) was being serialized in *Macmillan's Magazine* the editor wrote to Hardy: 'A gentle hint on one small matter—the affair between Miss Damson and the Doctor . . . I think, if you can contrive not to bring the fair Miss Suke to too open shame, it would be as well. Let the human frailty be construed mild.'[26] The implication here is that Suke Damson should not become pregnant by Fitzpiers.

Worse was to come with the publication of two of Hardy's late novels, *Tess of the d'Urbervilles* (1891) and *Jude the Obscure* (1895). By now Hardy was prepared to resist the censorship of sexual matters where previously he had bowdlerized for serial publications and restored something like their original form for the volume editions. This time Tillotson and Son had contracted to pay him one thousand guineas for what was to become *Tess* but which Hardy was then calling 'Too Late, Beloved!' When, having seen half the text, Tillotson asked him to delete or cut scenes such as Alec's rape/ seduction of Tess, Hardy refused. So anxious were the publishers to escape from their commitment that they risked losing their 1,000 guineas by cancelling the contract. Subsequently *Tess* was rejected by *Murray's Magazine* and then *Macmillan's Magazine*. Mowbray Morris, editor of the latter, now wrote bluntly to Hardy on lines similar to those in his letter about *The Woodlanders*, finding 'rather too much succulence' in the story:

It is obvious from the first page what is to be Tess's fate at Trantridge; it is apparently obvious also to the mother, who does not seem to mind, consoling herself with the somewhat cynical reflection that she may be made a lady *after* if not *before*. All the first part therefore is a sort of prologue to the girl's seduction which is hardly ever, & can hardly ever be out of the reader's mind. Even Angel Clare, who seems inclined to 'make an honest woman' of Tess, has not as yet got beyond a purely sensuous admiration for her person. Tess herself does not appear to have any feelings of this sort about her; but her capacity for stirring & by implication for gratifying these feelings for others is pressed rather more frequently & elaborately than strikes me as altogether convenient, at any rate for my magazine.[27]

Morris's letter is frank enough to reveal the precise nature of the standards he is applying. He does not accuse Hardy of moral indifference to the way that Alec treats Tess but objects to the fact that he gives prominence to the subject of seduction. Similarly it is the portrayal of sexual desire, however 'legitimate' it might be in the case of Angel Clare, who wishes to marry Tess, that he dislikes. So unpalatable would be the portrayal of such feelings in a woman that he simply overlooks any signs of it in Tess. But her physical attractiveness is regarded as itself a crime: she also is too succulent. Morris evidently preferred to read Tess's response as a cold gratification of Alec's lust.

After these rebuffs Hardy seems to have decided that if his novel was to be mutilated he would do it himself. He proceeded to carry out a process which he thought of literally as dismemberment: he removed the rape/seduction scene and the secret baptism of Tess's illegitimate son, Sorrow. He then arranged for the unobtrusive publication of these episodes as two short stories. Meantime he had agreed the publication of his bowdlerized *Tess* in the *Graphic* magazine. The text he presented to the editor was savagely cut. It exchanged the rape/seduction and its antecedents for a bogus marriage, and omitted the baby, the baptism, and the secret burial of the child. Other alterations included a ludicrous change in the scene where Angel Clare carries the four dairymaids one by one across a flooded lane. In the bowdlerized version he pushes them across in a wheelbarrow. Needless to say, Hardy restored a version of all the original events for the three-volume edition. He did so with a prefatory note in which he speaks of reassembling the murdered body of his text/Tess:

The main portion of the following story appeared—with slight modifications—in the *Graphic* newspaper: other chapters, more especially addressed to adult readers, in the *Fortnightly Review* and the *National Observer*, as episodic sketches. My thanks are tendered to the editors and proprietors of those periodicals for enabling me now to piece the trunk and limbs of the novel together, and print it complete, as originally written two years ago.[28]

The same bitter cynicism is evident in Hardy's brutal bowdlerizing of *Jude* for serialization in *Harper's New Monthly Magazine* (Dec. 1894–Nov. 1895). In this version Arabella does not seduce Jude; Sue and Jude do not become lovers and have children; Jude does not spend a night with Arabella when she returns after their separation. Possibly Hardy's keen sense of the grotesque led him to create such incongruities as Sue leaving her husband Phillotson for Jude but merely arranging to live on the opposite side of the street from her lover so that they can talk across it; or Sue referring not to her pregnancy when talking to Arabella but to her shame at selling gingerbread from a market stall. The inference that Hardy displayed a kind of satirical ludicrousness in these changes is made plausible by his stance in the public debate, fostered by external events, which was raging at this time.

The Battle Against Censorship

By the time of the publication of *Tess* (1891) a debate had been carried on publicly in the periodicals and in journalistic letter columns for over a decade on the question of unofficial censorship. The discussion focused on three issues: the anomalous sensation novels; the tyranny of the circulating libraries and periodicals; and the assessment of French 'naturalistic' or 'realistic' writers such as Gustave Flaubert and Émile Zola. Though literature was at issue, the debate involved broader questions of public propriety and decency as well as sexual morality; it culminated in what was sometimes described as a *fin de siècle* sexual anarchy.

The first of the literary sites of contest, the fast novels, were the predictable result of the exclusion from serious fiction of sexual matters generally. The potency acquired from taboo meant that adultery and bigamy had become the staple of such works. As early as 1866 the *Westminster Review* described bigamy in particular as 'Miss Braddon's big black baboon, with which she has attracted all the young girls in the country'.[29] Any radical treatment of such topics was precluded in the 1860s and 1870s by the combination of sensational and criminal events with a priggish narratorial commentary. A two-faced reader is inscribed in the text—ignorant, innocent, and high-minded, who wishes to know the sensational details of these events only in order to feel the appropriate surges of moral indignation. As one critic writes approvingly, 'All the crime is done under proper reprobation and yet the writer and readers have all the benefit of the crime'.[30] The opportunity offered by discussion of sensation novels, however, allowed liberals to argue for a future extension of acceptable limits of treatment. Justin MacCarthy wrote:

That sense of propriety which is satisfied by simply pretending that we do not see and hear things which no human precaution can shut out from our eyes and ears, is worthy of nothing but contempt. The innocence which is ignorance becomes impossible after a certain age, and if it were not impossible it would be merely despicable.

The reading of sensational fiction, MacCarthy here argues, can be educative. This is the case when a particular narrative of a fallen woman abandoned by her lover survives morally: 'The heroine sees and understands her risk, accepts it, suffers for her venture, and pays the penalty with a brave heart'.[31]

The opening made by such comments led in part to the attack in the 1880s on what came to be thought of by some novelists as Mudie's tyrannical censorship. This attack focused on the young girl-reader whom novelists were instructed to inscribe in their texts as pictorial artists were expected to inscribe a particular moral perspective in their paintings. It was a Royal Academy exhibition in 1877 which caused Henry James to complain 'Here, as throughout the field of English art and letters, the influence of the "young person" and her sensitive cheek is perceived to prevail'.[32] In the next decade criticism was extended and made more explicit by other novelists. Chief of these was George Moore who, in 1885, wrote 'Literature at Nurse or Circulating Morals'. His method of attack was not so much argument as deliberately suggestive derision of Mudie and other 'libraries':

Into this nursery none can enter except in baby clothes; and the task of discriminating between a divided skirt and a pair of trousers is performed by the librarian. Deftly his fingers lift skirt and underskirt, and if the examination proves satisfactory the sometimes decently attired dolls are packed in tin-cornered boxes, and scattered through every drawing-room in the kingdom, to be in rocking-chairs fingered and fondled by the 'young person' until she longs for some newer fashion in literary frills and furbelows. Mudie is the law we labour after; the suffrage of young women we are supposed to gain: the paradise of the English novelist is in the school-room.[33]

The third literary context for this long debate was the discussion of French realist novels. There was a belief dating back to the eighteenth century that French novels were salacious. Fielding writes ironically in *Tom Jones* in 1749: 'I am so far from wishing to exhibit such pictures to the Public, that I would wish to draw a Curtain over those in certain French novels' (*OED*). In 1850 the same significance attaches to Robert Browning's use of the adjective in 'Bells and Pomegranates': 'My scrofulous French novel' (*OED*: French a.2b). With the emergence in the mid-nineteenth century of a group of French realist or naturalist writers who dealt with physical aspects of life in a detailed and factual way, the impression of extreme salaciousness was heightened. The French treatment of crime and sexual matters avoids the didacticism of sensation writers. Consequent discussion focused on the relevance of naturalistic detail in literature. Flaubert's *Madame Bovary* (1857) dealt with the adultery of Emma Bovary, a country doctor's wife, and a clerk, Léon, in a totally unromanticized way. Zola's *Thérèse Raquin* (1867) was a meticulous account of passion and murder in the grimmest detail. The naturalists sought verisimilitude in presenting crime, sexual relations, and human inhumanity which they believed represented the 'reality', that physical facts were the causes of those events.

It is on this subject that Hardy is commenting when in a symposium or printed debate in the *New Review* in 1890 he writes in his 'Candour in English Fiction':

Life being a physiological fact, its honest portrayal must be largely concerned with, for one thing, the relations of the sexes, and the substitution for such catastrophes as favour the false colouring best expressed by the regulation finish that 'they married and were happy ever after', of catastrophes based upon sexual relations as it is. To this expansion English society opposes a well-nigh insuperable bar.

He adds on the subject of the readily blushing female reader:

Whether minors should read unvarnished fiction based on the deeper passions, should listen to the eternal verities in the form of narrative, is somewhat a different question from whether the novel ought to be exclusively addressed to those minors. The first consideration is one which must be passed over here; but it will be conceded by most friends of literature that all fiction should not be shackled by conventions concerning budding womanhood, which may be altogether false. It behoves us then to inquire how best to circumvent the present lording of nonage over maturity, and permit the explicit novel to be more generally written.[34]

Though Hardy claimed in a letter to Edmund Gosse in 1895 'I am read in Zola very little' (*Letters*, ii. 99), he had certainly read and noted Zola's story *Abbé Mouret's Transgressions*. The plot resembles the desertion of Tess by Angel Clare, and after Hardy had read it in 1886 or 1887 he began to write *Tess*. He also owned Zola's *The Downfall*, *The Dream*, and *Rome*. It was George Moore, however, who led and, as he believed, won the anti-censorship campaign. Unlike Hardy, he was open in his praise of French naturalism. He corresponded with Zola on that and on the circulating libraries. He modelled his own work on Zola's with the result that his *A Modern Lover* (1883) was banned by the libraries. So too was *A Mummer's Wife* (1884) in which Kate Ede, wife of a shopkeeper, is seduced by actor Dick Lennox who is her lodger. The scene in this novel that drew the libraries' fire was one in which Kate lets Lennox into the house late at night. Its mildness by today's standards shows the degree of censorship that was at issue, as Kate and Lennox go together up the stairs in the dark and past Lennox's bedroom:

Although she could not see his face she felt his breath on her neck. Strong arms were wound about her, she was carried forward, and the door was shut behind her.

Only the faintest gleam of starlight touched the wall next the window; the darkness slept profoundly on landing and staircase, and when the silence was again broken, a voice was heard saying—, 'Oh, you shouldn't have done this! What shall I tell my husband if he asks me where I've been?' (chapter 9)

Moore complained publicly to and about Mudie and succeeded in finding a publisher prepared to produce a cheap one-volume edition of *A Mummer's Wife* and so evade the libraries. By this time increasing numbers of other novelists had managed, with the help of hard-strapped publishers, to force their way into the market with novels for publication cheaply, often in one volume. These cheap editions had become popular and cut into the profits the libraries had made by their sell-off of three-deckers at the end of a year's moratorium on cheap sales. This commercial pressure combined with public criticism to bring about the fall of the three-decker novel. Libraries themselves made moves in 1894 to kill it off, thereby precipitating their own decline, which was also helped by the growth of free public libraries. This did not mean the end of censorship but it allowed for novels which were somewhat franker in their approach and for discussion for, as well as against, the changes.

Hardy, Naturalism, and Realism

Hardy may have denied that he was influenced (for the worse) by French naturalistic writing but he was always inclined to over-react to adverse criticism. Certainly the comparison with Flaubert and Zola must have seemed reasonable at the time. He, like George Moore, plainly treats sexual relationships in a more open, less sentimental way than had previously been done. Whether reviewers disapproved or, like Havelock Ellis, approved, they were not wrong in seeing a similarity between Hardy's novels and those of the French naturalists.

One who took the disapproving line was Margaret Oliphant, also writing on *Jude*, in *Blackwood's Magazine*. She condemns both Hardy and Zola: 'The present writer does not pretend to a knowledge of the works of Zola, which perhaps she ought to have before presuming to say that nothing so coarsely indecent as the whole history of Jude in his relations with his wife Arabella has ever been put in English print—'; she then adds a comment which is of interest: '—that is to say, from the hands of a Master. There may be books more disgusting, more impious as regards human nature, more foul in detail, in those dark corners where the amateurs of filth find garbage to their taste.'[35] This is presumably a reference to the abundant Victorian pornography and those 'amateurs' who sought it out. Such a reference helps to explain the assumed connection between the kind of mildly explicit treatment of seduction such as Moore presents in *A Mummer's Wife* and pornographic intent on the part of the author. It also throws light on Hardy's shrinking from the kind of abuse that Oliphant metes out.

Though Ellis, Oliphant, and other critics are not wrong to link Hardy with naturalist writers, his denial has its own rationale. He did not much theorize about literature separately from the other arts except for three articles: 'Candour in English Fiction' (1890), 'The Profitable Reading of Fiction' (1888), and 'The Science of Fiction' (1891). The last of these in fact engages with Zola's work on the *roman expérimental*. No writer, Hardy argues, even the 'sheerest naturalist',[36] can reasonably deny the manipulation and selection inherent in telling a story. Zola's own work, he asserts, contradicts the claim made in *roman expérimental* that in his own novels no such selection takes place. The rest of Hardy's essay is an expansion of the argument that so-called naturalistic 'realism' in novels is nothing of the kind. It is just another illusion created because 'Nothing but the illusion of truth can permanently please, and when the old illusions begin to be penetrated, a more natural magic has to be supplied.'[37] Experience itself is a phantasmagoria and the piling up of naturalistic detail in the interest of verisimilitude offered as truth is just one more necessary illusion. A deeper reality exists which the gifted author captures through their illusion.

This essay seems to have been much more than a polemic produced to order out of a wish to distinguish Hardy himself from the likes of Zola. It echoes many of the statements that Hardy made elsewhere about art generally, visual as well as verbal. Hardy's view implies that a keen grasp of the superficial details of sights, sounds, events, and people is only effective as art if it is the medium for an understanding (or questioning) of their intrinsic significance:

A sight for the finer qualities of existence, an ear for the 'still sad music of humanity', are not to be acquired by the outer senses alone, close as their powers in photography may be. What cannot be discerned by eye and ear, what may be apprehended only by the mental tactility that comes from a sympathetic appreciativeness of life in all its manifestations.

Characteristically he illustrates his point with images from painting and music:

to see in half and quarter views the whole picture, to catch from a few bars the whole tune, is the intuitive power that supplies the would-be storywriter with the scientific bases for his pursuit'.[38]

In effect Hardy, in denying that he is a naturalist, is denying his acceptance of Zola's belief that human life is determined entirely by physical externals. Later he copied into his notebook many passages from other writers who make this same point with what he presumably regarded as particular succinctness or vividness. He cites, for example, G. K. Chesterton on the dramatist Maeterlinck: 'The one real struggle in modern life is the struggle between the man like Maeterlinck, who sees the inside as the truth, and the man like Zola, who sees the outside as the truth.' Chesterton takes as an instance the event called 'falling in love'. In his view a Zola figure would describe this solely as 'an animal and sexual instinct designed for certain natural purposes'. A Maeterlinck man would dismiss this as a merely 'philosophical or zoological' explanation; and would see it as 'a divine and sacred and incredible vision'.[39]

These kinds of comments are copied increasingly in the later sections of Hardy's notebooks. A more telling expression than Chesterton's is one Hardy abridged from Ellis:

Zola's rule for novels—one must get one's human documents . . . frequent the society of people one is studying . . . record their surroundings. 'But have we got reality then? Does the novelist I casually meet . . . takes note of my cond[ition] . . . furniture &c. . . . know anything whatever of the romance or tragedy which to me is the reality of my life, these other things being but shreds or tatters of life. Or if my romance or tragedy has got into a law-court or a police-court, is he really much nearer then? The unrevealable motives, the charm, the mystery . . . were not deposed to.[40]

Wessex and 'Realism'

The fact that the many quotations referring to this conception of 'reality' or truth occur later rather than earlier in Hardy's notebooks is suggestive. It seems as though this account of it grew upon him gradually. A striking instance of how he put it into practice is given by the changes he made over time in the treatment of his 'Wessex'.

The name itself was used in Anglo-Saxon times, when England was divided into several separate kingdoms, for an area in the south-west populated originally by the West Saxon tribe. Its most famous ruler was Alfred the Great who held court at Winchester. The name for the region died out after the Norman Conquest but persisted as an adjective describing certain breeds of farm animals there. Hardy would have known it from them as well as from his gradually acquired knowledge of archaeology. In his first two novels the setting is identifiably Dorset, though the identity of places is concealed under entirely fictitious names which suggest associations with the area. These are Creston for Weymouth and Froominster for Dorchester in *Desperate Remedies*; and Casterbridge for Dorchester and Budmouth for Weymouth in *Under the Greenwood Tree*. The two names in the latter novel, Casterbridge and Budmouth, were to become fixtures in the landscape of Hardy's novels. In 1874 with *Far from the Madding Crowd* comes his first use of the name Wessex applied to the whole of Dorset: 'Greenhill was the Nijnii Novgorod of Wessex; and the busiest, merriest, noisiest day of the whole statute number was the day of the sheep-fair' (chapter 50).

Though he later claimed to have thought of the name 'Wessex' himself, it is predated by an earlier use by his admired friend, the Dorset poet William Barnes (1801–86). Barnes had learnt enough Old English to produce a primer on the subject *Se Gefylsta* (1849). So he was familiar with the source of the name and in addition he had published *Poems of Rural Life in the Dorset Dialect* (1844) and *Hwomely Rhymes* (1859). Then in his Preface to *Poems of Rural Life in Common English* (1868) he wrote: 'As I think that some people beyond the bounds of Wessex, would allow me the pleasure of believing that they deemed my homely poems to be worthy of their reading, I have written a few in common English.' Hardy met Barnes during his time in Hicks's office which was close to Barnes's house and he became a literary friend. So presumably Hardy forgot that, as is likely, he had read Barnes's Preface.

All the novels after *Far from the Madding Crowd* either refer to (*A Laodicean* and *Two on a Tower*) or are set in the same area. It is now regularly called 'Wessex' but in *The Trumpet-Major*, as it is a 'historical' account of an episode supposed to have taken place in the Napoleonic period, real-place names are used such as Weymouth, Dorchester, and Salisbury. The implication of this anomaly seems to be that a distinction is to be made between the real region (however defined—whether by the boundaries of Dorset or not) and the fictional Wessex. This is not incompatible with Hardy's later development of internal consistency in names and distances found in the two collected editions of his works. The first in 1895–6 was called the Wessex Novels, the grander one in 1912 was called the Wessex Edition. Each collected edition was revised by Hardy himself. Among the many changes he made were some to the names and details of Wessex which lent coherence to the complete editions. As with the first collected edition, the alternatives were aimed not at realism but at consistency. By this time 'Wessex' took in parts of Hampshire, Wiltshire, and Somerset.

From his earliest days as a novelist Hardy was praised as the creator of matchless pictures of rural life. Horace Moule, reviewing *Under the Greenwood Tree* speaks of 'the power and truthfulness shown in these studies of the better class of rustics' in 'the South-Western counties of England'.[41] Somewhat misleadingly in 1895 Hardy hints at the fulfilment of an early blueprint in the Preface to *Far from the Madding Crowd*:

The series of novels I projected being mainly of the kind called local, they seemed to require a territorial definition of some sort to lend unity to their scene. Finding that the area of a single county did not afford a canvas large enough for this purpose, and that there were objections to an invented name, I disinterred the old one.

In the Preface to *Tess* in the same collected edition he gives surprisingly clear details of this hypothetical design. In 'planning the stories', he says, 'the idea was that large towns and points tending to mark the outline of Wessex—such as Bath, Plymouth, The Start, Portland Bill, Southampton &c.—should be named outright'. For the rest he used fictitious names which 'seemed good at the time of

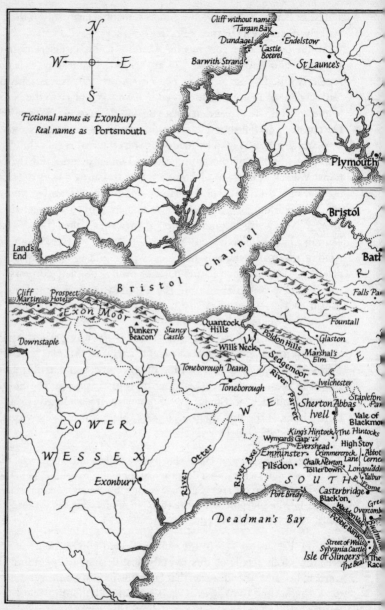

Map of Hardy's Wessex.

HARDY'S WESSEX
OF THE NOVELS AND POEMS

0   10   20
Miles

Christminster
Lumsdon
River Thames
NORTH
The Brown House
Alfredston
Cresscombe
Marygreen
MID-
River Thames
Castle Royal
Marlbury Downs
WESSEX
Gaymead
Aldbrickham
Kennetbridge
WESSEX
Inkpen Beacon
Stoke Barehills
Quartershot
The Great Plain
Weydon Priors
Icenway House
Stonehenge
Stour Head
UPPER
Wintoncester
Leddenton
Melchester
Fernel Hall
Shaston
Marlott
Wingreen
Deansleigh Park
The Chase
The Slopes
WESSEX
Trantridge Cross
Chaseborough
Stourcastle
Knollingwood Hall
The Great
Southampton
Bulbarrow
Shottsford
Lornton Inn
Portsmouth
Flintcombe Ash
Forum
Bramshurst
Yewsholt
Warborne
Chene Manor
FOREST
Weatherbury
Kingsbere
Welland R. Stour
Solentsea
WESSEX
Egdon Heath
Talbothays
Anglebury
Sandbourne
Dairies
Wellbridge
Nether Minton
The Island
Corvesgate
Knollsea
Lulwind Cove
Lightship

The   Channel

writing' and which as with 'Shaston' for Shaftesbury were easily identifiable or thought to be so.[42] In practice the rationalizing of a previously partly haphazard development of names, distances, and journey times was carried out in this revision for the 1895–6 Wessex Novels.

In the 1895 edition Hardy further improved on the consistency of the details of Wessex. Again in the Preface to *Far from the Madding Crowd* he describes Wessex as 'a merely realistic dream country'. He insists, and now more emphatically because of the change just referred to, that

the dream-country has, by degrees, solidified into a utilitarian region which people can go to, take a house in, and write to the papers from. But I ask all good and idealistic readers to forget this, and to refuse steadfastly to believe that there are any inhabitants of a Victorian Wessex outside these volumes in which their lives and conversations are detailed.

Despite the mild humour, Hardy is evidently claiming that his representation of the life and countryside of this region of south-west England is not naturalistic in the French sense but imaginative and impressionistic, involving its traditions and history in their essence. That is its reality and by 1912, in his version of the Preface to *Far from the Madding Crowd*, he characterized it as 'a partly-real, partly dream-country'.[43]

While writing *The Woodlanders* in 1886 he saw the controversial exhibition of impressionist paintings and wrote:

The impressionist school is strong. It is even more suggestive in the direction of literature than in that of art. As usual it is pushed to absurdity by some. But their principle is, as I understand it, that what you carry away with you from a scene is the true feature to grasp; or in other words, *what appeals to your own individual eye and heart in particular* amid much that does not so appeal, and which you therefore omit to record. (*Life*, p. 191)

This argument is precisely the one that Hardy uses to distinguish 'naturalism' from realism: there is always selection involved in description; and such selection is part of the method of distilling the essence of reality from what is being described. In *The Woodlanders* itself he had one hypothetical location in mind in the early versions but later made changes to a supposed 'location' which has somehow been seen as changing the location of the novel. Tellingly he wrote later to a correspondent of a village in the same novel:

As to the spot being the 'Little Hintock' of 'The Woodlanders'—that is another question. You will be surprised and shocked at my saying that I myself do not know where 'Little Hintock' is! Several tourists—mostly American—have told me that they have found it, in every detail, and have offered to take me to it, but I have never gone.

He adds, however, that

it has features which were to be found fifty years ago in the hamlets of Hermitage, Middlemarsh, Lyons-Gate, Revels Inn, Holnest, Melbury Bubb, &c.' (*Letters*, vii. 24)

It is the 'reality' of any and all of these.

In the evolution of Wessex over a twenty-five-year period Hardy was not merely creating a distinctive landscape. He was creating a mythical kingdom which dislocates not only place but time. It involves everything that was and is inscribed in the landscape: layers of history, events, and artefacts. To the extent that it involves an older and more stable community it is elegiac. But nostalgia is only a single element in a complex entity. Wessex is a place, a history, a celebration, an elegy; it is not merely a region, imagined or real.

CHAPTER 4

SOCIAL ISSUES: CLASS IN HARDY'S NOVELS

THE condition of England generally was not Hardy's concern but only, as was indicated in Chapters 2 and 3, the rural west of England. And the precise times to which the novels refer are in the main vague. Nonetheless the half-real, half-imaginary account of Wessex draws its factual basis from roughly contemporary conditions. He is a social novelist, but not in the usual sense. He is engaged with two interlocked subjects which become the almost obsessive focus of his later novels: what he comes to perceive as the similar injustice in the conventional treatment of the working classes and of women, both of which he relates to the question of social mobility. These finally become intertwined in two of his last novels, *Tess* and *Jude*. This does not mean that he is a chronicler of social conditions like Charles Dickens and Elizabeth Gaskell, who earlier offered a high degree of verisimilitude in descriptions of unhealthy and dangerous factories, long working hours, the exploitation of children and paupers, squalid living conditions, near-starvation. These and other condit-ion-of-England novelists would even draw details from government reports or Blue Books on these social ills. Hardy's novels were dis-tinctive as a group because, though dealing mainly with the working class, they were set almost exclusively in rural areas of the west country, a fact which became more striking with the emergence of 'Wessex'; and because they offered no easy resolutions.

The tendency to treat Hardy as a less than honest social critic grew up gradually, in part because he was assumed to be aiming at verisimilitude. Early in his career it became usual to praise his work for its descriptions of country life. This was so, even when the critic disliked other aspects of the novels. Henry James, for instance, wrote patronizingly of *Far from the Madding Crowd* in 1874: 'The most genuine thing in his book, to our sense, is a certain aroma of the meadows and lanes—a natural relish for harvesting and sheep-washings.' Not surprisingly, Hardy resented such trivializing of his work. Already in *Far from the Madding Crowd*, which harks back to a more happily ranked society, he had introduced darker elements in the shape of Gabriel Oak's misfortunes and loss of his farm as well as the death of Fanny Robin and her illegitimate baby in the workhouse. Those who most approved of this novel ignored blighted lives and agricultural disasters.

Hardy and Social Realism

As Chapter 2 showed, rural conditions in the west country from the mid-century onwards were those of extreme privation, and it has been argued by social historians that Hardy was not a social reformer but 'a detached and educated member of the Dorset market-town middle or professional class, with literary connections in London' who adopted an existing stereotype of the farm labourer. As a result Hardy's 'presentation of conditions in Dorset' is said to be 'unrealistic and evasive'.[2]

The account of life in Dorset on which these conclusions are based is unchallengeable; the assessment of Hardy is not. It overstates the level of the novelist's early social position and simplifies his ambiguous attitude to class. In addition it treats the novels as a 'presentation' not a 'representation', regarding them as would-be realistic depictions of a particular period of rural life, ignoring the partly imaginary nature of Wessex. 'Wessex' (which should always perhaps be in quotation marks), as Chapter 3 has shown, is not Dorset, whether the assessment is made in relation to the first editions of the novels between 1871 and 1895 or the tidied up versions of the collected editions in 1895–6 and 1912–13. In practice Dorset and Wessex became further removed from each other as Hardy revised his work. Like place or topography, time too is 'half-imaginary' as well as 'half-real'. Snell takes particular exception to Hardy's Preface to the 1912 Wessex Edition. He sees it as a demonstration of Hardy's false claims to realism. But careful attention to the wording of the Preface shows Hardy claiming something different from a socially realistic account of contemporary conditions. He claims vaguely to give only 'a fairly true record of a vanishing life' and says that 'At the dates represented in the various narrations things were like that in Wessex'.[3] This implies that Wessex is an amalgam in terms of time as well as place. Hardy reads into Wessex traces of a vanished agricultural community in the same way that he reads into it traces of vanished prehistoric, Roman, and historical life. Some positive aspects are evident but so are privation, misery, and natural disasters.

Nor can Hardy's novels be assumed to conform to Weber's chronology[4] as to 'dates represented'. *Under the Greenwood Tree* is blatantly no more datable in terms of when it is supposed to take place than an Elizabethan pastoral poem such as 'Come live with me and be my Love, | And we will all the pleasures prove | That woods and valleys, dales and fields, | Or woods or steepy mountain yields.' It represents a ranked society still carrying traces of a supposed idyllic lost world. Other novels suggest dates, sometimes in an authorial preface, sometimes by a reference within the text. In the 1895 Preface to the *Return of the Native* Hardy states:

The date at which the following events are assumed to have occurred may be set down as between 1840 and 1850, when the old watering-place called 'Budmouth' still retained sufficient afterglow from its Georgian gaiety and prestige to lend it an absorbing attractiveness to the romantic and imaginative soul of a lonely dweller inland.

The 'romantic and imaginative soul' is of course Eustacia Vye, and the date 'assumed' is determined by the need to locate her in a time when Budmouth was livelier than Egdon and not too far distant for her to yearn for. The permissive nature of the comment by Hardy suggests a fairly arbitrary way with time not an assurance that the narrative will be historically accurate in all its chronological details. Similarly *The Mayor of Casterbridge* is said in the opening chapter to begin 'before the nineteenth century had reached one-third of its span'. The Preface of 1895 gives a practical explanation: 'in the days recalled by the tale, the home Corn Trade, on which so much of the action turns, had an importance that can hardly be realized by those accustomed to the sixpenny loaf of the present date, and to the present indifference of the public to harvest weather.' In other words, the story is supposed to predate the repeal of the Corn Laws when the price of bread was kept artificially high. Dates are in effect dictated by the needs of the narrative, not by an anxiety to chronicle events precisely.

Such a way with time might be described as vague and the same is true of historical allusions within the texts which are supposed to date them. A pivotal matter in *The Woodlanders* is the divorce law which allows a husband to divorce his wife for adultery but would only allow Grace to gain a divorce if some further cause were added to Fitzpiers's adultery. This state of affairs was brought about by the Divorce Act of 1857 and allusions in the novel to a *recent* change in the law seem to refer to that year or the next. Another reference in the same novel to the arrival of Felice Charmond's ex-lover who has survived by some time the ending of the American Civil War of 1861–5, conflicts with the date suggested by the treatment of divorce. A quest to date each of Hardy's novels by this kind of allusion is as pointless as trying to read them biographically in terms of the author's life. All the references tell the reader is that Hardy wrote certain novels after certain dates when particular events had taken place. The most appropriate description of where in time Hardy sets his novels is Hardy's tendency 'to write not about the immediate present but about periods located somewhat vaguely in the recent past'.[5]

Within this context of the vaguely recent past there do occur instances of privation and oppression amongst the rural working class. But they are not sustained in Dickensian or Zolaesque detail throughout a narrative as is the case with city squalor in Dickens's *Bleak House* and other novels. Hardy is not offering a generic account of the working class as Dickens is. His only generic treat-ment of them is to be found in the highly stylized groups of rustics commenting chorus-like on the events which befall central char-acters. Specificity belongs to those central figures whose lives, like Tess's, are minutely observed in terms of adverse external condi-tions. Poverty becomes an issue for Clym Yeobright in *The Return of the Native* when failing eyesight compels him to abandon his ambition of studying to become a teacher. Its precise effect is to force him to take up what is seen as the low-class work of furze-cutting to support himself and Eustacia. The details of his drudg-ery are not omitted: the toil from the early hours of the morning till late at night; the beggarly payment of 2*s*. 6*d*. for every hundred faggots cut; the rough clothes; the monotony; his wife's resentment. Again, as with dates, it is the consequences not the simple facts that count. Eustacia's hopes of a glamorous social life as the wife of a successful teacher in Budmouth vanish. As a result she looks for excitement again with her former lover, Gabriel Wildeve, and finally commits suicide. The poor in Hardy's novels are not simply representative figures but individuals whose lives are largely shaped by the effect of poverty upon their temperaments as well as their circumstances.

In the same way Marty South's poverty is unsparingly described in *The Woodlanders* because of its results. Like Clym, she applies herself to menial and ill-paid drudgery when disaster strikes in the shape of her father's fatal illness. She takes over his work of splitting and shaping hazel rods into spars for roofing. It is difficult and painful work as Hardy makes clear when she looks at the ungloved hand holding her tool: 'The palm was red and blistering, as if her present occupation were as yet too recent to have subdued it to what it worked in' (chapter 1). The amounts paid for her work are, like Clym's, specified in detail. In a day she can make fifteen hundred spars, provided she works into the night. For this she is paid approximately 2s. 3d. The sum is provided as a contrast to the offer a local barber makes of a sovereign for the purchase of her abundant chestnut hair. He will pay her, he says, the equivalent of a week's wages (or of many thousands of spars) in order to provide the wealthy Felice Charmond with a hairpiece perfectly matching her own hair colour. The contrast in terms of the two women is sustained throughout the narrative; the chaste Marty deflowering herself of her sexual attractiveness on account of her poverty, and the idle *femme fatale*, Felice, who calmly buys the hair to attract her lovers. In addition, the purchase of Marty's hair has a significant and symbolic role in the plot. It provides Felice's new lover, Edred Fitzpiers, with an excuse to abandon her. Bored by her, he eventually uses the discovery that her beautiful hair is not entirely her own as a device to discard her. For Marty the loss of her hair implies her exclusion from a sexual life of her own.

Similarly the poverty of the over-fecund Durbeyfields is significant because of its consequences for Tess. The death of their only horse and the loss of their life-tenancy after John Durbeyfield's death determine her life. Certainly these details of privation, though they become more extensively described in *The Woodlanders* and in parts of *Tess* and *Jude*, are not there for the sake of chronicling them but have another function. In this way they are far removed from the comprehensive picture of urban misery in Gaskell's and Dickens's novels which do aim at description assumed to reveal to readers circumstances of which they are supposedly unaware and which for the characters involved are as unavoidable as the weather.

There is no sense that Hardy's novels are social tracts in the way that some of Dickens's and Gaskell's are. A few general issues are addressed but they arise naturally in the course of the narratives. They include the nature of working-class tenancies, rural immigration, and the impact of machinery on the nature of agricultural labour. The question of the type of tenure on which Giles Winterborne in *The Woodlanders* holds his properties for the duration of the named lives is a pivotal circumstance in the plot. His ownership depends on the life of John South:

It was the last of a group of lives which had served this purpose, at the end of whose breathings the small homestead occupied by South himself, the larger one of Giles Winterborne, and half-a-dozen others that had been in the possession of various Hintock village families for the previous hundred years, and were now Winterborne's, would fall in and become part of the encompassing estate. (chapter 13)

South's death leaves Winterborne at the mercy of Felice Charmond, the estate owner, who on a whim decides to pull down the cottages. Giles's resulting poverty proves the final straw that allows Melbury to tell his daughter that he can no longer accept Winterborne as a son-in-law. The marriage with the philandering Fitzpiers and all its consequences follow. The point about insecurity of tenure is made but apparently inevitably and not as part of a polemic.

The same issue is raised in *Tess* but there it is linked to the annual migrations from farm to farm on Lady Day when yearly contracts for labourers expired. As the narrator points out, not all migrations were voluntary and pleasantly exciting. Not all such moves originated in what he calls agricultural unrest: 'A depopulation was also going on.' This is seen as the result of the forced migration of the infrastructure of a rural village—the carpenter, the smith, the shoemaker, who serviced the needs of the villagers. These are usually life-holders, like Tess's father, or copy holders. As such holdings fell in 'they were seldom again let to similar tenants, and were mostly pulled down, if not actually required by the farmer for his hands' (chapter 51). This is seen as a crucial source of depopulation of the countryside of which the departure of the Durbeyfields from Marlott with no home in prospect is a single example. The legal facts as to tenancies like theirs is seen as contributing to a regrettable migration, usually from country to town. Only Alec's intervention saves Tess and her family from urban poverty.

The impact of machinery on the lives of rural labourers is a recurrent reference made by those who see Hardy as lamenting a lost world that was simpler, more natural, and happier. In practice the only really significant reference of this kind is the arrival of the mechanical threshing machine at Flintcomb-Ash. Even before its arrival Tess has found her life more and more arduous until she finally reaches the dreary terrain which is Groby's farm. Flintcomb-Ash is characterized by the narrator. Not only is it arid stony land but its tenure is held in the least desirable way: 'Of the three classes of the village . . . uncared for either by itself or by its lord—(in other words the village of a resident squire's tenantry, the village of free or copyholders, and the absentee-owner's village farmed with the land)—this place, Flintcomb-Ash was the third' (chapter 43). By implication such a farmer will be a slave driver. This is the nadir of Tess's privation and drudgery as she works in a cold stony field grubbing up the lower or earthy half of turnips with a hooked fork. The work is both hard and monotonous and when the steam threshing machine arrives, the women can no longer even work at their own pace. The monotony becomes mechanized and talk impossible. Tess is placed on the platform of the machine and unties the sheaves to be fed into the machine as it demands: 'for Tess there was no respite; for as the drum never stopped, the man who fed it could not stop, and she, who supplied the man with untied sheaves, could not stop either' (chapter 47). Deafened and exhausted, she is at Alec's mercy as he pursues her. The fact that this is a single episode revealing what the machine means to the worker, coming at this point in Tess's life when so much has gone wrong, means that it has no didactic overtones.

A more important contrast with didactic works like Gaskell's is provided by Hardy's avoidance of narrative closure: that resolution of conflict and reinstatement of an apparently harmonious society. Condition-of-England novels had deployed parallel public and private plots to prepare for an ending which offered such pseudo resolutions. On the one hand the public conflict was usually manifested in strikes, attacks on new machinery as in Charlotte Brontë's *Shirley* (1849), or in Gaskell's *Mary Barton* (1848) by John Barton's murder of the factory owner's son. Alongside this a personal and emotional discord mimicked the class conflict. This allowed for closure by offering individual reconciliations such as that between John Barton and the father of the man he has killed. A more usual resolution is that effected by a change of heart which converts a harsh employer to a more paternalistic approach, usually under the influence of a compassionate middle-class woman. These private events have a singular inappropriateness as the solution to a systemic disorder in society. Only Gaskell comes close to recognizing the radical nature of the social problem when her narrator in *Mary Barton* comments that the workers' misery in 'bad times' is made worse by the visible opulence of their employers. They are said to feel that they alone suffer. This dangerous comment, however, is swiftly neutralized as the narrator adds confusedly: 'I know that this is not really the case; and I know what is the truth in such matters: but what I wish to impress is what the workman feels and thinks. True, that with child-like improvidence, good times will often dissipate his grumbling, and make him forget all prudence and foresight' (chapter 3). The closure offered by industrial novels constitutes a blatant evasion of the real social issues momentarily glimpsed in this passage.

Such evasion is not Hardy's way despite one description of his novels as socially unrealistic and evasive.[6] It is the bypassing in condition-of-England novels of what creates poverty which is evasive. By contrast, Clym Yeobright is not restored to his former position; no paternalist superior allows him to leave his furze-cutting for a less arduous occupation. Marty loses both her father and the man she loves, as well as remaining penniless. Tess is not rehabilitated, Jude never achieves any of his aims. Hardy's preoccupation is with the damaging effect of social inequality, exploitation, and the imposition of rigidly authoritarian moral views upon individuals. In fiction verisimilitude does not necessarily lead to a probing of social problems in this way. But 'Wessex' is represented as a disordered society in its hierarchical organization and in the controlling limits it imposes on the lives of those who find themselves at the bottom of the social heap. Elsewhere in fiction these people are regularly represented as a group characterized by their common economic function—labour. Outside Hardy's novels fictional representations of working-class individuals are rare except as stereotypes, such as the anarchic trade unionist who crops up making trouble in several novels, for example in Dickens's *Hard Times* (1854). Major developments in Hardy's work are the increasing visibility and voice of individual working-class men, and, more significantly, individual working-class women such as Tess. What concerns Hardy is the pressure that society puts on such individuals through the class system as manifest in the law, access to education, and the Church. For these he offers no easy paternalistic change of heart. Instead his exploration of social conditions exposes the way that social class predetermines the possibilities open to individuals; the fuzzy nature of the criteria on the basis of which the class hierarchy is constructed; the corrosive effects it produces; and the flimsiness of the rationale offered for the system by such reflectors of current ideologies as Samuel Smiles. In his focus on individual women he reveals the crushing of potential (paralleling that effected by the class system) brought about by the contemporary construction of femininity described in Chapter 2. This focus leads on to a consideration of the specific issue of women's nature and place in society, marriage, and divorce law. Such topics are dealt with at a humanitarian level to examine the impact that they make on individual lives.

The ubiquitous and destructive nature of class gradation in the novels is perhaps most clearly illustrated by one which seems the most remote from such problems, *The Return of the Native*. The characters are few and the world they inhabit is largely cut off from outside. The opening chapter, devoted entirely to a description of Egdon Heath, insists on the primeval nature and timelessness of the place:

The great inviolate place had an ancient permanence which the sea cannot claim. Who can say of a particular sea that it is old? Distilled by the sun, kneaded by the moon, it is renewed in a year, in a day, or in an hour. The sea changed, the fields changed, the rivers, the villages, and the people changed, yet Egdon remained. (book 1, chapter 1)

The protagonists live in isolated dwellings—Bloom's End, Alderworth, Mistover, and the Quiet Woman Inn. The sense of their distance apart is figured by the journeys on foot that their occupants have to make in order to visit each other. Aside from the Mummers Play there are few social gatherings. It is made clear that not even the church serves as a focal point for the community: 'going to church, except to be married or buried, was phenomenal on Egdon' (book 1, chapter 10). There is little sense of social cohesion but Egdon proves to be a place riddled with and choked by class distinctions which make it a microcosm of the wider world. It is perceptions, judgements, and divisions, made largely on the basis of class, which form the dynamic of the narrative and lead to its disasters.

The functioning of the social order at Egdon is captured by the narrator's description of how its middle-class characters view their standing in society and the behaviour they consider appropriate. Captain Drew and his grand-daughter, Eustacia Vye, see themselves as 'the only genteel people of the district, except the Yeobrights, and though far from rich, they did not feel the necessity for preserving a friendly face towards every man, bird, and beast, which influenced their poorer neighbours' (book 1, chapter 10). This encapsulates both the arrogance of the Mistover pair and the deferential or even cringing behaviour imposed on the rest of the Egdon community. In doing so, it creates a pattern writ large in *Tess* and *Jude* where impoverished and unorthodox individuals are ostracized. The sense of superiority felt by Eustacia and her grandfather even over the Yeobrights is illustrated by the angry gibe which, in a jealous moment, she flings at her lover, the innkeeper, Wildeve. Contemptuously she tells him to marry Tamsin Yeobright if he wants her since 'she is nearer to your own position in life than I am!' (book 1, chapter 9). When she herself becomes infatuated with Clym Yeobright, her grandfather warns her against the match: 'Your town tastes would find them far too countrified. They sit in the kitchen, drink mead and elder-wine, and sand the floor to keep it clean' (book 2, chapter 3).

Nor do the Yeobrights accept their standing as subordinate to the Captain and Eustacia. Mrs Yeobright, on discovering that Clym is to marry the girl, dismisses her as 'a bandmaster's daughter'. She writes off the idea that Captain Drew is a man of rank: 'They call him Captain; but anybody is captain. No doubt he has been to sea in some tub or other' (book 3, chapter 5). Clym himself speaks to his cousin Tamsin when she wishes to marry the cleaned-up and prosperous ex-reddleman, Diggory Venn, as Drew spoke to Eustacia about Clym himself. He admits that Venn is honest and astute 'but not quite—'. Tamsin meekly completes his verdict—'Gentleman enough for me. That is just what I feel. I am sorry now that I asked you, and I won't think any more of him. At the same time I must marry him, if I marry anybody—that I *will* say' (book 6, chapter 3).

Far from being a timeless and class-free zone, Egdon is revealed as a place which shows that it is not only the physical privations created by the class system which cause society to malfunction but the corrosive effects on the minds and emotions of those involved. The novel is an analysis of the effects of the power relations that exist in Egdon as much as in urban settings.

Social Mobility and Marriage

A superficially logical argument for the justice of class-based Victorian society is that upward mobility is available to all who develop their talents to the full and persevere assiduously in using them. The case can then be made, as Smiles made it, from selected historical examples of those who began life in low-status occupations and then achieved inventions or creations that gave them high repute. Such an argument bypasses the fact that the criteria for assigning class status in the first place are fluid. The Smilesian version uses the simple test of original occupation to define social standing but assessment is not so straightforward. Obviously externals offered themselves for interpretation. Accents, clothes, type of housing, places in churches and trains poorer people were obliged to take might seem to have spelt out one's place in the world.

Provincial dialect is distinctively used in the novels as a marker of social class. Those who use it are marked out as poorer, less-educated country people, quite apart from the middle class: the farm workers in *Far from the Madding Crowd*, the Mixen Lane people in *The Mayor of Casterbridge*, Tess's parents and friends, Jude's grandmother and many others. The use of indicators of dialect is not, however, designed as a matter of accuracy in terms of the real world. Fiction had its own convention which Hardy manipulated with skill. He recognized explicitly, in response to a review of *The Return of the Native* (1878), that such language in his fiction 'is intended to show mainly the character of the speakers, and only to give a general idea of their linguistic peculiarities'. He adds that 'if a writer attempts to exhibit on paper the precise accents of a rustic speaker he disturbs the proper balance of a true representation'.[7] By the last phrase he means as usual to distinguish between a kind of phonetic accuracy and a significant belief that underlies the representation.

His alterations over various editions to the dialect forms in his novels bear this out. He increases the number of dialect markers for reasons that relate to particular effects in a given novel. When Gabriel Oak is warning Bathsheba against the seductions of Troy, later versions increase the dialect forms in his speech despite his original status as a farm-owner in his own right. The result is a sharper contrast with the smooth-talking dragoon he is criticizing than his normally less marked speech would be.

But Hardy's practice is far more complex than this. His own statements show that his view of the Dorset dialect is as ambiguous as his attitude to the social class it marks out. This ambiguity appears at moments when more central figures than the rustic groups are under the stress of strong emotion. In an earlier version of *Tess* than the final 1912 edition, he tells how her mother 'habitually spoke the dialect but her daughter . . . used it only when excited by joy, surprise or grief'.[8] This is a view of dialect held by several writers for whom it was a first language later discarded for a standard form of speech. What happens with Tess also occurs significantly with Marty South in *The Woodlanders*. Though at the bottom of the heap socially, she has an important role in the novel as a model of simple integrity. Consequently, for most of the narrative she uses few markers of dialect. But under the stress of a sudden emotion she reverts to dialect to express her feelings. Given a lift on the outside of Mrs Charmond's coach, she hears the occupant yawn. The coachman explains that Felice finds life dull. The girl responds in amazement at this insight into the life of a woman who has everything including the hair that Marty sold merely in order to survive: 'So rich, and so powerful; and yet to yawn! . . . Then *things don't fay* [*prosper*] *with her any more than with we*' (chapter 5; my emphasis).

More obviously, her native dialect is again wrung out of Marty when she utters her painful address to Giles over his grave: 'Now my own own love . . . you are mine, and only mine for she has forgot 'ee at last, although for her you died. But I—whenever I get up I'll think of 'ee, and whenever I lie down I'll think of 'ee again . . . I never can forget 'ee; for you was a good man, and did good things!' (chapter 48). This is an instance of a technique which occurs again in *Jude* in the exchange where Phillotson, the schoolmaster, is unburdening himself to his friend Gillingham about Sue wanting to leave him. Though he normally uses standard speech, he now speaks of how he *toled* or 'enticed' Sue when she was his pupil teacher. Gillingham bluntly tells him he is *rafted* or 'disturbed' (part 4, chapter 4). The lapse into dialect is explained as a reversion to the language of their boyhood but it has a disproportionate effect through its unexpectedness. In brief, Hardy has two contradictory ways of using dialect: one for the working-class Creedles of this world and one for Marty. The fact reflects a narratorial view of the working classes as inferior and mildly comic and at times a paradoxical view that they are profoundly valuable. Such a paradox is itself reminiscent of the differing visual and moral perspectives on humanity as typified by the different perspectives on *Tess*.

The other markers of social class, aside from accent—housing, occupation, and education are all convertible into size of income and are not definitive. Mobility is a real issue, however: it is possible to acquire money enough for a middle-class life-style without acquiring the status of a gentleman. Alec d'Urberville has the accoutrements of gentility without the status. His descent from a money-lender or loan-shark and his pseudo-aristocratic surname highlight the fact. Origins matter but Tess's blue blood is not sufficient to make her a lady in the eyes of the world, as Angel Clare's ambivalence about her lineage shows. A similarly complicated case is presented by the central female figures in *A Laodicean*—Paula Power and Charlotte De Stancy. Paula has inherited enough money from her railway tycoon father to buy the De Stancy castle and restore it lavishly. Charlotte, the blue-blooded but impoverished De Stancy, acts as a companion to Paula. Her origins and manners would seem to indicate a higher status but she treats Paula as a superior. Her lack of money has created a need for paid employment as a semi-servant. The impression is given that the world at large consequently sees her as declassed in the same way as governesses are if coming from a middle-class background: they are somehow middle class and yet not their employers' equals. Charlotte De Stancy's position is worse than this. Her lineage makes her the social superior of the woman who employs her and who has bought the De Stancy castle. But Paula accepts the new hierarchy, treating Charlotte (affectionately) as her poodle.

So the possession of refinement of taste and manners or even blue blood does not alone guarantee upper-class status, but the lack of them necessarily marks out individuals as lower-class. Even Elfride in *A Pair of Blue Eyes* thinks less of her lover Stephen Smith, an architect's assistant, because of his unskilled way of handling chess pieces which she recognizes as a social blunder. Like Estella noticing Pip's vulgar vocabulary in *Great Expectations*, she thinks his behaviour has an 'indescribable oddness': 'Antecedently she would have supposed that the same performance must be gone through by all players in the same manner; she was taught by his differing action that all ordinary players, who learn the game by sight, unconsciously touch the men in a stereotyped way' (chapter 7).

While representing the inconsistency of these *ad hoc* standards for deciding on someone's class, Hardy's early novels cut through them to the underlying fact that classing individuals is a matter of whether or not their 'superiors' find them acceptable members of the group they aspire to. An assessment as to acceptability is precisely what Elfride makes over the chess game. The distinction between professional recognition and social acceptability is revealing in this context. The issue which recurs repeatedly in Hardy's early novels is the question of whether working-class men of talent and diligence can arrive at a status which makes them 'acceptable' as husbands for middle- or upper-class women. Hardy's own marriage happens to have been cross-class, but the issue has wide implications as a possible counter to the glib Smilesian view that talent in the aspirant will create acceptability. The question of acceptability is put to the test in a series of varying contexts or what George Eliot might have called 'experiments in life'.

The belief seems to prevail among working-class characters in the early narratives that marriage can affect social standing. Ideas about how it works, however, differ. Stephen Smith's peasant mother sees a precise mechanism: 'I know all men move up a stage by marriage . . . parsons marry squires' daughters; squires marry lords' daughters; lords marry dukes' daughters. All stages of gentleman mate a stage higher' (*A Pair of Blue Eyes*, chapter 10). Grace Melbury's ambitious father takes an equally dogmatic but contradictory view that 'a woman takes her colour from the man she's walking with' (*The Woodlanders*, chapter 12). Such views are explored from Hardy's earliest days as a novelist.

The remnants of his first unpublished work, *The Poor Man and the Lady*, which appeared in 1878 as *An Indiscretion in the Life of an Heiress*, nakedly displays its subject in the title. The same pattern of a talented man of working-class origin aspiring to the hand of a woman of a superior class is found in *A Pair of Blue Eyes* and *Two on a Tower*. In later novels the handling of this issue becomes more complex. In *The Woodlanders* the superior status of Grace Melbury, a timber merchant's daughter, is itself uncertain. She has been educated beyond her station with middle-class girls, as she herself recognizes. After the discovery of Fitzpiers's infidelity, she tells her startled father 'I hate genteel life'. Such a life, she says, 'has only brought me inconveniences and troubles'. She wishes she had never been sent to 'those fashionable schools' on which Melbury lavished his money:

I have never got any happiness outside Hintock that I know of, and I have suffered many a heartache at being sent away. Oh the misery of those January days when I got back to school and left you all here in the wood so happy. I used to wonder why I had to bear it. And I was always a little despised by the other girls at school, because they knew where I came from, and that my parents were not in so good a station as theirs. (chapter 30)

Her father sees her as too good for her humble lover, Giles Winterbourne, while the local doctor, Fitzpiers, thinks a marriage to her socially dubious for him. Further complications arise with true and false d'Urbervilles in *Tess*. A pivot of the early narratives is the question of crossing class frontiers. The fact that the position of the talented but socially inferior man in the early novels corresponds to Hardy's own relationship with Emma Gifford's family is less significant than the fact that such a case questions the ideological argument for social mobility that Smiles's *Self-Help* crystallizes. Social acceptability as a member of the middle class is far more difficult to achieve than Smiles suggests.

A crucial factor in Hardy's treatment of class mobility is the implied placing of his narrators within the hierarchical world that they represent. The position of Dickens's and Gaskell's narrators, for instance, is the one usual in nineteenth-century narrators: securely fixed in the middle class and attempting to bring social ills to the attention of fellow class members. The narratorial aim is represented as a desire to bring about a similarly benign change of heart in the upper classes which will ameliorate things for the lower classes. By contrast Hardy's narrators by their reactions identify themselves as originally on the wrong side of the social divide but asserting a claim to have crossed the middle-class frontier (presumably by delivering a literary text). The ambivalence resulting from this position produces resentful generalizations against those whose sense of superiority offers not a frontier but a barrier to would-be immigrants. In *Desperate Remedies*, for instance, the landowner Miss Aldclyffe's treatment of her tenant, Edward Springrove, elicits a biting comment from the narrator:

like a good many others in her position, [she] had plainly not realized that a son of her tenant and inferior, could have become an educated man, who had learnt to feel his individuality, to view society from a Bohemian standpoint far outside the farming grade in Carriford parish, and that hence he had all a developed man's unorthodox opinion about the subordination of classes. (volume 2, chapter 3)

There is a similar reflection by the narrator when Elfride, in *A Pair of Blue Eyes*, casually deserts her working-class lover Smith and his family:

Few women of old family can be thoroughly taught that a fine soul may wear a smock-frock, and an admittedly common man in one is but a worm in their eyes. John Smith's rough hands and clothes, his wife's speeches, the necessary narrowness of their ways, being constantly under Elfride's notice were not without their deflecting influence. (chapter 27)

The narrators are visibly equating their own position with that of the man rejected.

It is made clear that the motives of Egbert Mayne (in *An Indiscretion*), Stephen Smith, and Swithin St Cleeve are disinterested. They love the women in question and, in this sense; for them class is not a consideration. But for each—and to a lesser extent for the musician, Christopher Julian, in *The Hand of Ethelberta* and the architect George Somerset in *A Laodicean*—an external constraint hinders their marriage and their consequent rise in the world. Their value and social status is predetermined for the upper classes by the category to which they belong by birth. Geraldine Allenville's father tells her that, however worthy Mayne may be, permission to marry him 'depends upon his rank and circumstances' (*An Indiscretion*, part 1, chapter 8). Elfride Swancourt's father reacts even more violently when told that Smith wishes to marry her: 'Foh! A fine story. It is not enough that I have been deluded by having him here—the son of one of my village peasants—but now I am to make him my son-in-law! Heavens above us, are you mad, Elfride?' (*A Pair of Blue Eyes*, chapter 9). Viviette Constantine in *Two on a Tower*, who thinks herself to be the widow of a baronet and so independent, will agree only to a clandestine marriage with her lover, St. Cleeve. But she also insists 'in consideration of my peculiar position in this county' that 'you will not put an end to the absolute secrecy of our relationship without my full assent. Also that you will never come to Welland House without first discussing with me the advisability of the visit, accepting my opinion on the point.' Swithin is quick to understand: 'It would be a humiliation to you at present that I could not bear if a marriage between us were made public' (chapter 15).

As Swithin's comment makes clear, the social constraints on their ability to join the class above them by marrying into it are recognized by the poor men as an inescapable fact. Mayne feels 'what a vast gulf lay between that lady and himself' (*An Indiscretion*, part 1, chapter 1). Smith tells his mother, who is hostile to the match with Elfride, 'Why, to marry her would be the great blessing of my life— socially and practically, as well as in other respects. No such good fortune as that, I'm afraid; she's too far above me. Her family doesn't want such country lads as I in it' (*A Pair of Blue Eyes*, chapter 10). The recognition of these social obstacles does not preclude resentment. Mayne recognizes the existence of the gulf between himself and Geraldine but is bitter: 'That the habits of men should be so subversive of the law of nature as to indicate that he was not worthy to marry a woman whose own instincts said he was worthy, was a great anomaly, he thought, with some rebelliousness' (*An Indiscretion*, part 1, chapter 8). Late in *A Pair of Blue Eyes* Elfride's new middle-class lover makes an excuse to his protégé Smith for not introducing him to such a lady. Stephen responds with 'dim bitterness': 'You should have said that I seemed still the rural builder's son I am, and hence an unfit subject for the ceremony of introductions' (chapter 27).

To an extent the women that these men love also collude with their humiliation. Geraldine is made less happy by noticing 'how little Egbert was accustomed to what is called society, and the polite forms which constant usage had made almost nature with her'. On such occasions 'Egbert would go away, wander about the lanes, and be kept awake a great part of the night by the distress of mind such a recognition brought upon him' (part 1, chapter 7). Elfride subjects

Stephen to the same kind of humiliation over the chess pieces and by allowing him to win a game before she realizes how she has dispar-aged him. Viviette, by insisting on a secret marriage, lays Swithin open to a rebuke from the bishop for apparently keeping a mistress. How could she reveal the marriage, asks the narrator ironically on Swithin's behalf, 'when her feeling had been cautiously fed and developed by her brother Louis's unvarnished exhibition of Swith-in's material position in the eyes of the world?' (*Two on a Tower*, chapter 29). Not only do the women collude with the devaluing of the socially inferior men whom they love but the latter do not achieve acceptance into the class they aspire to. Even when Geral-dine is dying, her father resents her husband: 'It was only when he despaired that he looked upon Egbert with tolerance. When he hoped, the young man's presence was hateful to him (*An Indiscretion*, part 2, chapter 7). Stephen is not accepted as an equal either by Elfride's parents or by Henry Knight. Clearly the experience of humiliation and devaluing that Mayne and St Cleeve undergo is exacerbated by the loss of normal male dominance. But paradoxically the recognition of this fact seems to effect an epiphany for them. It opens the narrators' eyes to the injustice of the conventional power relationship between men and women. In *A Pair of Blue Eyes*, after Elfride has humiliated Stephen over the chess game, Henry Knight does the same to her. She recognizes what Knight is up to and is affronted: 'I know what you are doing! . . . You were thinking of letting me win to please me! . . . I won't have it . . . It is insulting me' (chapter 18). This equivalence of the man humiliated because of his lower class and a woman humiliated because of her gender consti-tutes an epiphany for Hardy.

It reveals the fundamental parallel between the class system and the male–female hierarchy. By the end of the century it was a com-monplace among radicals that 'Both Labour and Woman are seeking to throw off slavery arising from economic dependence'[9] but this is an early recognition. The common feelings of humiliation are most explicitly represented in Viviette's reaction to a letter from Swithin's uncle cynically warning her lover against her. She is afraid that he will accept the view that she will blight his life:

The humiliation of such a possibility was almost too much to endure; the mortification—she had known nothing like it till now. But this was not all.

There succeeded a feeling in comparison with which resentment and mortification were happy moods—a miserable conviction that this old man who spoke from the grave was not altogether wrong in his speaking, that he was only half wrong, that he was, perhaps, virtually right. Only those persons who are by nature affected with that ready esteem for others' positions which induces an undervaluing of their own, fully experience the deep smart of such convictions against self, the wish for annihilation that is engendered in the moment of despair at feeling that at length we, our best and firmest friend, cease to believe in our cause. (*Two on a Tower*, chapter 35)

By now Hardy was aware that such persons as are brought up to such a self-effacing 'esteem for others' positions' as to undervalue their own are characteristically women. But he has also come to understand that such conditioning is also to be found in poor men. Stephen Smith, for instance, is said to respond to Henry Knight's patronizing treatment as a woman might by still retaining affection for him. The explanation given is that 'The emotional side of his constitution was built rather after a feminine than a male model; and that tremendous wound from Knight's hand may have tended to keep alive a warmth which solicitness would have extinguished altogether' (*A Pair of Blue Eyes*, chapter 38). It is almost as though, in a milder form, Smith reacts as a battered but faithful wife. In experiences like these, the lives of poor but talented men intersect with the lives of women, even those of the upper class. The intersection undermines the contemporary construction of gender as an unchangeable male–female hierarchy. An alternative division of semantic space is opened up in which gender boundaries are not always significant. Certainly a common humiliation transcends them. Consequently for Hardy 'woman' is now perceived as an appropriate figure for the poor man devalued on grounds of his class as women are devalued on the grounds of their gender. The equation of the two is at the same time radically subversive, a recognition that becomes more explicit in Hardy's later novels.

Already before this, in the first published novel *Desperate Remedies*, there is a glimpse of an emerging view which contradicts not only other comments in the early works but the standard view of women as given in Romanes's account' quoted in Chapter 2 above (see p. 50):

for in spite of a fashion which pervades the whole community at the present day—the habit of exclaiming that woman is not undeveloped man, but diverse, the fact remains that, after all, women are Mankind, and that in many of the sentiments of life the difference of sex is but a difference of degree. (volume 2, chapter 2)

A telling use of this equation of women and lower-class men is made when rejection by Elfride's father reveals feminine qualities in Stephen Smith. He shows that very plasticity in adapting to the demands of others displayed by Amy Dorrit in Dickens's novel and other similarly 'ideal' models of femininity: 'Quickly acquiring any kind of knowledge he saw around him, and having a plastic adaptability more common in woman than in man, he changed colour like a chameleon as the society he found himself in assumed a higher and more artificial tone' (*A Pair of Blue Eyes*, chapter 10). Plasticity in women of course is a facet of their powerlessness, a characteristic revealed by St Cleeve. When he changes from a masterful 'promising young physicist' to become the 'commonplace inamorato' of a titled woman he is left waiting 'as helplessly as a girl for a chance of encountering her' (*Two on a Tower*, chapter 14). This captures a further parallel between these unlucky suitors and the habitual position of women unable to profess their love or seek out its object. It is not only a sense of their own inferiority but powerlessness that the two have in common.

Such lack of power is the basis of a striking use of the figure of humiliated man as woman, pointed out by Elaine Showalter, in *The Mayor of Casterbridge*. When Henchard is overcome by womanly sentiments of 'shame and self-reproach' after his brutal attack on Donald Farfrae, the narrator comments: 'So thoroughly subdued was he that he remained on the sacks in a crouching attitude, unusual for a man, and for such a man. Its womanliness sat tragically on the figure of so stern a piece of virility' (chapter 38). Showalter reads this as the culmination of a pilgrimage of 'unmanning' which begins the restoration to Henchard of the feminine elements he has literally and metaphorically discarded by selling his wife.[10] But it is more significantly the culmination of the string of metaphors based on the powerful equivalences between lower-class men and all women which undermine contemporary construction of femininity.

Social Mobility and Education

The other obvious route to a higher class status in the Victorian period would seem to be education. Because the educational institutions were gatekeepers to many professions and because they were the preserve of the upper classes, it might seem that an ambitious man of the working class had an obvious route to social acceptability. It is likely that up to the early 1860s Hardy had seen a university education at Cambridge as a path he might follow. Certainly he had aspirations to do so. Though his ambition was fired by a love of learning for its own sake, it would, if fulfilled, theoretically have led to a change in his social status. The subject of education and its class implications for working men is dealt with in relation to Clym Yeobright in an early novel and more fully in relation to Jude Fawley in one of the very last that Hardy wrote.

Surprisingly, the limited educational possibilities for girls and women are not an issue that Hardy addresses. There are passing references to the educational standard of some of the women in the novels. Fancy Day in *Under the Greenwood Tree* is an apparently competent mistress of the village school. Tess Durbeyfield has 'passed the sixth standard in the National school under a London-trained mistress' (chapter 3). Sue Bridehead, after acting as a teaching assistant, follows part of the course at a teachers' training school. Other women seem to have educated themselves by wide reading. Ethelberta is familiar enough with the theory of Utilitarianism to marry a rich and lecherous old peer on the grounds that it will bring the greatest happiness to 'all concerned'. By this she means her large and lowly-paid family. Sue Bridehead can match Jude in discussing the history of Christianity and Greek civilization. She can also hurl a quotation from J. S. Mill as a brickbat at her husband when she wishes to leave him. Elfride Swancourt has read enough to write a romance which has been published and reviewed. But there is no serious concern with the nature of the education that girls receive despite the contemporary debate and the developments in new public schools providing for at least some daughters of the middle class.

The only occasion when a narrator generalizes on the subject is in reference to the Training School in *Jude*. The school is condemned for its rigid insistence on discipline and propriety which inhibits Sue's meetings with Jude and leads to her expulsion. The narrator suggests that even the education offered by such a school makes little impact on the women involved:

Half-an-hour later they all lay in their cubicles, their tender feminine faces upturned to the flaring gas-jets which at intervals stretched down the long dormitories, every face bearing the legend The Weaker upon it, as the penalty of the sex wherein they were moulded, which by no possible exertion of their willing hearts and abilities could be made strong while the inexorable laws of nature remain what they are. They formed a pretty, suggestive, pathetic sight, of whose pathos and beauty they were themselves unconscious, and would not discover till, amid the storms and strains of after-years, with their injustice, loneliness, child bearing, and bereavement, their minds would revert to this experience as to something which had been allowed to slip past them insufficiently regarded. (part 3, chapter 3)

The reference to the 'inexorable laws of nature' is one of the several contradictions in *Jude* as to the idea that women's nature is ultimately determined by their physiological characteristics. The implication here is that their capacity to benefit from education is limited by the existence of their maternal role and instincts. Elsewhere it is perhaps explicable as an illustration of how a wish to abandon the theory of essentialism is qualified by an inability to recognize where that ideology begins and ends. In the twentieth century was power-dressing by women a similar failure or a sign of advance?

By contrast, both Clym and Jude are potentially equipped to progress in life, given the education they crave. Both *The Return of the Native* and *Jude* make clear that such education was perceived as a marker of higher social standing than they currently experience. In the earlier novel the narrator comments on Clym's ambition to learn enough to become a teacher:

Yeobright loved his kind. He had a conviction that the want of most men was knowledge of a sort which brings wisdom rather than affluence. He wished to raise the class at the expense of individuals, rather than individuals at the expense of the class. What was more, he was ready at once to be the first unit sacrificed. (book 3, chapter 11)

Such an altruistic view of the value of education is seen as distinctive and unusual in its detachment even from a secondary aim of increasing status:

In passing from the bucolic to the intellectual life the intermediate stages are usually two at least, frequently many more; and one of these stages is almost sure to be worldly advance. We can hardly imagine bucolic placidity quickening to intellectual aims without imagining social aims as the transitional phase. Yeobright's local peculiarity was that in striving at high thinking he still cleaved to plain living. (book 3, chapter 11)

This generalization is strangely borne out by Jude in a novel where the fate of both central characters is inextricably dominated by the institutional Church. Sue, despite her atheism, is controlled by the Church through the institution of marriage and Jude by his educational ambitions. From the start Jude confuses his intellectual ambitions with the social. This is understandable at a time when education at the older universities authenticated class and produced well-paid clergymen 'like radishes'. Before he meets Arabella his confessed yearning for Christminster as a place of beauty, religion, learning, and social prestige is ironically outlined by the narrator:

[He] thought he might become even a bishop by leading a pure, energetic, wise Christian life. And what an example he would set! If his income were £5,000 a year he would give away £4,500 in one form and another and live sumptuously (for him) on the remainder. Well, on second thoughts, a bishop was absurd. He would draw the line at an archdeacon. Perhaps a man could be as good and as learned and as useful in the capacity of archdeacon as in that of bishop. Yet he thought of the bishop again. (part 1, chapter 6)

As Jude's painful progress in learning to read Latin and Greek indicates, he does not lack talent nor does he lack perseverance. On the basis of Samuel Smiles's account, this should be enough to guarantee upward advancement. But the education that Jude aspires to is the form most difficult of access for the working man as the tiny numbers of those who succeeded in attaining it show. The older universities remained a virtually impregnable bastion of the upper classes. The obstacles are those already described in Chapter 2: money and the requirement for a considerable knowledge of Greek and Latin texts. The latter was routinely drilled into boys at expensive public schools. Jude's sustained and strenuous efforts at self-instruction have not, he realizes, brought him near to this standard:

he soon perceived clearly, what he had long uneasily suspected, that to qualify himself for certain open scholarships and exhibitions was the only brilliant course. But to do this a good deal of coaching would be necessary, and much natural ability. It was next to impossible that a man reading on his own system, however widely and thoroughly,—even over the prolonged period of ten years, should be able to compete with those who had passed their lives under trained teachers, and had worked to ordained lines. (part 2, chapter 6)

The scholarships referred to which might provide Jude's only means of financing a university course were by the 1890s open to all including public schoolboys instead of reserved solely for poor boys as they had originally been.

The letter of rejection that Jude receives from the Master of Biblioll College echoes the comments of those who explicitly opposed access to Oxford and Cambridge for working men: 'judging from your description of yourself as a working-man, I venture to think that you will have a much better chance of success in life by remaining in your own sphere, and sticking to your trade than by adopting any other course. That, therefore, is what I advise you to do' (part 2, chapter 6). Like the poor men of talent in the early novels, Jude internalizes the criticism implicit in this letter. He is prevented by convention from reacting emotionally—whereas 'If he had been a woman he must have screamed under the nervous tension he was now undergoing' (part 2, chapter 6). Most importantly, however, woman-like he begins to disparage himself and to accept his ambition as flawed and even hypocritical:

The old fancy which had led on to the culminating vision of the bishopric had not been an ethical or theological enthusiasm at all, but a mundane ambition masquerading in a surplice. He feared that his whole scheme had degenerated to, even though it might not have originated in, a social unrest which had no foundation in the nobler instincts; which was purely an artificial product of civilization. (part 3, chapter 1)

He sees himself as subject to the vice of social restlessness that the Master's letter hints at.

Smiles had urged that 'patient purpose, resolute working and steadfast integrity' would necessarily produce 'an honourable competency and a solid reputation'.[11] Since this was an important argument for the existence of social mobility in a necessarily hierarchical society, Jude's failure was significant. Some critics were quick to see its subversive nature. The nature of Jude's story led R. Y. Tyrell into a vicious personal attack on Hardy as one of those who, having risen to the top of 'young Ambition's ladder' now 'kick away the ladder of lowliness'. To damn the novel itself he produces a dogma apparently intended as universal: 'When Nature implants in a young man eager desires for a certain career, such as those which animated Jude, she generally gives him the powers and the resolution by which he may achieve his ambition'.[12] This is an interesting variation on Smiles's view that talent and perseverance are certain to bring advancement in the chosen career. It follows, according to Tyrell, that the litmus test of worthiness to progress upwards is shown by the result of the working man's effort. Failure to succeed is itself an indication of the lack of 'powers' or of 'resolution'. For Hardy, however, the point of the events in this narrative is that they show the fictitious nature of supposed social mobility through education as surely as the failed attempts at cross-class marriages do.

CHAPTER 5

SOCIAL ISSUES: WOMEN AND SOCIETY

THE status and position of women in Victorian society was based on the account of them as described, for instance, by Romanes and outlined in Chapter 2, which indicated that they were by nature inferior, more like children than men. This picture of them was inscribed in the law, particularly after marriage, in their non-status as voters, in the kind of limited education provided for them, and in literature. Novels both reflected and 'confirmed' the conventional account of women as essentially different from men and inferior to them. Consequently when Hardy began to write novels which increasingly focused on what he called the 'woman interest' he did so in a language which was already highly constrained. Yet from the beginning in his fiction, when treating the 'woman interest', he shows surprising signs of unconventionality. At first these are occasional but later his acceptance of equality between the sexes becomes paramount, despite his unhappy first marriage.

Certain stereotypes of ideal or of unreconstructed deviant women were handed on as literary currency in the mainstream (three-decker) fiction to which he aspired. Changing this aspect of the medium was not easy: a writer can deviate from the mainstream to produce anomalous figures but whether or not that change is accommodated by becoming part of novelistic language is generally dependent on other factors. Hardy clearly wished for professional success and yet the language he was obliged to use entrapped him, as his subtitle to *Tess of the d'Urbervilles*, 'A Pure Woman', shows. In adding this, he was attempting to subvert the conventional terminology in which 'pure' was the highest term of approval for a woman. The accolade was considered appropriate only if she was a virgin or a chaste wife: it depended on her sexual status. The consequent argument that ensued with critics consisted of wrangles over the 'true' meaning of the term and over the natural feeling that in applying it to Tess Hardy was misusing language. In the end, however, Hardy's late novels helped to alter the ways of constructing women in fiction because they were written at a time when other forces combined to effect a breaking down of available literary stereotypes or *signs* for women. In particular, they helped to break the convention which required that the images of ideal and of deviant women should be sharply separate and without an overlap. The only literary alternative was the 'New Woman' who flourished for a brief period in fiction of the early 1890s such as Sarah Grand's *The Heavenly Twins* (1893), Mona Caird's *The Daughters of Danaus* (1894), Grant Allen's *The Woman Who Did* (1895). More subtle than any of these; and much admired by Hardy was *Keynotes* (1893), a set of short stories by 'George Egerton' (Mary Chavelita Clairmonte, née Dunne, 1859–1945). The latter keenly interested Hardy who carried on a discussion with Florence Henniker in its margins. Egerton's subversive account of women and sexuality is captured in her story 'A Cross Line': 'the woman who tells the truth and is not a liar about these things is untrue to her sex and abhorrent to man, for he has fashioned a model on imaginary lines, and he has said "so I would have you".'[1]

Earlier Novels

Overtly, nonetheless, Hardy's early texts are characterized by a partial acceptance of 'woman' generically viewed as inferior to 'man', physically, emotionally, and intellectually. Conventional accounts provided a source of dogma from which generalizations could be drawn to explain the conduct and reactions of individual women. Such a practice is common in most periods and certain generalizations persist. Anyone can cry operatically 'La donna è mobile' and accuse all women of instability, whether a change of mind is rational or pure whimsy. In *Desperate Remedies*, *A Pair of Blue Eyes*, and *Far from the Madding Crowd* the perceived need of the narrator for explanations of women's behaviour is strong. Hardy from the first is preoccupied by such a need, out of which his later progressive attitudes grew, and all three novels draw on a contemporary account of the nature of women which is inherently ambivalent. The ambivalence resulted from a construction of the potentially ideal woman as selfless, maternal, the guardian of family morals, happy, and effective in a domestic sphere. But such an ideal was allegedly built out of characteristic features which involved irrationality, emotionalism, and a kind of childishness. These negative characteristics were assumed to be capable of becoming positive through strenuous efforts by individual women towards selfless plasticity in responding to the needs of others. So the balance-sheet that Hardy keeps from the first by generalizing from the behaviour of individuals about women in general, fluctuates and contradicts itself. These generalizations are what he was looking back to when he wrote of the 'woman interest' in his early novels. Because the account contains contradictions there is no straight chronological development in the comments of women in these works.

The much-noticed generalizations in the early novels, which led some early feminists to regard Hardy as a misogynist, disappear in the middle-period novels such as *The Trumpet-Major*, *A Laodicean*, and *The Mayor of Casterbridge*. In the late novels, as will be shown, Hardy creates his own kind of general comments on the nature of women. The early explanations of why women behave as they do are sometimes invoked where the text reveals a difference of behaviour between a man and a woman or when a woman acts in a way that is superior, not inferior. When Cytherea and her brother are forced to take menial jobs as a lady's maid and as a draughtsman, she is the resilient one: 'We can put up with being poor . . . if they only give us work to do . . . be cheerful'. Her stoicism is explained away as a mark of inferiority:

In justice to desponding men, it is as well to remember that the brighter endurance of women at these epochs—invaluable, sweet, angelic, as it is—owes more of its origin to a narrower vision that shuts out many of the leaden-eyed despairs in the van, than to a hopefulness intense enough to quell them. (*Desperate Remedies*, volume 1, chapter 3)

The admonition to 'remember' this fact implies a pre-existing incontrovertible account of what women are like. This account is also called on when Miss Aldclyffe acts deceitfully by lying to Springrove about Cytherea's feelings for him. The general feminine interest in ends not means is 'recognised' by the narrator as the cause:

A fiery man in such a case would have relinquished persuasion and tried palpable force. A fiery woman added unscrupulousness and evolved daring strategy; and in her obstinacy and to sustain herself as mistress, she descended to an action the meanness of which haunted her conscience to her dying hour. (volume 2, chapter 3)

Similarly, Elfride's greater efficiency in planning an elopement with Stephen in the face of her father's disapproval is explained as only a meretricious superiority:

Either from lack of the capacity to grasp the whole *coup d'œil*, or from a natural endowment for certain kinds of stoicism, women are cooler than men in critical situations of the passive form. Probably, in Elfride's case at least, it was blindness to the greater contingencies of the future she was preparing for herself, which enabled her to ask her father in a quiet voice, if he could give her a holiday soon, to ride to St Launce's and go on to Plymouth. (*A Pair of Blue Eyes*, chapter 11)

When torn between her two lovers, Stephen Smith and Henry Knight, her behaviour is attributed not to a divided heart but to something more well known: 'Woman's ruling passion—to fascinate and influence those more powerful than she—though operant in Elfride, was decidedly purposeless' (chapter 20).

Likewise Bathsheba's dealings with her suitors, Oak and Boldwood (whom she does not love) merely demonstrate a cardinal feminine characteristic: 'La donna è mobile'—'Women are never tired of bewailing man's fickleness in love, but they seem only to snub his constancy' (*Far from the Madding Crowd*, chapter 24). Her dealings with the worthless man she does love, Sergeant Troy, indicate of course feminine irrationality: 'Bathsheba, though she had too much understanding to be entirely governed by her womanliness had too much womanliness to use her understanding to the best advantage' (chapter 29). The two-sidedness of supposedly womanly intuitiveness shows through here in the use of *womanliness* not for intuitive understanding but for intuitiveness as the irrational pursuit of whim.

But even in the three early novels the disparaging aspects of the conventional account on which they draw do not dominate. The generalizations constitute one discourse among several and so are set in a context that creates unease with the stereotype of 'woman'. Emma Hardy once asserted that her husband only understood the women he created. These texts reveal that understanding as it develops within each of them. For they show that women internalize the view of themselves as narrow, limited, and less than rational. They are consequently haunted to the point of pathos by a felt need to shape themselves so as to conform to ideals of femininity. Somehow, they feel, they have to convert what they have been taught to think their inborn weaknesses into womanliness. All three heroines in the early novels have a strong sense of a contour to be conformed to which has been created by the choosing male whom in theory they have chosen as their partner. It is the recognition of this pressure to conform—even to the man's preference as to physical appearance—that begins to change Hardy's account. Both Cytherea and Elfride are anxious to match their lovers' wishes even to the hopeless extent of providing the preferred eye colour or physical features. Cytherea anxiously asks her brother what Edward Springrove's specifications for a wife are. She learns that he has particular requirements as to 'temper, hair, and eyes' (*Desperate Remedies*, volume 1, chapter 2). Already the narrator is indicating that the anxiety to provide a perfect match for the lover's ideal is debilitating and constricting: Cytherea is 'timidly careful what she says and does, lest she be misconstrued or under-rated to the breadth of a shadow of a hair' (volume 1, chapter 3). When Elfride is told by Knight that he prefers black hair to her own brown and hazel eyes to her own blue, she is 'thoroughly vexed' but the more his opinions go against her 'the more she respected them' (*A Pair of Blue Eyes*, chapter 3). But this is explained by Hardy as more than vanity, as a deep sense of inferiority: 'Elfride's mind had been impregnated with sentiments of her own smallness to an uncomfortable degree of distinctness, and her discomfort was visible in her face' (chapter 19).

Hardy recognizes such discomfort as Elfride's as caused by a gap or slippage between an individual woman's sense of self and what she feels is required of her by those around her. Elfride's authorship of a published romance represents her only autonomous life and she feels that it gives her an identity. Knight's criticism of it, published in a journal, is highly disparaging. His review begins by telling how, having opened the book with the hope of something pleasurable, 'Instead of this we found ourselves in the hands of some young lady, hardly arrived at years of discretion, to judge by the silly device it has been thought worthwhile to adopt on the title page, with the idea of disguising her sex' (chapter 15). Her work, he says, lacks inventiveness and spirited descriptions of human passions. Knight's only positive comment is that she is occasionally felicitous when dealing with matters of 'domestic experience' which by implication are all she knows about. Since her talent is irrelevant to what Knight requires in a woman, she questions herself as to what he thinks of her as 'a woman apart from an author: whether he really despised her; whether he thought more or less of her than of ordinary young women who never ventured into the fire of criticism at all' (chapter 16). Even Bathsheba Everdene, that cool negotiator in the market place and fearless rider, is alarmed by her maid's accurately 'Amazonian picture' of her and asks anxiously whether she is too bold and 'mannish' (*Far from the Madding Crowd*, chapter 30).

The same narratorial ambivalence is evident also in the main area where society demands impossibilities from women. As sexual beings, women in Victorian fiction (though not always in medical literature) are assumed to know themselves only through male desire. This dogma is casually accepted by the narrator in *Far from the Madding Crowd* as an explanation of Bathsheba's attitude to Boldwood:

Boldwood as a means to marriage was unexceptionable; she esteemed and liked him: yet she did not want him. It appears that ordinary men take wives because possession is not possible without marriage, and that ordinary women accept husbands because marriage is not possible without possession. (chapter 30)

Yet the three heroines in question are ardent in their response to the men who attract them. Elfride feels that Smith's 'inflammable' disposition is exactly like her own. After the famously phallic scene of Troy's sword-play in *Far from the Madding Crowd*, Bathsheba feels 'powerless to withstand or deny him'. As he kisses her, her blood beats in her face and sets her 'stinging as if aflame to the very hollows of her feet, and enlarged emotion to a compass which quite swamped thought' (chapter 28). Significantly, however, she feels 'like one who has sinned a great sin' (chapter 28).

These accounts of individual women's reactions constitute alternative discourses which serve finally to oust the use of conventional explanations of them as a species. Strikingly, it is in the first published novel that momentarily a woman steps far enough outside the conventionally accepted view to speak of her desire for autonomy. It is when Cytherea is driven into a loveless marriage by the financial needs of her brother, although she loves Springrove:

Yes—my duty to society . . . But ah, Owen, it is difficult to adjust our outer and inner life with perfect honesty to all! Though it may be right to care more for the benefit of the many than for the indulgence of your own single self, when you consider that the many, and duty to them, only exist to you through your own existence, what can be said? What do our own acquaintances care about us? Not much. I think of mine . . . they will pause just for an instant, and give a sigh to me, and think, 'poor girl', believing they do great justice to my memory by this. But they will never, never realize that it was my single opportunity of existence, as well as of doing my duty, which they are regarding; they will not feel that what to them is but a thought, easily held in those two words of pity, 'Poor girl' was a whole life to me . . . Nobody can enter into another's nature truly, that's what is so grievous. (*Desperate Remedies*, volume 2, chapter 5)

Such slippage between a woman's outer actions in the interests of conformity and her inner feelings is forcibly expressed also by Bathsheba and Elfride. Their perceptions create a powerful alternative account of women's nature which ultimately sweeps away the kind of easy generalities of a relatively misogynistic view. Both women recognize that the language they are offered in which to describe their feelings is essentially the language of men. Bathsheba in *Far from the Madding Crowd* articulates this unambiguously when Boldwood offers her a choice of states of mind, 'Do you like me, or do you respect me?' This is a choice and no choice: it assumes no other reactions are possible. Surprisingly she rejects these options: 'I don't know—at least, I cannot tell you. It is difficult for a woman to define her feelings in language, which is chiefly made by men to express theirs' (chapter 51). For her the valentine she sends him is a joke; he insists on taking it seriously and insists that she ought to do the same.

Elfride too recognizes a gap between her inner life and the language she has to use, though she does not ascribe it to men. When Knight accuses her of vanity she replies 'Well, you know what I mean, even though my words are badly selected and commonplace . . . Because I utter commonplace words, you must not suppose I think commonplace thoughts' (*A Pair of Blue Eyes*, chapter 19). But the ultimate entrapment for women in men's control of language is the assumption for which Tess rebukes Alec d'Urberville: that a woman's 'no' can be read as 'yes'—a belief which Clare also accepts. Conformity to male reality is thus ensured. In *The Hand of Ethelberta* (1875), the novel which followed *Far from the Madding Crowd*, Ethelberta coolly demolishes the public proverbs about women on which Hardy's narrators intermittently draw. She passes on her wisdom to her sister Picotee: 'But don't you go believing in sayings, Picotee: they are all made by men, for their own advantages. Women who use public proverbs as a guide through events are those who have not ingenuity enough to make private ones as each event occurs' (chapter 22).

Aside from these central figures of women aspiring desperately to the ideal of femininity as conventionally constructed are a handful of examples of the unfeminine fallen woman who has sinned sexually. Society and literature encodes such women as full of guilt, self-hatred, and remorse. The nearest Hardy comes to creating such a figure is the hapless Fanny Robin, seduced by Troy, in *Far from the Madding Crowd*. But Fanny is represented externally only—her self-perception is never revealed. She is trusting, affectionate, stoical, an emblem of victimized womanhood struggling to the poorhouse where she dies in childbirth. The other two fallen women are even more anomalous in that they feel no guilt, shame, or remorse. Neither has lost her respectable place in society. Miss Aldclyffe in *Desperate Remedies*, despite her illegitimate son, has established herself as a wealthy and respected figure. Though, like Fanny, she dies, this is a random event, unconnected with her past.

Most unorthodox of all is Eustacia Vye. She can be seen as attempting to break free from the contemporary construction of femininity in her spiritedness and independence but mainly in her passionate desire which is spontaneous, not vicarious: 'To be loved to madness—such was her great desire . . . And she seemed to long for the abstraction called passionate love more than for any particular lover' (*The Return of the Native*, book 1, chapter 7). She chooses her lovers, not they her. She has of course given herself to Wildeve and threatens to withhold the gift: 'I won't give myself to you any more' (book 1, chapter 9). She refuses to be either a victim or a complaisant mistress. Even though she marries Clym, she does not accept the role of submissive wife but tries to dominate and remould him. When this fails, she again chooses her own way and returns to Wildeve as a lover. Yet the narrator gives her none of the trappings of fallen women. Hardy will not give her those of the angel in the house. Instead he describes her as an anomaly having 'the raw material of a divinity' (book 1, chapter 7) and represents her as a goddess: 'On Olympus she would have done well with a little preparation. She had the passions and instincts which make a model goddess, that is, those which make not quite a model woman'. The whole of chapter 7 is given over to loading her with seductive and pagan images in what represents a kind of eulogy to a woman whose development is limited only by her lack of power in the place where she finds herself:

Her presence brought memories of Bourbon roses, rubies, tropical midnights, and eclipses of the sun; her moods recalled lotus-eaters, the march in *Athalie*, her motions, the ebb and flow of the sea; her voice, the viola. In a dim light, and with a slight rearrangement of her hair, her general figure might have stood in for that of either of the higher female deities.

The implication of pent-up and frustrated power here suggests a deeply 'unfeminine' longing to be a free agent. She is given something of the menace of a Lady Audley. Though she meets the usual fate of a fallen woman, death by drowning, she chooses it out of rage, not shame. It is a choice as deliberate and grandiose as Tess's death on the gallows. As an anomaly falling within the acceptable range for a *femme fatale*, she does not initiate a subsequent change in the literary treatment of women.

Women in the Later Novels

By the 1880s Hardy recognized explicitly his desire to change novelistic language as it related to women. As he later told a journalist and editor in 1891—

Ever since I began to write—certainly ever since I wrote 'Two on a Tower' in 1881—I have felt that the doll of English fiction must be demolished, if England is to have a school of fiction at all: & I think great honour is due to the D: Chronicle for frankly recognizing that the development of a more virile type of novel is not incompatible with sound morality. (*Letters*, i. 250)

What the reference to the *Daily Chronicle* makes clear is that by this time the weakening of the power of the circulating libraries and the more open climate for the discussion of sexuality were creating conditions which could further the literary changes that Hardy and others had initiated. He speaks approvingly later in the same letter of the 'distinct advance in journalism' represented by making literature an important topic for a newspaper. For it was the subject of sexuality in women which clashed with the view of them as potential moral angels which was the chief focus of the anti-censorship feeling amongst writers. In practice what it meant in Hardy's later novels was that he took up the topics he had dropped after *Desperate Remedies* which had been made familiar by the sensation novels: adultery, marital breakdown, divorce, and bigamy. His treatment, however, was now very different. It was more direct and abandoned the usual hypocritical approach to such subjects to deal with 'sexual relations as it is (*sic*)'.[2]

By the 1880s resistance to the censorship imposed by the circulating libraries was beginning to open up possibilities for more frankness. The increased freedom of publication interacted with developments which by this time had moved women from the legal status of non-persons to that of half-persons. Divorce had become easier and less expensive after 1857, though the law still discriminated against women. Further changes in 1884 made it possible to obtain a divorce without waiting for a two-year period of desertion to elapse. The Infant Custody Act of 1873 gave a mother rights in certain circumstances to claim custody of children up to the age of 16 rather than 7. The Married Women's Property Act of 1870 protected a wife's earnings and gave her some claim to her own property. The identically named Act of 1882 went further: wives could now acquire, hold, and dispose of any real or personal property exactly as unmarried women could.

But such events merely prepared the way for a change in the construction of femininity by creating new material to draw on. Different interpretations of legal changes and their consequences were still available and proliferated in articles in periodicals, such as those of Eliza Lynn Linton. Defences of the old ideal suggested that the virtues of 'the Desdemonas and Dorotheas, the Enids and Imogens' were to be abandoned in favour of a 'masterful Domina'—a female tyrant demanding 'absolute independence coupled with supreme power over men'.[3] This was a defence that worked by insisting on an absolute separation of the ideal woman and the deviant one. More obliquely, the image of a wilful, irrational Eve tempted by the attractions of a dangerous autonomy is hinted at in an article in 1889 on 'The Apple and the Ego of Woman'. Like Linton's article, this one connects the increased independence of women with 'social insurgency': 'So accustomed are we to consider the feminine element as the conservative, fruitful passive side of nature, that we never connect the idea of destruction with it.[4] This is not altogether true: the ideal woman was supposed to emerge by restraining her irrationality and fickleness which were allegedly innate and destructive.

On the other hand, women who expressed approval of these legal and other changes such as the increase in secondary and tertiary education could be represented as 'New Women'. In the brief flourishing of the New Woman in literature the figures represented are largely new in their attitudes to the options in life, including sexuality and marriage. So in Sarah Grand's *The Heavenly Twins* (1893) the heroine Evadne Frayling refuses to consummate her marriage because she discovers her husband's sexual history. Fearing venereal disease, she 'declines to live with' him—an episode that reverses the conventional view that prostitutes are the source of such diseases. Hadria Fullerton in Mona Caird's *The Daughters of Danaus* (1894) deserts her blameless husband and child to study music in Paris. This she describes as overcoming 'a sickly feminine conscience'. What *The Woman Who Did* (1898), Herminia, does (in Grant Allen's best-seller of that name) is refuse to marry the man she loves because she hates 'monopolist physical instincts' and regards marriage as degrading. Despite their apparent radicalism these novels effect a compromise in two ways: by their insistence on the high-mindedness of their heroines, who in the end conform or die, and by their gingerly handling of any reference to sexuality.

This description of the New Woman is paralleled by that of the 'New Man' at the end of the twentieth century. The comparison is illuminating. 'New Man' was originally the term used approvingly to describe a man who, as a result of accepting male–female equality in partnership and marriage, is prepared to take on a share of what was traditionally feminine domestic work including childcare. But while some groups saw the phrase as approving, others interpreted such men as unmasculine wimps. A range of variants in these two perspectives on the 'New Man' also existed. Similarly 'New Woman' was the phrase used to describe middle-class women who took advantage of their improved legal position and new opportunities for education. But to traditionalists, as happened later with the 'New Man', the expression became one of abuse. Such women were trying to become men. They were likely to dress like men, smoke like men, reject marriage or if married neglect their duties as a mother. If they developed their intellectual faculties too far they would impair their reproductive function. This in turn would physically affect them and cause neurosis and instability.

Hardy was one of those prepared to accept a different construction of femininity which would rewrite both the ideal womanly woman and her reinforcing opposite, the fallen woman as well as the New Woman. This is evident in Grace Melbury and Sue Bridehead on one hand, and Tess and Arabella Donn on the other. These women are all subject to feelings and actions previously excluded by literary taboos but which are now explicitly articulated. Yet they are not, like the wicked Lady Audley, freaks beyond the pale; nor do they, like those in the New Woman novels, repent or die. They are struggling to achieve a certain autonomy for themselves of a kind that baffles the men they are involved with and even the narrators who describe them. Hence the contradictions within the novels' accounts of Grace, Tess, Sue, and Arabella.

Central, therefore, to the change which gives Hardy's heroines glimmers of a possible new self is the existence of spontaneous sexual attraction felt by Grace Melbury, Tess, and Arabella towards Edred Fitzpiers, Jude Fawley, Angel Clare, and even, to an extent, Alec d'Urberville. With Grace Melbury, her physical reaction to Fitzpiers is what undermines the traditional pictures of the pure middle-class girl. Her father of course reads her as a delicate, refined, and sexless being who will obediently marry Giles Winterborne, the husband whom he originally chooses for her as an act of reparation to Giles's father. But when a new desire arises in Melbury to raise his daughter to a class above his own, fitted to her middle-class manners, he brings, as new choice of husband, the local doctor, Edred Fitzpiers. The commercial nature of the transaction is made clear: 'if it costs me my life you shall marry well! To-day has shown me that whatever a young woman's niceness, she stands for nothing alone' (*The Woodlanders*, chapter 12). Melbury is even gratified at the idea of Grace 'making havoc in the upper classes' (chapter 22). She accepts her new suitor with apparent meekness but her reasons in this context are subversive. The doctor arouses her physically, stirs her 'indescribably':

That Fitzpiers acted upon her like a dram, exciting her, throwing her into a novel atmosphere which biassed her doings until the influence was over, when she felt something of the nature of regret for the mood she had experienced—could not be told to this worthy couple in words. (chapter 22)

Significantly, the nature of her feelings for Fitzpiers is not recognized by her father. It falls outside his expectations for a well-bred, womanly girl: 'She could not explain the subtleties of her feeling as clearly as he could state his opinion, even though she had skill in speech, and her father had none' (chapter 22). The language of men has no room for such feelings as hers in a well-bred girl. Similarly, when she learns of Fitzpiers's infidelity she has no language in which to express her feelings. Her husband is surprised by her silence on the subject: 'He expected a scene at breakfast—but she only exhibited an extreme reserve' (chapter 30). In attributing this to what he has said of regretting his marriage, he misconstrues her as surely as her father does later. When Melbury sees her indifference to Fitzpiers's adultery he wants 'to ask her a dozen questions: did she not feel jealous, was she not indignant . . . ' He reproaches her by saying: 'You are very tame and let-alone, I am bound to say.' Her astonishing reply, 'I am what I feel' (chapter 30), represents a claim to feel and to mean something individual to her not covered by routine generalizations about jealous wives. To her surprise, the purely physical nature of her feelings for Fitzpiers seems to preclude even jealousy: 'she was quite sure he was going to Mrs Charmond. Grace was amazed at the mildness of the anger which the suspicion engendered in her: she was but little excited, and her jealousy was languid even to death' (chapter 28). From the 1895 version of the novel onwards, she puts her full realization of Fitzpiers's affair into words of a shattering simplicity to Felice Charmond: 'He's had you! Can it be . . . !' (chapter 33). But she accepts the fact to the point of feeling sisterly sympathy with Fitzpiers's old and new mistresses, Suke Damson and Felice Charmond, when they rush to what they believe is his sick-bed in her house. With laconic irony she invites them in 'Wives all, let's enter together!' But the moment of irony passes and 'The tears which his possibly critical situation could not bring to her eyes surged over at the contemplation of these fellow-women whose relations with him were as close as her own without its conventionality' (chapter 35). A 'tenderness' spreads over her 'like a dew' and she rejects the language of men designed to dismiss such women: 'It was well enough, conventionally, to address either one of them in the wife's regulation terms of virtuous sarcasm, as woman, creature, or thing' (chapter 35).

Her 'illicit' love for Giles later shows the same sexual dimension as her infatuation with Fitzpiers. It grows more explicit when she asks him with an 'agonizing seductiveness' in an addition made in 1895 'why don't you do what you want to?' (chapter 39). The long embrace and passionate kiss that result are something she looks back on with gratitude when hope of divorce from Fitzpiers collapses. Though she mentally blames her ignorance at the time about the likelihood of divorce, 'yet in the centre of her heart she blessed it a little for what it had momentarily brought her' (chapter 39). Her well-known refusal at first to allow Giles to sleep in the hut where she shelters after running away from Fitzpiers deflects attention from the addition to the text in 1895 of an extended expression of desire when she finally invites him in: '*Come to me dearest!* I don't mind what *they say or think of us any more*' (chapter 41).

Grace is not the ideal 'pure' woman she seemed at first and this is disturbing to the men around her. Fitzpiers is titillated by the idea that she committed adultery when she allows him to believe that Giles was her lover: 'the man whom Grace's matrimonial fidelity could not keep faithful was stung into passionate throbs of interest concerning her by her avowal to the contrary' (chapter 44). Giles on the other hand resists the idea that she is physically attracted to him. He is 'pure' and womanly on her behalf in rejecting the invitation to spend the night in the hut with her. In doing so he is clinging to a reading of her which is obviously no longer accurate.

Tess Durbeyfield, by contrast with Grace, represents a reshaping of the fallen woman—one with illicit sexual experience. She undergoes a metamorphosis from the stereotype to someone extraordinary. Sometimes the narrator of *Tess* points this out directly, as after her affair with Alec:

Let the truth be told—women do as a rule live through such humiliations, and regain their spirits, and again look about them with an interested eye. While there's life there's hope is a conviction not so entirely unknown to the 'betrayed' as some amiable theorists would have us believe. (chapter 16)

At the same point it is asserted that Tess again feels her 'invincible' instinct 'towards self delight'. Like Grace, she is an explicitly sexual being, with her appearance described in erotic terms by the men around her, including the narrator.

She had an attribute which amounted to a disadvantage just now; and it was this that caused Alec d'Urberville's eyes to rivet themselves upon her. It was a luxuriance of aspect, a fulness of growth which made her appear more of a woman than she really was. (chapter 5)

This description is, as Dolin notes, a coded reference to her breasts, 'consistently the most privileged feature of her appearance'.[5] The allusion is not missed by the censorious reviewer who wrote this passage:

the story gains nothing by the reader being let into the secret of the physical attributes which especially fascinated him in Tess. Most people can fill in the blanks for themselves, without its being necessary to put the dots on the i's so very plainly; but Mr. Hardy leaves little unsaid.[6]

Though Tess learns from circumstances to feel shame at her 'fall', as society instructs her, she finally shakes this off. Under the shock of Angel Clare's finding her living with Alec, she can assert (according to an insertion made by Hardy in 1912) with the directness that marks Grace's later utterances that a woman's first lover possesses her. She tells Clare, in an allusion to their unconsummated marriage, that the step back to Alec 'was not so great as it seems. He had been as husband to me: you never had!' (chapter 55). With the final consummation of their marriage she becomes free not only of sexual guilt but of guilt for the murder. And this to Hardy is evidently 'the moral woman' since 'The beauty or ugliness of a character lay not only in its achievements but in its aims and impulses; its true history lay not among things done but among things willed' (chapter 49).

But Hardy goes much further than asserting the rights of women to be sexual beings. He examines the social issues involved in the sexual relationships in these novels. Grace wishes to divorce her unfaithful husband and is led to think she can because of his adultery. This allows her a respite during which her love for Giles returns. It is only then she learns that though, if she were the unfaithful one, Fitzpiers could divorce her, she cannot divorce him without some further aggravating cause. But this is not a simplistic picture of a failed marriage. Under the persuasions of a Fitzpiers stirred by the thought of her supposed adultery, added to the physical attraction he holds for her, she returns to him. There is no happy ever after. This diminished second union with Fitzpiers is represented not as a new stability but as the beginning of a cycle of infidelities on his part which will recur, presumably followed by successive reunions. As Hardy puts it in a letter which catches the sense of diminishing returns, 'In the story the reunited husband & wife are supposed to live ever after *un*happily!—or at any rate not quite happily' (*Letters*, i. 196). In a recursive process of insertion in the text itself that mimics what it describes, Hardy makes two telling additions. In 1895 he adds to the earlier version of Melbury's final thoughts on his daughter's return to Fitzpiers: 'Well, he's her husband . . . but it's a forlorn hope for her; and God knows how it will end!' In 1895 this was changed, after 'her husband' to:

. . . and let her take him back to her bed if she will! . . . But let her bear in mind that the woman walks and laughs somewhere at this very moment whose neck he'll be coling next year as he does hers to-night; and as he did Felice Charmond's last year; and Suke Damson's the year afore! . . . It's a forlorn hope for her; and God knows how it will end! (chapter 48)

The prediction of the recurrence of Fitzpiers's infidelity and Grace's compromises with it represents the instability of the legal institution of marriage as much as the marital merry-go-round in *Jude*. Along with this, *The Woodlanders* indicates the speciousness of using marriage in fiction as closure and a signal that all is now well. It also shows how superficial is the idea that women could choose a husband. Grace twice 'chooses' Fitzpiers but in both instances the lack of alternatives on which she might exercise her free will is evident. Her middle-class education, her father's pressure, the instilled sense of duty, and Fitzpiers's wide experience virtually determine what is acquiescence rather than choice. The source of her original engagement to him is captured in an exchange with her father:

'I needn't tell you to make it all smooth for him.'
　'You mean, to lead him on to marry me?'
　'I do. Haven't I educated you for it?' (chapter 22)

In the second 'choosing' there is little scope for a refusal to return to her husband. Her very identity is compromised by her status as neither wife, widow, nor unmarried girl. The social pressure to conformity is evidenced by her rereading of the marriage service and her convenient recognition of the 'awfully solemn promises she made' when marrying Fitzpiers.

The same sophisticated treatment of social issues is found in *Tess*. In this instance also there are several threads to disentangle. It is important not to assume that Tess is as pure as the subtitle claims because she is the victim of outright rape by Alec d'Urberville. There is an ingenious argument that as the law stood and as Hardy (who was a Justice of the Peace) would have known, even if Tess were asleep during the episode, Alec's actions would legally constitute rape. But though for the 1891 edition Hardy included a reference to Alec as 'the spoiler' which was later omitted, and he included one to Tess being overheard sobbing on the night of the scene in the Chase, other later revisions render the scene more ambiguous. They suggest co-operation from Tess. For instance, in 1892, Hardy removed the reference to 'the spoiler' and to Alec drugging Tess with cordial or (earlier) spirits which had been in the text from the manuscript stage. Alec says to her in an early version, as she is leaving Trantbridge: 'You didn't come for love of me . . . '. She then replies "Tis quite true . . . If I had ever really loved you, if I loved you still, I should not so loathe and hate myself for my weakness as I do now!' (chapter 12). In 1892 'really' was changed to 'sincerely' and Tess concluded 'My eyes were dazed by you for a little, and that was all'. Similarly an increased implication of involvement is added to a narratorial description of her thoughts when confessing to her mother: 'She had dreaded him, winced before him, succumbed to a cruel advantage he took of her helplessness; then, temporarily blinded by his flash manners, had been stirred to confused surrender awhile, had suddenly disliked and despised him, and had run away' (chapter 12). And as many have pointed out, the scene in the Chase is followed by 'some few weeks' in which Tess remains as Alec's mistress before returning home.

It is clear that the episode in the Chase is on any count to be seen as questioning the line between seduction and rape; and Tess's response is crucial to this issue. Given her economic dependence and that of her family on Alec, given her innocence and his experience, and the absence of anyone she can turn to, this event is as much rape as it would have been had Alec used violence or had Tess been drugged or asleep. Alec's act is culpable, Tess's response is not. His culpability is, strangely, signalled in the first edition of 1891 in two sentences that persist through all Hardy's revisions:

Doubtless some of Tess d'Urberville's mailed ancestors rollicking home from a fray had dealt the same measure even more ruthlessly towards peasant girls of their time. But though to visit the sins of the fathers upon the children may be a morality good enough for divinities, it is scorned by average human nature; and it therefore does not mend the matter. (chapter 11)

In a bold move Hardy extends the concept of rape to take in forms of seduction while simultaneously making an even more provocative point. This is that the physical attraction that Tess feels towards Alec is natural. Hardy then develops a strand of thought about sexuality and naturalness that urges the exclusion of sexual relationships from the sphere of moral judgement. In a less artificial world Tess might have regarded her relationship with Alec as a freely available option. As the narrator says: 'But for the world's opinion those experiences would have been simply a liberal education' (chapter 15).

The same point is made about the stigma imposed on illegitimacy. The condemnation is seen as a social artifice. Hardy sets aside the conventional figure of the unmarried mother, the 'magdalen', who by convention is rightly and naturally dishonoured and ashamed. He says of Tess

If she could have been but just created, to discover herself as a spouseless mother, with no experience of life except as the parent of a nameless child, would the position have caused her to despair? No, she would have taken it calmly, and found pleasures therein. Most of the misery had been generated by her conventional aspect, and not by her innate sensations. (chapter 14)

By her 'conventional aspect' Hardy means the social conventions as to pre-marital sex that Tess has accepted and internalized. He also castigates the stigmatizing of an illegitimate child by this hypocritical society. The vicar of Marlott refuses to allow her dead child a Christian burial although validly baptized by Tess. His overt reason is bureaucratic: that 'he could not allow the plea of necessity for its irregular administration'. In reality it is because 'Having the natural feelings of a tradesman at finding a job he should have been called in for had been unskilfully botched by his customers among themselves, he was disposed to say no' (chapter 14). This attack on the consequences of branding a child illegitimate had implications beyond the contemptible nature of doing so. It suggested what Hardy spelt out later when he referred to 'the present pernicious conventions in respect of manners, customs, religion, illegitimacy, the stereotyped household (that it must be the unit of society), the father of a woman's child (that it is anybody's business but the woman's own, except in cases of disease or insanity)' (*Letters*, iii. 238). As this makes clear, Hardy is moving towards beliefs subversive of the whole of established society as constructed by the State, the Church, and other institutions.

The other fallen woman, Arabella Donn in *Jude*, is what might be called a New Fallen Woman. Her openly sexual innuendo in attracting Jude's attention by throwing a pig's penis at him rapidly leads to her seducing him. As she says to her woman companions 'I want him to more than care for me: I want him to have me; to marry me! I must have him. I can't do without him. He's the sort of man I long for. I shall go mad if I can't give myself to him altogether!' (part 1, chapter 7). This she says 'in a curiously low, hungry tone of latent sensuousness'. She either feigns pregnancy to bring him to marriage; or, if the female pills she procures from the quack doctor are abortifacient, procures an abortion when she has achieved her aim. When, bored and disappointed, she leaves Jude, she calmly enters into a bigamous marriage in Australia. She is active, robust, resourceful, and at ease with herself and her own sexuality and quite unmaternal towards her son.

The shock to much public taste of a relatively promiscuous woman is captured by Margaret Oliphant's description of Arabella as 'a woman so completely animal that it is at once too little and too much to call her vicious. She is a human pig . . . quite without shame or consciousness of any occasion for shame.'[7] The nub of this criticism is Oliphant's final remark. Hardy's representation of Arabella shows no trace of the crucial remorse, shame, and self-loathing of the stereotypical working-class fallen woman of fiction and painting in this period. The fate of such women is characteristically suicide by drowning. Such a death serves to represent at once a punishment and a cleansing. When Jude dies after their second marriage, Arabella does head for the river but it is in search of Vilbert, the chosen candidate for her third husband, not to attempt suicide. Since the disease-bringing promiscuous woman was frequently the figure for the social disorder that the working class threatened, this characterization was an affront to Oliphant and the class she belonged to.

Further, the whole novel of which Arabella is a part questions an institution which helped to underpin the stability of society and the power of the establishment's clerical arm. The marriages in the narrative represent a kind of merry-go-round which trivializes them. Jude marries Arabella because he wrongly believes her pregnant; Arabella leaves Jude and contracts a bigamous marriage; Sue marries Phillotson partly to spite Jude for concealing his marriage to Arabella; Phillotson divorces Sue out of kindness on spurious grounds, after she leaves him; Jude divorces Arabella to enable her to marry her bigamous husband; Sue, as a self-punishment for her children's death, remarries Phillotson who is physically repugnant to her; Arabella gets the sick and wretched Jude to remarry her when drunk. In addition to these events relevant to the narrative, the text includes cameo descriptions of two extraneous weddings observed by Jude and Sue. One is that of a 'sullen and reluctant' soldier to a bride 'soon, obviously to become a mother' and with a black eye. The other is that of a well-to-do middle-class couple at which the bride is visibly trembling with fright (part 5, chapter 4).

This repetition of marriages contracted or dissolved for the wrong reasons figures the institution as a farcical game. Again, one reviewer noted this: 'The crowning absurdity of the double re-marriage makes the whole book appear dangerously near to farce.'[8] But farce, as Hardy saw it, is really the point. As Hardy wrote at this time to his friend Edward Clodd, 'What you say is pertinent & true of the modern views of marriage [as] a survival from the custom of capture & purchase, propped up by a theological superstition' (*Letters*, ii. 92). Later still Hardy published an attack on marriage entitled 'Laws the Cause of Misery' in *Nash's Magazine* for March 1912:

As the present marriage laws are, to the eyes of anybody who looks around, the gratuitous cause of at least half the misery of the community, that they are allowed to remain in force for a day is, to quote the famous last word of the ceremony itself, an 'amazement', and can only be accounted for by the assumption that we live in a barbaric age, and are the slaves of gross superstition.

He is equally critical of divorce laws which allow Jude and Arabella to connive in a divorce and for Phillotson to divorce Sue on the grounds of her (non-existent) adultery. But the objections go further than this. Some of them are stated by the narrator at the time of Jude's wedding to Arabella:

And so, standing before the aforesaid officiator, the two swore that at every other time of their lives till death took them, they would assuredly believe, feel, and desire precisely as they had believed, felt and desired during the few preceding weeks. What was as remarkable as the undertaking itself was the fact that nobody seemed at all surprised at what they swore. (part 1, chapter 9)

Here Hardy clearly makes the point which this particular marriage goes on to show: that individuals can reasonably promise to do things; but they cannot reasonably promise to feel and desire things for an unlimited period. By this time of course he could speak from experience.

There are other objections to the institution of marriage even beyond this which are articulated shockingly for the time by a woman—Sue Bridehead. When both she and Jude find themselves divorced from Phillotson and Arabella and free to remarry, she decides that if they married

[We] Should be two dissatisfied ones linked together, which would be twice as bad as before . . . I think I should begin to be afraid of you, Jude, the moment you had contracted to love me under a Government stamp and I was licensed to be loved on the premises by you—Ugh, how horrible and sordid! Although, as you are, free, I trust you more than any man in the world. (part 5, chapter 1)

This sounds like a plea for free love but there is a major inconsistency in the narrative here. The idea of a contrast between legalistic and natural marriage has already been expressed at Jude's first wedding by the narrator's comment on the impossibility of making a promise to love someone for ever. Yet what Jude and Sue represent is not a sexual freedom where only passion justifies the act, but a marriage-like monogamy. The narrative implies throughout that these two will feel the same for ever.

Hardy offers no solution to what he sees as the problem of how to arrange the relationships between the sexes in the interests of society. But he complicates that issue as well as the question of women's role in a partnership by his representation of Sue. She is presented as an opalescent figure whose contradictions have baffled critics. She would have been readily identifiable by contemporary readers as a New Woman through her rejection of marriage. This was typical of the fictional type but she differs from the stereotype by not speaking euphemistically of her sexual life. She speaks as frankly as Grace Melbury in talking to Jude: 'I have never yielded myself to any lover . . . I have remained as I began . . . People say I must be cold-natured—sexless on account of it. But I won't have it!' (part 3, chapter 4). Yet after leaving her husband to live with Jude, she refuses to become his lover. She gives at least four different reasons for her refusal:

Put it down to my timidity, . . . to a woman's natural timidity when the crisis comes. I *may* feel as well as you that I have a perfect right to live with you as you thought—from this moment. I *may* hold the opinion that, in a proper state of society, the father of a woman's child will be as much a private matter of hers as the cut of her underclothes, on whom nobody will have a right to question her. But partly, perhaps, because it is by his generosity that I am now free, I would rather not be other than a little rigid . . . But don't press me and criticize me, Jude! Assume that I haven't the courage of my opinions. I know I am a poor miserable creature. My nature is not so passionate as yours! (part 4, chapter 5)

But her uncertainty as to her motive for refusing Jude is not seen by her as entailing uncertainty as to her absolute right to say no. She claims, as Penny Boumelha pointed out, 'her right to a non-sexual love and her right to a non-marital sexual liaison'.[9]

She is aware of herself not just as an oppressed individual but as a member of a gendered group rightly seeking autonomy. In this she resembles Jude, the last representative in Hardy's fiction of the talented working man barred from his hoped-for course by a rigid class system. Hence the bond between them that is recognized in Hardy's earliest titles for this novel: 'The Simpletons' and 'Hearts Insurgent'. It is characteristic of Hardy's ambivalence in this novel that he attaches to it a final title which does not acknowledge the fact that in this narrative humanity is represented not solely by a man but equally by a woman. Of all the women in Hardy's novels Sue Bridehead goes furthest in claiming autonomy of a distinctive kind. She does not wish, like earlier women, merely to have a truly free choice of husband. She claims for herself a right to override the traditional claims of husband, children, and society. As she tells Jude

I have been thinking, ... that the social moulds civilization fits us into have no more relation to our actual shapes than the conventional shapes of the constellations have to the real star-patterns. I am called Mrs Richard Phillotson, living a calm wedded life with my counterpart of that name. But I am not really Mrs Richard Phillotson, but a woman tossed about, all alone, with aberrant passions and unaccountable antipathies. (part 4, chapter 1)

In this way she is a hybrid developed from the blending of the characteristics of the two stereotypes, the womanly ideal and the fallen woman. As such she was a shocking figure for contemporaries.

But her resolution withers under the impact of an event that relates directly to her being female: the deaths of her and Jude's children. The suicide and murders are triggered in part by her ineptness in explaining her new pregnancy to Jude's son. Her ill-thought-out answer to his questions leads him to the fatal conclusion that 'If we children was gone there'd be no trouble at all!' (part 6, chapter 2). In consequence she later sees a causal link between the deaths and her own unconventional behaviour. She attributes the catastrophe to her sexual immorality in leaving Phillotson and producing illegitimate and doomed children: 'I have thought that we have been selfish, careless, even impious, in our courses, you and I. Our life has been a vain attempt at self-delight. But self-abnegation is the higher road. We should mortify the flesh—the terrible flesh—the curse of Adam!' More than this, she feels she should suffer self-mutilation: 'I should like to prick myself all over with pins and bleed out the badness that's in me!' (part 6, chapter 3).

So by a mad logic she concludes that her necessary punishment is a return to the husband whom she finds so physically repugnant that at one stage she leapt from their bedroom window to escape him. Her reaction leads also to a guilt-induced collapse into the religiosity she has so scornfully abandoned earlier.

The transformation in Sue is to an extent ambiguous. It can be read as the New Woman's stereotypical return to conventionality which usually takes place in such narratives unless the heroines die. This would be a return on Hardy's part to a traditional view of women as a second and inferior sex: irrational creatures dominated by their emotions (and in particular a maternal instinct) which, uncontrolled, lead them into mental instability. A more convincing reading sees Hardy's account as capturing a crucial stage in the change in the position of women in society. Sue has advanced intellectually in a way not matched by her emotions because society reinforces its ideology by fostering guilt. It is her conditioning to feel guilt that hinders and destroys Sue: her self-inflicted punishment is represented as a terrible mistake. Such an interpretation shows a new subtlety not found in other New Woman novels. At the same time the final characterization of the Phillotson marriage as a self-inflicted form of punishment for the woman serves as yet another attack on the institution. Hardy was not the only one to represent it in this way, though those who did so were very few. Phillotson is not a bad—and certainly not a violent—man; but he and Sue are incompatible. Their marriage is finally something worse than the legalized prostitution that George Egerton had described.

Yet one more complication is found in the novel in the account of the relationship between Jude and Sue. Jude, now living platonically with Sue Bridehead, uses Arabella's unexpected return to coerce Sue into a sexual relationship. Arabella is, he insists, despite their divorce, still his real wife and he will go to see her. He chooses this moment to refer to his own lack of a physical relationship with Sue when he calls Arabella coarse:

Perhaps I am coarse too, worse luck! . . . I have the germs of every human infirmity in me . . . I do love you Sue, though I have danced attendance on you for so long for such poor returns . . . It is all very well to preach about self-control, and the wickedness of coercing a woman. But I should just like a few virtuous people . . . to have been in my tantalizing position with you through these late weeks! (part 5, chapter 2)

Sue is distressed by the combination of this and Jude's imminent visit to Arabella: 'I can't bear it, I can't! If she were yours it would be different!' (part 5, chapter 2). To which he replies 'Or if you were', and Sue yields. This emotional blackmail is accepted without comment by the narrator. This slide into an orthodox view of a man's rights which makes male desire paramount goes by unnoticed. It is now next morning and Jude who did not go to see Arabella is arranging to marry Sue. Such a shift enacts Hardy's attempts to break free of the orthodoxy of his day. It is—as often with him—a struggle full of inconsistencies.

CHAPTER 6

HARDY AND SCIENCE: SPACE, TIME, EVOLUTION, AND THE HUMAN RACE

Space and Time

DURING Hardy's long life, a bewildering range of technological advances took place: a railway network, bicycles, cars and aeroplanes, the electric telegraph and the telephone. Photography had been developed in the 1820s and 1830s and by the early twentieth century so had motion pictures. The impact of these on the everyday life of the middle classes must have been enormous. But Hardy seems to have been unmoved by most of them, apart from the bicycle.

What really affected his ideas profoundly were scientific discoveries of a broader and more remote kind in astronomy, geology, and evolution. For him speed of travel, ease of communication, and developments in the visual medium were as nothing compared with the shattering implications for humanity of what scientists like Herschel, Lyell, and Darwin had discovered. Hardy's earliest visual horizons were narrowed to the area of Dorset over which he could walk and of which he perceived every detail. What he saw went through seasonal changes which he observed minutely. From the beginning he saw the world as a changing place and as he grew older he learnt more of the nature of change and how it came about. By contrast, in the novels he wrote from the late 1870s onwards his perspective on the physical world had been magically transformed. The discoveries of astronomers translated for him into a tangible sense that the world was a pinprick in a universe that was limitless. This knowledge did not displace the narrower vision but created a visual dialectic with it.

Astronomical discoveries and their significance are explicitly displayed in *Two on a Tower* where the tower of the title is the old building from which the amateur astronomer, Swithin St Cleeve, directs his telescope towards the heavens. After making the acquaintance of the local lady of the manor, Lady Viviette Constantine, he reveals to her and the reader what his telescope shows. At first he exhibits only those features that lie *within* the solar system. First he points the telescope towards Jupiter and exhibits 'the glory of that orb'. Next he shows the planet Saturn and 'a world which is to my mind by far the most wonderful in the solar system. Think of streams of satellites or meteors racing round and round the planet like a fly-wheel, so close together as to seem solid matter.' Heedless of Viviette's desire to turn to more personal matters, he moves outwards 'to get outside the solar system altogether—leave the whole group of sun, primary, and secondary planets quite behind us in our flight—as a bird might leave its bush and sweep into the whole forest' (chapter 4). Up to this point all the stages in Swithin's journey by telescope are described as objects of wonder. But now, against a tension created by the woman's increasingly urgent wish to speak of her own affairs, he shows her a more alarming vision.

As a kind of reproof he makes her 'travel' with him to the

mysterious outskirts of the solar system; from the solar system to a star in the Swan, the nearest fixed star in the northern sky; from the star in the Swan to remoter stars; thence to the remotest visible, till the ghastly chasm which they had bridged by a fragile line of sight was realized by Lady Constantine. (chapter 4)

As St Cleeve explains, wonder has turned to horror. Awe is inadequate as a reaction to the world *beyond* the solar system. Wonder and admiration are only possible with an 'imaginary picture of the sky as the concavity of a dome whose base extends from horizon to horizon of our earth'. This is 'grand, simply grand, and I wish I had never gone beyond looking at it in that way'. The grandeur, he claims, is the result of an optical illusion that the sky is an enclosing ceiling to our habitat, the roof of our home. Instead in reality it reveals monsters of a terrible enormity: 'Immensities. Until a person has thought out the stars and their interspaces he has hardly learnt that there are things much more terrible than monsters of shape; namely, monsters of magnitude without known shape. Such monsters are the voids and waste places of the sky.' What seem to be 'pieces of darkness' are 'deep wells for the human mind to let itself down into, leave alone the human body!' Those who, like St Cleeve, 'exert their imaginative powers to bury themselves in the depths of that universe merely strain their faculties to gain a new horror'. The effect of all this on Viviette is to make her feel, naturally enough, that 'it is not worth while to live—it quite annihilates me'. She finally understands what Swithin means when he declares that of all the sciences astronomy alone deserves 'the character of the terrible' (chapter 4).

Individuals in Hardy's novels are like the uninitiated Viviette in seeing cosmic space as 'grand'. For them the 'dome' above, though distant, is not a threat but a wonder. They are seen to experience it as thrillingly awesome. The first glimpse is given in the scene of Gabriel Oak alone at night on Norcombe Hill in *Far from the Madding Crowd*:

To persons standing alone on a hill during a clear midnight such as this, the roll of the world eastward is almost a palpable movement. The sensation may be caused by the panoramic glide of the stars past earthly objects, which is perceptible in a few minutes of stillness; or by the better outlook upon space that a hill affords, or by the wind; or by the solitude; but whatever be its origin the impression of riding along is vivid and abiding. (chapter 2)

A similar but individualistic experience is described by Tess Durbeyfield in a way that first stirs Angel Clare to see her as different from the other dairymaids. She explains what she means by saying that 'our souls can be made to go outside our bodies': 'A very easy way to feel 'em go . . . is to lie on the grass at night, and look straight up at some big bright star; and by fixing your mind upon it you will soon find you are hundreds and hundreds o' miles away from your body' (chapter 18).

Viviette, Gabriel Oak, and Tess are all looking outwards into space with a sense of enlargement, not realizing that the actual sky is a horror and by contrast diminishes humanity. But the perspective of the narrators in many of Hardy's novels is at times the reverse of this: they see the reduction in size of the human world. Their inescapable perception of the stellar universe leads them to take a bird's-eye view of the world, an idea that Hardy himself uses. As if in anticipation of aerial photography, the narrators frequently see the world as a panorama viewed from above. Typical is the description of Egdon Heath, 'that grand inviolate place', already quoted, from which the narrator gradually focuses in (as so often in opening scenes) on a road. And in looking down, the narrator sees immense time written into the sight by history and geology:

With the exception of an aged highway, and a still more aged barrow presently to be referred to—themselves almost crystallized to natural products by long continuance—even the trifling irregularities were not caused by pickaxe, plough, or spade, but remained as the very finger-touches of the last geological change. (*The Return of the Native*, book 1, chapter 1)

There is a similar bird's-eye view of Casterbridge in *The Mayor*. As Elizabeth-Jane and her mother are approaching on foot, it is seen not through their eyes alone: 'To birds of the more soaring kind Casterbridge must have appeared on this fine evening as a mosaic-work of subdued reds, browns, greys, and crystals, held together by a rectangular frame of deep green' (chapter 4). In a later description which refers back to this passage, the aerial view predominates and the scale suggests a distant viewer:

Casterbridge, as has been hinted, was a place deposited in the block upon a cornfield. There was no suburb in the modern sense, or transitional intermixture of town and down. It stood, with regard to the wide fertile land adjoining, clean cut and distinct, like a chess board on a green table-cloth. (chapter 14)

Bleak winter weather in *Tess* sends the narrator flying to its source, charging distance with a sense of doom:

strange birds from behind the north pole began to arrive silently on the upland of Flintcomb-Ash; gaunt spectral creatures with tragical eyes—eyes which had witnessed scenes of cataclysmal horror in inaccessible polar regions, of a magnitude such as no human creature had ever con-ceived, in curdling temperatures that no man could endure; which had beheld the crash of icebergs and the slide of snow-hills by the shooting light of the Aurora; been half blinded by the whirl of colossal storms and terraqueous distortions. (chapter 43)

Such recurrently panoramic perspectives alternate with a micro-scopically detailed focus famously illustrated by the contrast between the description of Tess seen from so close that the strands of colour in her irises are visible to the narrator and the view of her standing upon 'the hemmed expanse of verdant flatness, like a fly on a billiard table of indefinite length, and of no more consequence to the surroundings than that fly' (chapter 16). There is a profound dichotomy implicit in this double vision of human beings that will emerge later.

The first of these two perspectives, the microscopic, is however by no means static. Where the panoramic view changes in a way that extends space, this detailed view dissolves into its past state in a way that visibly extends time. As a man like Gabriel Oak looking at the night sky is drawn outwards into the universe, the observer of, say, the bonfire on an ancient burial mound in *The Return of the Native* is drawn back and back into layers of past history. The bonfire springs up briefly as a 'tall flame' which subsides; to be followed by some less, then greater flares. These latter light up the heath below only to leave it in a darkness so intense as to look like Dante's Limbo in his *Inferno*. Then the fire dissolves into all those earlier fires built upon this ancient mound:

The ashes of the original British pyre which blazed from that summit lay fresh and undisturbed in the barrow beneath their tread. The flames from funeral piles long ago kindled there had shone down upon the lowlands as these were shining now. Festival fires to Thor and Woden had followed on the same ground, and duly had their day ... such blazes as this the heathmen were now enjoying are rather the lineal descendants from jumbled Druidical rites and Saxon ceremonies than the invention of popular feeling about Gunpowder Plot. (book 1, chapter 3)

The pattern illustrated by this account is one in which scrutiny of detail becomes so intense that it sees through the present into what it records of the past. When Hardy's narrators describe a scene they read into it traces of the recent past which may remain in the folk memory, as well as earlier Roman and Saxon history, the traces of prehistoric people and the geological formations which have shaped it. The birds'-eye view of Casterbridge already described is paralleled by a contrasting view of detail which reaches back into the past:

Casterbridge announced old Rome in every street, alley, and precinct. It looked Roman, bespoke the art of Rome, concealed dead men of Rome. It was impossible to dig more than a foot or two deep about the town fields and gardens without coming upon some tall soldier or other of the Empire, who had lain there in his silent unobtrusive rest for a space of fifteen hundred years. He was mostly found lying on his side, in an oval scoop in the chalk, like a chicken in its shell; his knees drawn up to his chest. (chapter 11)

But further layers of history are visible to the narrator that are nearer to the present: the woman hanged and burnt in Casterbridge's

Roman amphitheatre in the eighteenth century; and the witnesses of this lurid episode are seen in their later everyday lives where they never 'cared particularly for a hot roast after that' (chapter 11). The narrative moves back over these centuries of history into the depths of prehistoric time just as St Cleeve's telescope moves gradually further into space.

As the narrator moves back in time, he observes the geological conditions that aeons of time have produced. Tess's story involves her movement from Marlott to Talbothays and then Flintcomb-Ash. In both these locations the geology of the landscape literally shapes her life and metaphorically figures it. The rich alluvial soil in the valley of the Var creates the lushness that confronts Angel Clare when he returns from visiting his austere family to Talbothays: 'that green trough of sappiness and humidity, the valley of the Var or Froom' (chapter 27). The physical succulence helps to nurture the feverish sexual desires that develop in all the dairymaids there. It can also be seen to represent passions as the women 'writhed feverishly under the oppressiveness of an emotion thrust on them by cruel Nature's law—an emotion which they had neither expected nor desired'. Even the very air of the sleeping chamber seems 'to palpitate with the hopeless passion of the girls' (chapter 23).

At Flintcomb-Ash where Tess labours in a bitter winter the privations she and others endure are determined by the geology of the place—signalled by its name. With all the precision and language of a geological textbook, the narrator describes the scene. Tess and her companion are set to work hacking in a swede field—a 'stretch of a hundred odd acres, in one patch, on the highest ground of the farm, rising above stony lanchets or lynchets—the crops of siliceous veins in the chalk formation, composed of myriads of loose white flints in bulbous, cusped, and phallic shapes'. This close perspective on what the women see as they grub up the remains of swedes is transformed to a distant view of them:

these two upper and nether visages confronted each other, all day long, the white face looking down at the brown face, and the brown face looking up at the white face, without anything standing between them but the two girls crawling over the surface of the former like flies. (chapter 43)

The aeons of history, both human and geological, shake belief in the overriding significance of human beings whose lives are so brief and this view of them as insignificant is reinforced by the recurrent idea that the emotional lives of individual men and women are the only things that do not leave their mark on the landscape. To those who experience love, loss, and grief, the sites of these emotions have powerful associations. But for those who succeed these people, there are no traces left: the most passionate of human dramas are forgotten and leave no fossils in the landscape where they were enacted. But in accordance with the cyclic pattern of evolution, Hardy believes that dramas of the kind found in ballad stories—involving love, betrayal, revenge—are generic experiences repeated over and over again. In *Jude* the newly seeded, ploughed field where Jude is employed to act as a human scarecrow frightening away birds with a rattle is a brown surface marked with lines like a new piece of corduroy but revealing nothing else. Yet, says the narrator, it has been 'the site first or last of energy, gaiety, horseplay, bickerings, weariness' (part 1, chapter 2). In keeping with the varying perspective on human life in the novels, these events are referred to as narrowly domestic or as the ingredients of high tragedy. It is against fluctuating and contradictory perspectives on time, on space, and on the importance or unimportance of human beings, that the narratives take place.

Evolution and the Human Race: The Descent of Man

Darwin, in *The Origin of Species*, did not touch the subject of the human race. This absence is significant since his central argument has unmistakeable implications for the whole of humanity. He draws on Malthus's assertion that many more individuals are born into each species than circumstances will allow to survive. The number is reduced by the survival only of those who by chance are best adapted to their environment and so are naturally selected. Darwin also makes the point that the excess of individuals is to be found throughout 'the whole animal and vegetable kingdoms'.[1] Consequently natural selection takes place 'in each species in that kingdom'. The natural inference from this is that human beings are a product of this relatively automatic process, like other animals. Later, in *The Descent of Man* (1871), he did argue that men and women had evolved from the higher primates.

So natural selection in all species requires the transmission by heredity of characteristics which favoured survival. Darwin found difficulties with the question of hereditary features but decided to conclude that 'Perhaps the correct way of viewing the whole subject, would be, to look at the inheritance of every character whatever as the rule, and non-inheritance as the anomaly'.[2] This means that characteristics distinctive of the human race must be of the kind that have favoured survival. Darwin was speaking of physical survival but when contemplating human beings it was impossible to ignore less measurable features. He confesses that 'The high standard of our intellectual powers and moral disposition is the greatest difficulty which presents itself' after reaching the conclusion that human beings are descended from the higher animals.[3] What he is particularly concerned with is altruism in human beings. Such selflessness clashes with the ruthless self-interest and indifference to others which the struggle for existence requires. How can altruism really be a characteristic that favours the survival of the selfless agent and so persists in humanity?

But Hardy and many others did not need the publication of *The Descent of Man* to include humanity in the evolutionary picture. Already by the end of 1872 he had written the famous scene in *A Pair of Blue Eyes* where Henry Knight, out walking with Elfride Swancourt, slips over the edge of the Cliff Without a Name and hangs precariously with his foot on 'a bracket of quartz' (chapter 21). What he then experiences draws directly on a passage in Gideon Mantell's *The Wonders of Geology* (1838). It is quite clear from the pictures that fill his mind that humanity's place in the evolutionary chain is an accepted fact. Immediately opposite his gaze is 'an imbedded fossil, standing forth in low relief from the rock'. As an amateur geologist he recognizes 'one of the early crustaceans called Trilobites'. Even in these desperate circumstances he sees a painful irony in the fact that the creature represents 'but a low type of animal existence'. It is lower even than zoophytes, mollusca, and shell-fish of those ancient times. Never 'in their vernal years had the plains indicated by numberless slaty layers been traversed by an intelligence worthy of the name'. Yet Knight's intelligence cannot save him. It seems to be an evolutionary redundancy. This reflection of Knight's draws on Mantell's precise vocabulary with its use of the terms crustacean, trilobites, zoophytes, and mollusca which are drawn from the geologist's glossary. The times when such creatures were alive were, Knight thinks, grand in some sense but 'mean' in others, 'and mean were their relics. He was to be with the small in his death' (chapter 22). The conclusion seems to be that he too is insignificant in spite of his intelligence and intense consciousness. Knight's retrospective view here is based on Mantell's *Retrospect* at the end of a lecture on the geology of south-east England. Mantell imagines some higher intelligence speaking, giving a historical survey of evolution:

'Countless ages ere man was created,' he might say, 'I visited these regions of the earth . . . and I saw monsters of the reptile tribe, so huge that nothing among the existing races can compare with them, basking on the banks of its rivers, and roaming through its forests; while in its fens and marshes, were sporting thousands of crocodiles and turtles. Winged reptiles of strange forms . . . fishes, shells, and crustacean. And after the lapse of many ages I again visited the earth . . . And its waters teemed with nautili, ammonites, and other cephalopoda . . . innumerable fishes and marine reptiles . . . And thousands of centuries rolled by . . . and dry land had again appeared . . . different in character [from] . . . the vanished Country of the Iguanadon. And I beheld, quietly browsing, herds of deer of enormous size, and groups of elephants, mastodons, and other herbivorous animals of colossal magnitude. And I saw in its rivers and marshes the hippopotamus, tapir, and rhinoceros, and I heard the roar of the lion and the tiger, and the yell of the hyena and the bear. And another epoch passed away . . . And I beheld human beings, clad in the skins of animals, and armed with clubs and spears; and they had formed themselves habitations in caves, constructed huts for shelter . . .'[4]

At what he imagines to be the moment of his death, this chronological account compressed and then reversed in order of time forces itself upon Knight's mind. He sees first his cavemen ancestors and then falls back through time to their origins and the origins of their ancestors back to the humble trilobite.

Time opens up like a fan before him to reveal the true 'descent of man', with his useless sense of supreme difference from the rest of creation. He is descended from strange beings who are described in terms that are a mixture of literary and scientific:

Fierce men, clothed in the hides of beasts, and carrying, for defence and attack, huge clubs and pointed spears, rose from the rock, like the phantoms before the doomed Macbeth . . . Behind them stood an earlier band. No man was there. Huge elephantine forms, the mastodon, the hippopotamus, the tapir, antelopes of monstrous size, the megatherium, and the mylodon—all, for the moment, in juxtaposition. Further back, and overlapped by these, were perched huge-billed birds, and swinish creatures as large as horses. Still more shadowy were the sinister crocodilian outlines—alligators and other uncouth shapes, culminating in the colossal lizard, the iguanadon. Folded behind were dragon forms and clouds of flying reptiles; still underneath were fishy beings of lower development. (chapter 22)

The nightmarish account of humanity as a part of the evolutionary animal chain raises the question captured by the alternating perspective on characters like Tess. Are human beings more significant than their non-human predecessors? Do they represent evolutionary progress? Are they the apex of existing life?

Darwin had attempted in *The Origin of Species* to be strictly neutral on the question of whether survival was to be equated with improvement. But, as Beer points out, 'the hope that "improvement" will be the outcome of the process he names "natural selection" and sets in opposition to artificial selection still haunts his vocabulary and argument'.[5] Also, by later adding Herbert Spencer's phrase 'survival of the fittest' to his chapter title 'Natural Selection', he allows the implication that those who survive are the fit, the superior examples. Spencer's development of Darwin's ideas into his 'Social Darwinism' consolidated this implication. This theory, popular in the late nineteenth century, argued that social life was a struggle for survival in which the fittest or rightly superior survived. Spencer's successors developed the theory to justify *laissez-faire* capitalism, where competition excluded the inferior members of society from worldly success indicated by wealth.

At about this time, in *The Descent of Man*, Darwin was struggling with aspects of human nature which do not fit readily into his accounts and fit even less well into Spencer's. In relation to the moral disposition, Darwin tries to explain why a man should be 'bitterly regretful, if he has yielded to a strong sense of self-preservation and has not risked his life to save that of a fellow creature'.[6] Since altruism can scarcely be seen as an advantage in a ruthless struggle for survival so its continuing presence in human beings constitutes a problem.

In *The Woodlanders* Hardy confronts this problem of the nature and significance of man in an evolutionary world by setting up what appears to be represented as an experiment in social evolution. He first explicitly integrates humanity into the great evolutionary web by equating the woods and the woodlanders. He does this moreover in the context of a literal struggle for survival in the landscape which itself takes on human characteristics. As Grace and her father walk unheeding through the wood, they take for granted what is going on around them: 'They went noiselessly over mats of starry moss, rustled through interspersed tracts of leaves, skirted trunks with spreading roots whose mossed rinds made them like hands wearing green gloves ... On older trees still than these huge lobes of fungi grew like lungs.' The Melburys carelessly push these things aside but the narrator observes the battle going on and its consequences for the weaker growths: 'The leaf was deformed, the curve was crippled, the taper was interrupted; the lichen ate the vigour of the stalk, and the ivy slowly strangled to death the promising sapling' (chapter 7).

Later Grace, sheltering in Giles's hut after running away from Fitzpiers, is in a state of anxiety that triggers a receptiveness to the struggle taking place in the world of nature:

From the other window all she could see were more trees, in jackets of lichen, and stockings of moss. At their roots were stemless yellow fungi like lemons and apricots, and tall fungi with more stem than stool. Next were more trees close together, wrestling for existence, their branches disfigured with wounds resulting from their mutual rubbings and blows. It was the struggle between these neighbours that she had heard in the night. Beneath them were the rotting stumps of those of the group that had been vanquished long ago, rising from their mossy setting like black teeth from green gums. (chapter 42)

In this way humanity is included in the struggle for existence and is equated with the natural world, of which it becomes one more aspect. Even more plainly in the first of the two passages just quoted, natural deformities, the crippled curve and the strangled sapling, are shown to be paralleled in human life: 'Here, as everywhere, the Unfulfilled Intention, which makes life what it is, was as obvious as it could be among the depraved crowds of a city slum' (chapter 7). This pattern points to the nature of the experiment that the narrative represents: a test of human 'fitness' evaluated in terms of survival or worldly success along with an emphasis on the usefulness or otherwise of altruism. Not only the involvement of human nature in the natural struggle but also an earlier title of the narrative,

'Fitzpiers at Hintock', points to a shaping of the story as an exploration of 'social evolution'. The juxtaposition of an urban stranger with an aristocratic name and a rural location implies what Grace refers to when she thinks of Fitzpiers as a 'tropical plant in a hedgerow' (chapter 6). He is an exotic in a temperate setting to which perhaps he is unadapted. Giles Winterborne by contrast is recurrently shown to be at one with the environment, able to read the 'hieroglyphs' of nature 'as ordinary writing' (chapter 44).

Fitzpiers is quite unsuited to Little Hintock. He finds the customs, habits, and manners of the woodlanders so alien to him that he is bored and indifferent. His practice flags and he lacks curiosity about the place. But the expectation that he will not thrive in his new location is overturned by the fact that his outstanding characteristic is his sexual predatoriness. The very boredom he experiences drives him to divert himself with a series of sexual encounters marked by ruthless self-interest. The first of these is a random union with a flirtatious country girl, Suke Damson, whom he chases into a hayfield. He then employs himself in a careful courtship of Grace Melbury whose unwilling reaction to his mere presence captures his irresistible powers of seduction. His physical magnetism allows him even in this lonely place to find three sexual partners who between them span the whole social hierarchy at Little Hintock: Suke Damson, Grace Melbury, and the local lady of the manor Felice Charmond.

Fitzpiers, despite his desertion of Suke and the ruin of her marriage, his infidelity to Grace, and his abandonment of his pregnant mistress Felice, secures a newly reconciled wife, the prospect of inheriting Melbury's money, and a medical practice bought with an inheritance from a relative who is, of course, female. The troublesome Suke has left the country/county; and the troublesome Felice is dead. In terms of the worldly struggle, Fitzpiers's success is so striking that it provoked hostility from a typical contemporary critic who did not expect sin to pay—not, at least, in fiction: 'Mr Hardy ought not to have allowed this sensual and selfish liar, good-natured in an easy way though he certainly was, to be received back into his wife's favour and made happy on terms so easy as are here imposed on him'.[7]

It is true that the terms for Fitzpiers are easy, not least because he ends up with a rich wife who will turn a blind eye to his future liaisons. What his career as an urban transplant in a remote rural setting demonstrates is that a disregard of morality and ruthless self-interest can, if accompanied by sexual attractiveness, produce financial and social success. Fitzpiers does not merely survive—he thrives, illustrating the fact that, as Darwin himself pointed out, 'the power to charm the female has sometimes been more important than the power to conquer other males in battle'.[8] In the second edition of *The Descent of Man* he quotes approvingly from Schopenhauer on this subject: 'the final aim of all love intrigues, be they comic or tragic is really of more importance than all other ends in human life'.[9] By contrast the native plant in Hintock, Giles Winterborne, has all the woodland skills as well as the altruism that Fitzpiers lacks. In this environment he is the superior male but he lacks not only Fitzpiers's physical attraction but also his ruthlessness. His selflessness is his undoing: it leads to his renunciation of the promised marriage to Grace when he loses his house, although such a union would recover his financial position. His altruistic concern for her and her reputation leads him to sacrifice his life by withdrawing from the hut where she shelters in violent weather. The result of his principled decision to put her welfare first leads to an avoidance of action when a more selfish choice would lead to success. In the struggle for a mate, predatoriness pays and Giles has none.

What the two male figures in the experiment with social evolution show is that the moral sense here is at odds with sexual and worldly success. Yet Hardy, like Darwin, cannot but admire the very characteristic that leads to failure. The final scene of *The Woodlanders* spells out this admiration in Marty South's eulogy over Giles's grave:

Now, my own own love . . . you are mine, and only mine; for she has forgot 'ee at last, although for her you died. But I—whenever I get up I'll think of 'ee, and whenever I lie down I'll think of 'ee again. Whenever I plant the young larches I'll think that none can plant as you planted; and whenever I split a gad, and whenever I turn the cider-wring, I'll say none could do it like you. If ever I forget your name let me forget home and heaven . . . But no, no, my love, I never can forget 'ee; for you was a good man, and did good things! (chapter 48)

In this scene Marty is transfigured like the girl in Wordsworth's 'The Solitary Reaper': 'the marks of poverty and toil' are 'effaced by the misty hour'. More significantly she is said to have 'touched sublimity at points' and to have rejected 'the attribute of sex for the loftier quality of abstract humanism' (chapter 48). The last phrase suggests tellingly the valuing of the inexpedient quality of fidelity and self-lessness over competing qualities that might result in sexual and worldly success.

The painful consequences of an acute moral sensibility seen in Giles are also found in Sue Bridehead in *Jude*, though in very different circumstances. Here renunciation of self-interest comes in a form warped by her grief after the violent deaths of her children. She feels that somehow she is responsible for what has happened and therefore deserves punishment. This and her separation from the man she loves seems to her an act of atonement for her earlier self-ishness. It is at this point that the narrator suggests ironically the idea that such an acute sensibility, 'a development of emotional percep-tiveness among the creatures subject to those conditions as that reached by thinking and educated humanity', is an evolutionary aberration (part 6, chapter 3). Like many such ideas which are mere suggestions of an ironic kind in the novels, this one is captured fully in a poem 'The Aërolite' (the title is a scientific term for a meteoric stone which falls to earth):

> I thought a germ of Consciousness
> Escaped on an aërolite
>   Aions ago
> From some far globe, where no distress
> Had means to mar supreme delight . . .
>
> And that this stray, exotic germ
> Fell wanderingly upon our sphere,
>   After its wingings,
> Quickened, and showed to us the worm
> That gnaws vitalities native here,
>
> And operated to unblind
> Earth's old-established ignorance
>   Of stains and stingings,
> Which grin no griefs while not opined,
> But cruelly tax intelligence.
>
> *(Poems*, iii. 86)

Of course the theory expressed in this poem and in *Jude* that moral sensibility is an evolutionary mistake offers a way for Hardy to express with bitter irony the sense that the qualities he most admires are the source of the worst human suffering. For those evolutionary errors Giles Winterborne, Michael Henchard, and Tess Durbeyfield have a stoicism that turns profound failure into what seems at times to Hardy the only significant form of success: moral survival. This consists in an ability to sustain the consequences of following the dictates of their moral sense without breaking beneath them. Winterborne characteristically has no dying words but silently endures a painful death. Henchard is transformed into a King Lear figure, separated from the daughter he loves. He sees himself in his loneliness as Cain, an 'outcast, an encumberer of the ground' (*The Mayor of Casterbridge*, chapter 44). But, like Lear defying the storm with 'Pour on—I will endure!', he insists; 'my punishment is *not* greater than I can bear!' (chapter 43). Tess accepts her arrest for murder with a grand calm in a majestic setting at Stonehenge: 'It is as it should be! . . . Angel—I am almost glad—yes, glad! This happiness could not have lasted—it was too much—I have had enough; and now I shall not live for you to despise me' (chapter 48). The representation of these individuals illustrates a generalization by John Morley of which Hardy indicated approval by copying it into one of his later notebooks: 'Those who no longer place their highest faith in powers above and beyond men, are for that very reason more deeply interested than others in cherishing the integrity and worthiness of man himself.'[10] Though Morley's phrasing ('for that very reason') suggests that admiration of integrity is a rational consequence of the lack of belief in a divine power, the statement is a paradox. Evolution implied that there was no such power, that humanity was not the highest point of divine creation but a routine part of animal development. Morley's assertion is based on emotion rather than logic: in the long perspective, human beings *are* flies on a billiard table; in close-up, for others who are emotionally attached to them, they fill the whole picture. The alternation between the two views remains unresolved in Hardy's novels. So too does the fact that on one reading what he shows as integrity in the downtrodden can be interpreted as collusion with the social status quo.

Heredity

In the chapter on 'Classification' in *The Origin of Species* Darwin insists that 'the natural system is genealogical in its arrangement, like a pedigree; but the degrees of modification which the different groups have undergone, have to be expressed by ranking them under different so-called genera, sub-families, families, sections, orders, and classes'.[11] He goes on to point out how the origins and development, say, of languages are also best represented by a genealogical pedigree. This is not surprising since the questions, such as his, being asked in the nineteenth century lent themselves to an answer in the shape of a family tree. Hardy accepts the centrality of genetic inheritance as described by Darwin which resonated with his early interest in the genealogy of human families. His attitude to this subject was part-antiquarian, part-romantic and was fed by his preoccupation with social class. So he took an approach to noble or 'ancient' families which for most of the time was worlds away from the Darwinian account. It belongs to a narrower construction of society as a hierarchy in which some blood is bluer or nobler than other blood and only some families are ancient. Hardy begins his *Life*, which Millgate believes had its roots in the winter of 1912–13, more than a decade after the completion of his novels, with an account of his own family tree. In part this is an attempt to link his family with the 'Jersey le Hardys' who had 'the characteristics of an old family of spent social energies'. He adds, speaking of himself in the third person, 'Hardy often thought he would like to restore the "le" to his name, and call himself "Thomas le Hardy"; but he never did so' (*Life*, p. 9). The novels too are studded with individuals of a lineage that was at some stage aristocratic, to whom a certain glamour seems to attach.

In *A Pair of Blue Eyes* some such cachet surrounds Elfride Swancourt as a distant relative of Lord Luxellian whom she eventually marries as his second wife. Yet paradoxically this is found in a text which attacks her father's snobbery as well as her own which leads her to reject a working-class lover. Nonetheless, after her premature death, her burial in the Luxellian family vault is referred to in romantic terms: 'She had herself gone down into silence like her ancestors, and shut her bright blue eyes for ever' (chapter XL). This leaves her two suitors, significantly named Smith and Knight, feeling 'like intruders' as they find a grieving peer embracing Elfride's coffin. In death, evidently Elfride has taken her proper place with the nobility. A few years later, in *A Laodicean*, Charlotte De Stancy may be declassed by the necessity of taking paid employment but that does not prevent her very rich friend, Paula Power, from wishing passionately that she were a De Stancy too, or at least that she could marry one.

By this time the attractions of the aristocracy are less evident to the narrator than to his characters, but the interest persists. The attractions of Fitzpiers as a prospective husband are enhanced for Grace Melbury's father by the fact that his family were once lords of the manor in the neighbourhood 'for I don't know how many hundred years' (*The Woodlanders*, chapter 23). In *Tess* it turns out that she is not the only dairymaid whose ancestors were aristocrats. Dairyman Crick mentions that Retty Priddle is one of the Paridelles, an old family 'that used to own lots o' the lands out by King's-Hintock now owned by the Earl o' Wessex' (chapter 19). He mentions six other families (including the Hardys) who have similarly declined socially. The ambivalence revealed in such accounts, wavering between ideas of ancient families as worthy of respect or manifestly worn out and effete, is recognized in Angel Clare's views on the subject. Though he has claimed to have nothing but contempt for the aristocracy, once in love with Tess he clarifies his position to his father differently: 'Politically I am sceptical as to the virtue of their being old. Some of the wise even among themselves "exclaim against their own succession" as Hamlet puts it, but lyrically, dramatically, and even historically, I am tenderly attached to them' (chapter 26).

It is not until *Tess*, in fact, that Hardy fully explores the question of heredity in a Darwinian sense of inherited characteristics. But significantly he chooses to do so in the familiar context of ancient families. As with other issues, some of the poems allow him to take a single perspective on issues that are dealt with more ambivalently in the novels. The poem 'Heredity', for instance, asserts the primacy of inherited physical features as the speaker appears to look in a mirror:

> I am the family face;
> Flesh perishes, I live on,
> Projecting trait and trace
> Through time to times anon,
> And leaping from place to place
> Over oblivion.

The years-heired feature that can
In curve and voice and eye
Despise the human span
Of durance—that is I;
The eternal thing in man,
That heeds no call to die
(*Poems*, ii. 166–7)

The extension of the idea of heredity to the transmission of traits other than the physical fascinates Hardy because it involves the question of free will, an aspect of causality which preoccupies him. With non-physical characteristics the possibility arises that someone's action may be, like their facial features (at least before the development of cosmetic surgery) determined solely by heredity. This theory was already used in the nineteenth century to account for such things as alcoholism, sexual promiscuity, and criminal tendencies which were said to be recurrent amongst the 'undeserving poor'. Again in a short poem, 'The Pedigree', it is possible for Hardy to give voice to such a view in an unqualified form with claims that all action is genetically determined. The pedigree in question is a copy of the speaker's own family tree. As he surveys it a cold thought strikes him that, though 'thinking, *I am I,* | *And what I do I do myself alone*', he is really the 'merest mimicker and counterfeit' of his ancestors. He too seems to look into a mirror:

And then did I divine
That every heave and coil and move I made
Within my brain, and in my mood and speech,
    Was in the glass portrayed
As long forestalled by their so making it;
(*Poems*, ii. 198)

The validity of this belief is raised in a dramatic form in *Tess*. She herself seems to feel trapped like the speaker in 'The Pedigree' after the affair with Alec. When Angel in his efforts to 'improve' her socially suggests that she read history, she replies 'what's the use of learning that I am one of a long row only—finding out that there is set down in some old book somebody just like me, and to know that I shall only act her part; making me sad, that's all' (chapter 19). She is of course part of a long line of seduced girls whose path downwards seems determined but her words, taken together with her name and subsequent events, take on a new force.

One of the many contradictions within the text is the varying implications attached to the fact that Tess is a d'Urberville. At the beginning of the novel, the narrative offers an apparent contrast between the revelation of her blue d'Urberville blood and Alec d'Urberville's origins as the son of a money-lender, prosaically named Stoke. The point of the contrast appears to be that she is a true (and, as the reader has already been told, a pure) d'Urberville and Alec a false and treacherous one. From the start his appearance and behaviour label him clearly 'a cad'. Certainly this is how a contemporary critic Mowbray Morris, interpreted the meaning of Tess's lineal descent from 'an ancient and knightly race of Norman warriors who once held large possessions in the West Country'. It is, he supposes, 'designed to account for a certain superiority claimed . . . for Tess over her rustic associates' in the opening scenes. He derides what he sees as Hardy's attempt here to illustrate 'the great principle of Heredity' which makes Tess a pure woman despite the offences that she commits. Morris insists that a girl 'unconsciously raised by the mixture of gentle blood in her veins to a higher level of thought and feeling would never have acted as Tess acted'. Finally he asks indignantly 'Has the common feeling of humanity against seduction, adultery, and murder no basis in the heart of things? It is the very foundation of human society.'[12] Certainly, on the face of it, an act of murder committed by stabbing a man to death seems difficult to defend as the act of a pure woman. Hardy appears to be compounding his own problem by adding Alec's death to Tess's supposed sexual aberrations.

But the story of Tess's actions raises in an acute form the question of causality and its workings. Hardy was always fascinated by accounts of real or fictional events of a sensational kind which involved the utterly improbable actually happening. 'The Convergence of the Twain', his poem on the sinking of the unsinkable *Titanic*, is a perfect example of this. The story of the ship has been given many fictional and dramatic treatments focusing on the passengers and their sufferings. Hardy's poem is remarkable for the total absence of any reference to the people on board. In what is from a humane point of view a coolly detached tone, the emphasis is laid on the unlikelihood of the convergence of the great iceberg and the great ship, and the apparent inevitability of the collision. It occurs in a way suggesting mathematical precision mixed with magic. The poem tells how, while this 'creature of cleaving wing' was being fashioned, 'The Immanent Will that stirs and urges everything | Prepared a sinister mate'. This is 'A Shape of Ice', for the time far and dissociate:

> Alien they seemed to be:
> No mortal eye could see
>
> The intimate welding of their later history,
> Or sign that they were bent
> By paths coincident
> On being anon twin halves of one august event.
>
> (*Poems*, ii. 12)

In the novel, when examining the causes (*not* who is to blame) for Tess's actions, the narrative is overdetermined as all possibilities are explored. Many sequences of right wrong circumstances combine to produce the rape/seduction by Alec: her father's discovery of his ancestry just when Tess reaches adulthood, Alec's assumption of the d'Urberville name, the death of the Durbeyfield's horse on which their livelihood depends, Tess's inexperience and guilelessness, the fact that Alec is a practised seducer, Tess's quarrel with the other women while returning home on the fatal night, Alec's fortuitous arrival on horseback. A similar web of circumstances causes her return to Alec, the prelude to his murder: her father's death, the nature of the family's tenancy which results in their homelessness and poverty, Tess's compassionate nature, the recognition of that nature by Alec who works on it by offering a financial way out, the belief of both Alec and Angel that Alec is her 'real' husband. The idea that the first physical 'possessor' of a woman owns her for life is one familiar to Tess from the society that she lives in.

And for the murder itself the same fuzzy account of causality appears: any one of several things could be offered as 'the cause'. In fact, all the series of circumstances leading to the rape/seduction and adultery could be seen as causes of the deed. Further, a recurrent factor in events is Tess's willingness to accept instruction from others—from her parents when they wish her to visit the d'Urberville house, from Alec, and above all from Angel (whose hypocritical disposition might itself be seen as causal in her life). It is Clare who has taught her to abandon religion, even though she does not really understand his arguments for doing so. He has also explained to her when refusing to consummate their marriage why this is impossible for him: 'How can we live together while that man lives?—he being your husband in Nature and not I. If he were dead it might be different' (chapter 36). The phrasing of this statement might have taken different form: 'If you were widowed . . . ', or 'It would be like bigamy for you and me to live together'. But Clare chooses a form of words which evidently sticks in Tess's mind. When Angel, whose views have been transformed by his experiences in Brazil, returns to her convinced that all will now be well, she knows what to do to make things 'different'. She acts to achieve the state of affairs that Angel spoke of on their wedding night by stabbing Alec to death. As she tells Clare after the murder, 'It came to me as a shining light that I should get you back that way'. To his amazement she rests on his shoulder guilt-free and 'weeping with happiness' (chapter 48). Angel feels that her affection for him has extinguished her moral sense. But in terms of her own newly forged morality, murder leaves her still a pure woman, or so Hardy seems to assert.

However, the picture is complicated by lineage and by heredity. What part do they play in Tess's actions? As has been said, the title of the novel has directed readers from the start to understand that great significance attaches to the fact that she belongs rightly to the ancient family of d'Urberville, as Elfride belonged rightly to the Luxellians. An innocent reading of the title and subtitle suggests the interpretation of the two together as 'Tess—of gentle blood and noble character'. She herself expects the d'Urberville family to be noble in every way. She is struck when she sees Alec, whom she believes to be a d'Urberville relative, by his unaristocratic appearance—'the touches of barbarism in his contours' and his 'bold rolling eye'. She had expected something different: 'an aged and dignified face, the sublimation of all the d'Urberville lineaments, furrowed with incarnate memories, representing in hieroglyphic the centuries of her family's and England's history' (chapter 5).

This is the beginning of a questioning in the narrative of the idea that there is 'virtue' in ancient families. There are two allusions to the story of the ghostly d'Urberville coach which foretells a murder either by a d'Urberville or of a d'Urberville. This is a typically ambivalent prediction of the murder of Alec which is in a sense a killing both by and of a d'Urberville. Shortly before Tess's confession to Angel they see in the house where they spend their wedding night, portraits of two of her female ancestors. Though Tess is repelled by them, Angel reluctantly finds that her fine features were unquestionably traceable in these exaggerated forms. As the narrator independently describes them they are strangely unflattering, even malign: 'The long pointed features, narrow eye, and smirk of the one, so suggestive of merciless treachery; the bill-hook nose, large teeth, and bold eye of the other, suggesting arrogance to the point of ferocity, haunt the beholder afterwards in his dreams' (chapter 33). Still, Tess herself is represented throughout the text as an exemplar of someone whose aims and impulses are pure, free from the evil ferocity of earlier d'Urbervilles.

Perhaps the most striking clash of these two views of the ancient family comes at the moment of Alec's rape/seduction. The narrator, following the recurrent insistence on Tess's purity, laments the imprinting of Alec's 'coarse pattern' upon such 'beautiful feminine tissue'. Why, he asks, was this doomed to happen, and refers to Tess for the first time as d'Urberville not Durbeyfield. The answer he gives to his own question is a startling one: 'One may, indeed, admit the possibility of a retribution lurking in the present catastrophe. Doubtless some of Tess d'Urberville's mailed ancestors rollicking home from a fray had dealt the same measure even more ruthlessly towards peasant girls of their time' (chapter 11).

From the publication of *The Origin of Species* onwards, nineteenth-century scientists and writers had continued Darwin's discussion of inherited characteristics. In the 1890s a recent theory was that of 'germ-plasm', thought to transmit physical and mental characteristics unchanged from generation to generation. What is suggested by the reference in the rape scene, by the account of the pictures of the two d'Urberville women, and the legend of the coach is that the characteristic transmitted through the d'Urberville line is ferocious violence in the pursuit of individual aims. Eventually at Flintcomb-Ash Tess herself is momentarily implicated in the family trait. While working on the rick she is pursued by Alec, intent on winning her back. In doing so, he insults her absent husband in a way that transforms Tess into a violent male d'Urberville:

One of her leather gloves, which she had taken off to eat her skimmer-cake, lay in her lap, and without the slightest warning she passionately swung the glove by the gauntlet directly in his face. It was heavy and thick as a warrior's, and it struck him flat on the mouth. Fancy might have regarded the act as the recrudescence of a trick in which her armed progenitors were not unpractised. (chapter 47)

This identification of Tess as a d'Urberville warrior occurs at a crucial moment in the narrative—just before her return to Alec— and it happens when the hereditary violence is directed towards him. It is a shadow version of what is to happen later. This is how Tess herself sees it when she tells Angel Clare that she has murdered Alec: 'I feared long ago, when I struck him on the mouth with my glove, that I might do it some day for the trap he set for me in my simple youth, and his wrong to you through me.' She feels also that 'I owed it to you, and to myself, Angel'. Even Clare sees it as the result of an hereditary characteristic. He wonders 'what obscure strain in the d'Urberville blood had led to this aberration, if it were an aberration. There momentarily flashed through his mind that the family tradition of the coach and murder might have arisen because the d'Urbervilles had been known to do these things' (chapter 57).

It is only by ignoring the meanings that gradually accrue to the d'Urberville family that it remains possible to read the narrative as an unqualified assertion that Tess is a pure and noble woman. Certainly she is noble in the sense of belonging to a once aristocratic family but equally undeniably the references to the d'Urbervilles depict them as rapists, warriors, given to 'merciless cruelty' and 'arrogance to the point of ferocity'. These are the characteristics they have to transmit to a true descendant. How can this be reconciled with the aggressive defence of Tess mounted by the narrator and continuing after the murder? Since that defence rests on things willed not things done, on intention not on the raw deed, they cannot be reconciled with hereditary violence. If Tess simply acts out the part determined for her by heredity, then her intentions are irrelevant and she has no free will, no choice.

At this point the narrator is merely offering an alternative reading which he does not fully assent to. It is typical of Hardy to take another perspective on events and ask here: What if the cruellest joke of all in a world full of cruel jokes is that Tess, despite her determination to take a moral course and despite all her painful struggles, is in the end only able to act a part predetermined by the genetic line that she belongs to? The simple directive given by the title to read the narrative as a defensive eulogy proves inadequate to what the whole text signifies.

Though the narrator, as has been said, does not cling to this narrow view of Tess, the very raising of it creates a certain symmetry in the novel. It has been noticed by critics that the narrator, like Alec and Angel, is enamoured of Tess. Hardy himself seems to have been similarly infatuated to the extent that he saw Agatha Thorneycroft, of whom he was enamoured, as the incarnation of her. The parallel between Alec, Angel, and the narrator goes further than this. First, Alec and Angel are similar in their attitudes to Tess. When Tess seeks a new life at Talbothays she tries to forget the past and leave Alec behind. She finds in the true 'gentleman' Angel Clare a tenderer and more considerate lover. He is evidently the 'guardian angel' so sadly absent on the night in the Chase (chapter 11). But ironically Angel reveals himself as merely a more refined version of Alec. He too takes her 'no' to mean 'yes' when he offers marriage, seeing the negative as 'nothing more than the preface to the affirmative' (chapter 28). Like Alec, he exploits her economic dependence: he gets Dairyman Crick to confirm that her employment is about to end and uses the fact to pressure her into marriage. Finally, he ruins her life as effectively as Alec did by deserting her after they have gone through a wedding ceremony. Now her last defender temporarily doubts her, completing the pattern of male betrayal by attributing her act of murder to an irresistible instinct imposed on her by her heredity.

Yet in a different mood Hardy was quite capable of constructing a sequence of events which forcefully denied the importance of a blood relationship. This represents a radical attack on the idea of its crucial significance which underlay both the double standard in sexual morality as it affected men or women and the divorce law based on the need for certainty of paternity. Its primacy is challenged in *The Mayor of Casterbridge* when the issue is raised of who is Elizabeth-Jane's biological father—Newson or Henchard. For much of the novel the truth is concealed both from Henchard and the reader. When it is revealed to be Newson, it is eventually made plain that the physical fact is irrelevant. The ties of affection that develop and bind Henchard to her make it so. And Henchard alone shows the unconditional parental love that sends him to exile and death.

Perceptions of the Future

Gillian Beer points out that *The Origin of Species* 'did not admit of a foreknown perfection towards which organisms were moving'.[13] It could be said, however, that there are some suggestions in the tone of such statements as that in the final chapter which suggest that evolution is a progress towards improvement: 'Thus, from the war of nature, from famine and death, the most exalted object which we are capable of conceiving, namely, the production of the higher animals, directly follows.'[14] This is found even in the first edition. In *The Descent of Man* there are even more explicit references to 'man' as 'the very summit of the organic scale'. It is added that 'the fact of his having thus risen, instead of having been aboriginally placed there, may give him hope for a still higher destiny in the distant future'.[15]

There was also the cultural inheritance of Christianity with its promise of ultimate justice and an eternity of bliss which facilitated an expectation of progress through evolution. When Herbert Spencer applied the evolutionary model to society he developed an essentially optimistic theory of the future despite hitches on the way. He predicted that eventually individualism would triumph, though after some turmoil. It is almost as though he were reworking Karl Marx's prospect for the future with a right-wing colouring. Marx, in the final words of *The Communist Manifesto* (1848), had predicted turmoil and the overthrow of the bourgeoisie: 'Its fall and the victory of the proletariat are equally inevitable.'

But by the mid-century a gloomier picture of the future was emerging and gaining currency. This picture depended on the theory of another group of scientists, physicists, who argued that the sun did not renew its energy and would gradually grow cold and leave the earth uninhabitable. The popular spread of some version of this theory is evidenced in the opening chapter of Dickens's *Bleak House* (1853) which describes a fog over London: a London 'pea-souper' or 'peculiar': 'Smoke lowering down from chimney-pots, making a soft black drizzle, with flakes of soot in it as big as full grown snow-flakes gone into mourning, one might imagine, for the death of the sun.' Though estimates varied of how long it would take for the sun to die, those who accepted it as a fact believed an end was certain. Some did not accept the idea that the sun would grow cold. T. H. Huxley, for instance, argued that possibly evolution might come to mean 'adaptation to a universal winter, and all forms of life will die out, except such low and simple organisms as the Diatom [tiny one-cell alga] of the arctic'.[16] By the 1890s, however, some popular understanding of the idea that one day the sun might not rise was widespread. The belief in such a disaster, however remote, fed the typical *fin de siècle* pessimism. This has a long history: as far back as the year AD 1000 approached, the monk Wulfstan, in his hell-fire address to his fellow Englishmen, warned them to repent of their sins before the Armageddon in which the Danes overran England in an orgy of pillage, fire, and death. A similar end-of-millennium fever fostered the expectation, in spite of satisfactory reassurances, that the end of the year 1999 would bring a millennium computer bug that would cause computers to crash in certain areas. This would result in global disasters raging from disruption of aircraft, traffic lights, water and electricity supply to riots in the streets. Similarly the end of the nineteenth century was thought to be, as the tenth century had been thought to be, a time of moral decay and social dissent. This belief also nurtured a fear of the future.

No doubt those of gloomy disposition and of a certain age were more affected by impending doom than others. Whatever the reason, from the 1880s onwards Hardy's view of the future was too bleak for him to contemplate—or so his novels suggest. He had written, or was to write, several poems in which he decisively turns his back on the idea of the future. Of these the most extreme are 'To an Unborn Pauper Child' and 'The Unborn'. The first addresses the child urgently:

> Breathe not, hid Heart: cease silently,
> And though thy birth-hour beckons thee,
> Sleep the long sleep:
> The Doomsters heap
> Travails and teens around us here,
> And Time-Wraiths turn our songsingings to fear.
>
> (*Poems*, i. 163)

Nonetheless, the speaker adds he knows 'Thou wilt thy ignorant entry make | Though skies spout fire and blood and nations quake' (*Poems*, i. 163). This is exactly what the crowds of the unborn in the second poem are seen to do. When a poem does project into the future nothing is revealed. This is so in the poems '1967' and

'The Strange House (Max Gate AD 2000)'. Their titles suggest some glimpses of what is to come but in each the future serves only as a mechanism to turn the poet-speaker's present into the past. Speaking in 1867 of '1967', he imagines it only as a time when, as he tells his lover, there will be 'nothing left of me and you' except 'a pinch of dust or two' (*Poems*, i. 269). 'The Strange House' summons up Max Gate in the year 2000 where the new occupants hear ghostly sounds of a piano being played and of invisible figures moving. They guess that what they hear is special—'But we—we do not care | Who loved, laughed; wept, or died here, | Knew joy, or despair' (*Poems*, ii. 347).

Though less bluntly than in the poems, it is also true that there is in effect no future in the late novels. In this they differ from what Catherine Belsey calls the 'classic realist novel', the dominant narrative mode in the nineteenth century. By this she means novels which offer apparent verisimilitude and a final closure which gives the illusion that order or a harmonious world is reinstated.[17] Hardy's novels resist this form and offer no reinstatement of harmony. They end with a bleak world where the heroic figures are physically defeated and die as do Giles, Henchard, and Tess. Even as early as *The Return of the Native* this pattern is emerging. The only large-scale figure, Eustacia Vye, commits suicide and her lover dies. There remain only Wildeve's widow, Tamsin, who makes a compromise marriage with Diggory Venn; and Clym Yeobright whose hope of transforming lives by becoming a teacher is reduced to the lonely life of an itinerant preacher. The same massive diminution of hope is evident in *The Mayor of Casterbridge*. With its hero dead along with Lucetta, Elizabeth-Jane—now knowing herself second-best for him—marries Farfrae. Though newly married, Elizabeth-Jane foresees the future and the way of facing it in a manner appropriate to someone who has been told that they have a fatal illness. She will practise what she has learnt, how to make 'limited opportunities endurable'. She will do this by 'the cunning enlargement by a species of microscopic treatment, of those minute forms of satisfaction that offer themselves to everybody not in positive pain'. She knows that life and the future offer only 'the occasional episode in a general drama of pain' (chapter 45). It is only the compromisers, the pragmatists, those who adapt, who survive the losses that life inflicts. Farfrae, for instance, consoles himself for the death of his first wife with the cool recognition that 'by the death of Lucetta he had exchanged a looming misery for a simple sorrow' (chapter 42).

The last few novels are those most reductive of the prospects for the future. Life together for the Fitzpiers couple holds only the prospect of his recurrent adultery and her self-deceiving compromise. *Tess* ends with her death by hanging and a suggestion that Angel Clare may be able to console himself by an illegal union with her (so far characterless) younger sister. Jude dies a wretched death, leaving Sue sentenced to a loveless marriage which, mentally and physically, is a torture to her. Only Arabella, who is prepared to lower her sights continually, settles for the quack doctor, Vilbert.

There are few children in the childless Hardy's novels: Fanny Robin's baby who, like Tess's son, dies; Arabella and Jude's son, who murders Jude and Sue's children and kills himself. The younger generation, who in some narratives represent a hope for a better future, do not survive. This idea of the genetic line dying out is captured by the speaker in Hardy's poem 'Sine Prole'—Childless. He sees nothing but extinction:

> Forth from ages thick in mystery,
> Through the morn and noon of history,
>   To the moment where I stand
> Has my line wound: I the last one . . .
>   (*Poems*, iii. 30)

Late in the narrative Jude tells Sue what the doctor has said of his son's death:

The doctor says there are such boys springing up amongst us—boys of a sort unknown in the last generation—the outcome of new views of life. They seem to see all its terrors before they are old enough to have staying power to resist them. He says it is the beginning of the coming universal wish not to live. (part 6, chapter 2)

Nothing could capture more graphically than this statement the sense that for Hardy there is no future for humanity.

CHAPTER 7

RELIGIOUS ISSUES

The Institutional Church and the Erosion of Belief

THOUGH it was learning about the discoveries of geologists and evolutionists which undermined religious belief for Hardy, his outlook was more ambivalent than the label 'agnosticism' suggests. He feels an irresistible need for an alternative explanation of human life now that the comforting Christian belief in ultimate justice is removed. He deals with the problem from a variety of angles. He records the way religious belief evaporates in a relatively educated individual who is left hopeless. He parallels this with religion dissolving into a fairly untroubled superstition among the 'country folk'. And in the late novels and the poems he abandons logic with a series of imaginative explanations offered speculatively as ways of making sense of life's random cruelty and lack of justice.

The Church as an institution underpinning established society was something from which Hardy gradually detached himself. Surprisingly, the novels reverse this process in terms of how preoccupied he is with the subject: he is most engaged when he has moved furthest away. In some of the early novels churches and vicars do play a very modest role. In *Tess* and *Jude*, both published in the 1890s, the institution and its failings loom large. Matters of doctrine are not an issue in the early texts with the strange exception of the subject of baptism in *A Laodicean*. In the early chapters the rights and wrongs of infant versus adult baptism are raised since the heroine, Paula Power, is a nominal member of the local Baptist chapel and has been prepared as usual for adult baptism by immersion. At the very last moment she rejects it during the ceremony and this paves the way for a long debate on the two kinds of baptism in chapter 7. The topic, which preoccupied Hardy as a very young man, is largely irrelevant to the narrative. Its only connection with Paula Power is that it allows the admirable Baptist minister, Woodwell, (based on an individual known to Hardy) to castigate Paula as 'A Laodicean'. This is a reference to the citizens of Laodicea condemned in the Bible as lukewarm—or half-hearted. Her half-heartedness, however, is chiefly addressed in the novel in relation to the way she blows hot and cold with her lover George Somerset.

Apart from this, other early novels involve not Christian beliefs but Anglican vicars and their flocks. None of these men is the subject of savage criticism on specifically religious grounds. Maybold in *Under the Greenwood Tree* is somewhat snobbish; and Swancourt in *A Pair of Blue Eyes* is even patrician in his outlook. But Maybold at least is represented as honourable in his acceptance of Fancy Day's preference for another man. The vicar, Thirdly, in *Far from the Madding Crowd* is virtually invisible except in the scene where he accepts the task of burying Fanny Robin and her illegitimate baby. There is a marked contrast here with the priest in *Tess* as Thirdly responds to Bathsheba's offer to shelter Fanny's corpse in her house overnight with at least routinely Christian sentiments:

Perhaps Mrs Troy is right in feeling that we cannot treat a dead fellow-creature too thoughtfully. We must remember that though she may have erred grievously in leaving her home, she is still our sister; and it is to be believed that God's uncovenanted mercies are extended towards her, and that she is a member of the flock of Christ. (chapter 42)

In *Desperate Remedies*, the parson Raunham is described approvingly in secular terms as a man of 'good taste and good nature' (volume 3, chapter 3). More than this, he is not merely a clergyman but a 'magistrate, and a conscientious man' (volume 3, chapter 5). This dual role allows him to act as *deus ex machina* and first tangle up and then resolve the plot by acting as confidant to both the villainous Manston and the virtuous Graye siblings. He finally intervenes in the mystery by hiring a detective who finds out that Manston is a murderous bigamist and so frees Cytherea from her loveless marriage to him. Just as the electric telegraph serves in *A Laodicean* to bring about many events of the novel, Raunham serves as its human equivalent here.

A more serious engagement with the established Church is found in *Tess*. In the narration, along with the condemnation of what the narrator calls ironically civilization (as opposed to nature) goes a damning judgement of the current representatives of institutional Christianity. It spans the whole range of that vauntedly broad

Church in the persons of Angel Clare's father, the Reverend James Clare, and Angel's elder brothers, Cuthbert and Felix, who are also clergymen. Cuthbert is a scholar and a fellow of a Cambridge college; Felix a curate in a small town. The picture is almost completed by the recently converted Alec d'Urberville who sets up as a travelling preacher.

The two Clare brothers represent the orthodox and conservative wing of the Anglican Church. Theirs is an orthodoxy caricatured in their appearance which, like silver, is hall-marked for genuineness:

After breakfast [Angel] walked with his two brothers, non-Evangelical, well-educated, hall-marked young men, correct to their remotest fibre; such unimpeachable models are turned out yearly by the lathe of a systematic tuition. They were both somewhat shortsighted, and when it was the custom to wear a single eyeglass and string they wore a single eyeglass and string; when it was the custom to wear a double glass they wore a double glass; when it was the custom to wear spectacles, they wore spectacles straightway, all without reference to the particular variety of defect in their own vision. (chapter 25)

To Angel, Felix seems 'all Church' and Cuthbert 'all College': the purest of stereotypes.

This self-regarding pair form a marked contrast with their father who, unlike his two elder sons, belongs to the Low Church. Consequently he is hostile to ritual and ceremony, insistent on the need for personal experience of conversion involving choosing Christ and redemption and repentance for sin: 'Old Mr Clare was a clergyman of a type which, within the last twenty years, has well-nigh dropped out of contemporary life. A spiritual descendant in the direct line from Wycliff, Huss, Luther and Calvin; an Evangelical of the Evangelicals, a conversionist' (chapter 25). While his sons are self-indulgent, he is austere. He is a 'man of Apostolic simplicity in life and thought'. It is an irony that he is the one who, if he had heard the true story of Tess, would have received and helped her. As one of life's sinners, she is suitable for him to work on. Only intolerance mars his virtue.

Ironically, one of his converted sinners is Alec who, since he enjoys extremes of sensation, throws in his lot when born-again with the extreme wing of ardent Christian believers. He becomes a hell-fire preacher or 'ranter', travelling the countryside to chasten incorrigible backsliders like himself until the novelty of his position wears off. The attack on the varying forms of Anglicanism is completed by the callous vicar of Marlott, too mean-minded to baptize Tess's baby. The total picture portrays all the different camps in the Church failing in their individual ways to live up to the Christian ideal. So much for the representatives of organized religion as Hardy saw them by the 1880s.

There is not much in any of this to suggest a serious engagement in these novels with religious beliefs and their significance. Only a single passage in *Far from the Madding Crowd* takes up in earnest the issue of the value of the institutional Church to which Hardy had once belonged. This is done not in terms of the clergy or the events they participate in but in the form of a commentary from the narrator in chapter 22 triggered by a detailed architectural description. On the first of June, Bathsheba's labourers are shearing sheep in the Shearing Barn 'which on ground plan resembled a church with transepts'. With the eye and language of a skilled architect, the narrator expands the comparison of this ancient building with the local church:

The vast porches at the sides, lofty enough to admit a waggon laden to its highest with corn in the sheaf, were spanned by heavy pointed arches of stone, broadly and boldly cut . . . The dusky, filmed chestnut roof, braced and tied in by huge collars, curves, and diagonals, was far nobler in design because more wealthy in material than nine-tenths of those in our modern churches. Along each side wall was a range of striding buttresses, throwing deep shadows on the spaces between them, which were perforated by lancet openings combining in their proportions the precise requirements of both beauty and ventilation.

This cathedral of labour is then politicized by the narrator as the positive image of which the village church is the negative. The description quickly becomes explicitly symbolic:

One could say about this barn, what could hardly be said of either the church or the castle, akin to it in age and style, that the purpose which had dictated its original erection was the same with that to which it was still applied. Unlike and superior to either of those two typical remnants of mediaevalism, the old barn embodied practices which had suffered no mutilation at the hands of time. Here at least the spirit of the ancient builders was at one with the spirit of the modern beholder.

The account manages to turn architectural description into a radical critique of what is seen as the decline and corruption of Church and State. Both are portrayed as parodies of this wonderful creation of human hands: the barn is 'immutable', a substitute church of humanity. It conveys unlike church and castle a 'satisfied sense of functional continuity throughout, a feeling almost of gratitude, and quite of pride, at the permanence of the idea which heaped it up'. It is not 'founded on a mistake'; it has not inspired any hatred of its purpose; it has not been crushed by any reaction to what it stands for. By implication all these negatives match features of Church history: the Church has inspired hatred, been crushed by reaction to what it stands for. Unlike the barn, it has neither repose nor grandeur. The barn is both beautiful and unshakeable:

For once Mediaevalism and Modernism had a common standpoint. The lanceolate windows, the time-eaten arch stones and chamfers, the orientation of the axis, the misty chestnutwork of the rafters, referred to no exploded close up fortifying art or worn out religious creed. The defence and salvation of the body by daily bread is still a study, a religion and a desire.

The idealistic conclusion to this account is that 'the barn was natural to the shearers, and the shearers were in harmony with the barn'. This humanistic credo contrasts secularism with religion in terms of human happiness. It attributes the latter to a life of communal and harmonious labour. The subject of secularism is not again dealt with in an expanded form until much later, in *Jude*, where it is given a different and more complex form relating to individuals' loss of faith. At the beginning of the novel it is articulated by Sue Bridehead, an avowed and enthusiastic humanist, who has discarded Christianity for what she calls Hellenism. She sees Christianity as essentially Hebrew or Hebraic: grim, life-denying, punitive. In a symbolic gesture she secretly buys statues of her 'gods' Venus and Apollo. In a scene which points the same contrast as the barn/ church description, she places the statues on either side of a picture of the Crucifixion. Before these images of the goddess of love and the sun god of beauty and light she reads Swinburne's 'Hymn to Proserpine'. This poem cites what were said to be the dying words of the Emperor, Julian the Apostate, a convert to paganism 'Vicisti Galileae!' This Swinburne expands to 'Thou hast conquered, O pale

Galilean: | The world has grown grey from thy breath' (part 2, chapter 3).

It is not until the time of dismissal from the Training School that she begins to reveal the nature of her pagan secularism to Jude. She quotes more of the 'Hymn to Proserpine' which characterizes Christianity as 'ghastly glories of saints, dead limbs of gibbeted Gods!' She tells her unwilling listener how she detests Christian attempts to falsify the meaning of biblical texts by, for instance, plastering over the Song of Songs with 'ecclesiastical abstractions' when its real meaning is the expression of 'ecstatic, natural, human love'. At this stage Jude refuses to reject the Church and its beliefs. Like the rustics in earlier novels, he clings to tradition: 'I suppose one must take some things on trust. Life isn't long enough to work out everything in Euclid's problems before you believe it. I take Christianity' (part 3, chapter 4). His change from this position is marked by a series of mental and emotional states which are fully mapped.

After Sue's loveless marriage to Phillotson, although Jude does not abandon his faith, it takes on the grim, life-denying force that she has attributed to it. Somewhat ludicrously he spends his time conscientiously 'mortifying by every possible means' his wish to see her. In the attempt to suppress his 'passionate tendency' to love her he nearly starves himself. In auto-didactic fashion he reads 'sermons on discipline' and hunts up 'passages in Church history that treated of the Ascetics of the second century' (part 3, chapter 9). At this point in his failure to crush his feelings, he seems to apply himself laboriously and literally to the letter of the law in an illustration of the novel's epigraph, 'The letter killeth'.

It takes only a mild form of passionate physical contact with Sue when they kiss 'close and long' to win him over emotionally to her wish for Hellenic naturalness:

The kiss was a turning-point in Jude's career. Back again in the cottage, and left to reflection, he saw one thing: that though his kiss of that aerial being had seemed the purest moment of his faultful life, as long as he nourished this unlicensed tenderness it was glaringly inconsistent for him to pursue the idea of becoming the soldier and servant of a religion in which sexual love was regarded as at its best a frailty, and at its worst damnation. (part 4, chapter 3)

It is still left ambiguous as to how much this erodes his belief in the central tenets of Christianity: 'He might go on believing as before, but he professed nothing and no longer owned and exhibited engines of faith which, as their proprietor, he might naturally be supposed to exercise on himself first of all'.

There is a contrast here with the variety of humanism symbolized by the barn in *Far from the Madding Crowd*. That embraced secularism as a life of integrity which depended on community, labour, and continuity. What Sue claims to believe in is humanism centred on personal freedom and the naturalness of erotic love which Jude finds himself accepting. The central fact in this acceptance of ideas contrary to his previous religious belief is his feeling that a night spent legitimately with his estranged wife Arabella is 'instinctively a worse thing' than his passion for another man's wife (*Jude*, part 3, chapter 10). Yet the Church would insist that a relationship with anyone other than Arabella would be adultery. His moral instinct is now not to accept this view.

The idea that marriage in the legal and ecclesiastical sense rules out 'Nature's law' becomes more central to the narrative than Jude's failed academic ambitions. There is some attempt to present the non-religious stance as a return to 'Greek joyousness' which involves a happy blindness to 'sickness and sorrow' and what twenty-five centuries of post-Greek history have 'taught the race' (part 5, chapter 5). But there is little sign of such joy in the text, though Sue retrospectively refers to it in these terms. The focus is constantly on the evils of what 'civilization' has imposed rather than the happiness of those who escape it. Indeed, in a passage unprinted in Hardy's lifetime, Jude expresses this sense of failure:

When men of a later age look back upon the barbarism, cruelty, and superstition of the times in which we have the unhappiness to live, it will appear more clearly to them than it does to us that the irksomeness of life is less owing to its natural conditions, though they are bad enough, than to those artificial compulsions arranged for our well-being, which have no root in the nature of things.[1]

In the narrative, what dominates is hostility to a society which is seen as largely held in place by the established Church. It is clear that doctrines are not an issue. Jude's faith is a combination of superstition and a pleasure in church music and biblical texts. The two are combined early on when he visits the cathedral at Christminster where he sees Sue. He hears the choir chanting a psalm which begins 'Wherewithal shall a young man cleanse his way?' (part 2, chapter 3). Since he is aware of the disastrous consequences of his 'animal passion' for Arabella, he interprets the choice of psalm as a sign from Providence. But, as the narrator is careful to point out, it is the ordinary psalm for the twenty-fourth evening of the month. This scepticism is emphasized by the additional comment that 'the atmosphere blew as distinctly from Cyprus as from Galilee' (part 2, chapter 3): from the home of Aphrodite, goddess of love, rather than of Christ. Even in his desperate state when he is trying to suppress his passion for Sue, Jude is deeply moved by a contemporary hymn called 'At the Foot of the Cross'. His circumstances and the title suggest that the hymn admonishes human beings to accept whatever suffering life inflicts on them. Again, Jude interprets it as a message directed to him personally and seeks out the composer for guidance as one might approach a soothsayer. Superstitiously also he feels, when he discovers that Sue has tried to visit him in his absence, that there has been 'another special intervention of Providence to keep him away from temptation' (part 3, chapter 10).

Ironically the very event, the death of the children, which releases him from his belief in an intervening Providence, recaptures Sue for the superstition he is rejecting. She lapses back into what she once described as the religion of 'fetishists and ghost seers' (part 3, chapter 4). She explicitly rejects the natural joyousness of Greek civilization; the belief that 'Nature's intention, Nature's law and *raison d'être* [was] that we should be joyful in what instincts she afforded us—instincts which civilization had taken upon itself to thwart'. She now believes in an interventionist God as Jude has previously done: he must exist because he is punishing her. She embraces a Hebraic attitude: 'Fate has given us this stab in the back for being such fools as to take Nature at her word!' (part 6, chapter 2). She herself recognizes that she is becoming 'as superstitious as a savage' (part 6, chapter 3). But clinging now to the letter of the law, as Jude did formerly, she tells him: 'Arabella's child killing mine was a judgement; the right slaying the wrong' (part 6, chapter 3). Evidently this refers to the fact that little Jude, who killed his half-siblings, was the product of a legitimate marriage—which they were not. The children were taken from her, she believes, to 'show' her that Arabella is still Jude's wife and, in spite of their divorce, Phillotson is her real husband. Allegedly because of this but manifestly as a punishment for her sexual sin, she decides she must return to Phillotson.

It is Sue's reversal as well as the children's deaths, which causes Jude to make explicit his rejection of Christianity:

After converting me to your views on so many things, to find you suddenly turn to the right-about like this—for no reason whatever, confounding all you have formerly said through sentiment merely! You root out of me what little affection and reverence I had left in me for the church as an old acquaintance. (Part 6, chapter 3)

He no longer rejects only the established Church but any form of religion—'You make me hate Christianity, or mysticism, or Sacerdotalism, or whatever it may be called'. He is convinced that what has happened to them is merely the work of 'man and senseless circumstance'.

This feeling that belief in a divine power is a kind of primitive insurance against further calamity is found, as usual, in an unmodified form in Hardy's poem 'A Plaint to Man'. In this, God asks

> Wherefore, O Man, did there come to you
> The unhappy need of creating me—
> A form like your own—for praying to?

God envisages humanity's answer in terms which capture Jude's final belief:

> 'Such a forced device', you may say, 'is meet
> For easing a loaded heart at whiles:
> Man needs to conceive of a mercy-seat
>
> 'Somewhere above the gloomy aisles
> Of the wailful world, or he could not bear
> The irk no local hope beguiles'
>
> (*Poems*, ii. 33)

Jude has abandoned his superstitious belief in a watchful Providence and, confronted by relentless disappointment and catastrophe, sees no justification for Christian belief in a just God. But the imaginative power of the Bible still holds him—that he cannot erase any more than Hardy could. At his period of deepest distress he finds a surrogate for his black misery in the Old Testament Book of Job. Most notably he identifies himself with the central figure Job, whom God allows Satan to deprive of riches, health, and (like Jude) his children. Job rails vehemently against these unjust afflictions and the delirious Jude, on the deathbed he has wishes for, repeats his cries: '*Let the day perish wherein I was born . . . Why died I not from the womb? . . . Wherefore is light given to him that is in misery, and life unto the bitter in soul?*' (part 6, chapter 11). Job, too, was a man whose faith in a benign and just God was overturned by 'the only problem': that of how to reconcile this conception of Him with life's evidently random cruelty to the just. The novel finally seems to assert not only that Christianity is a myth or a crutch but so too is the idea that by discarding it a life of natural joy becomes possible. The strongest statement it makes is that the random cruelty of life is made worse by the social machinery of a community supposedly based on a Christian religion of love.

Hardy's Rustics: Christianity and Magic

Those left behind in the group to which Jude was born are what Hardy call workfolk and what critics have come to refer to as rustics, a somewhat derogatory term when applied to people rather than landscape. They are the work people who would theoretically make up the congregations of the churches and parsons described in the novels. They have usually been treated as a comic chorus detached from the rest of the characters in the narratives. But when their relationship to religion is examined in detail it is clear that they perceive themselves as operating in a framework which in its essentials matches that of Jude—though in a weaker, more confused form. It too is a combination of superstition and biblical texts. The co-ordinates are the same but the viewpoint is different. Religion for this group, to whom it is filtered down in a bastard form through services and the Bible, is a matter of the same dogged pragmatism as that with which they treat the weather: nominally they accept it; practically they ignore it.

The services of the church and Sunday school have acquainted them fairly well with the Prayer Book and with biblical texts rather than with doctrine. The contemporary statement that working-class people do not regularly go to church is largely the case in Hardy's early narratives. As already noticed, it is said that people at Egdon Heath go to church only to be married or buried and attendance at any other time is phenomenal. Characters in the narrative admit as much. Grandfer Cantle confesses to not have been 'to-year'. The furze-cutter Humphrey, who becomes Clym's fellow-worker, explains why he has not been for three years: 'for I'm so dead sleepy of a Sunday; and 'tis so terrible far to get there . . . that . . . [I] don't go at all' (*The Return of the Native*, book 1, chapter 3). Joseph Poorgrass in *Far from the Madding Crowd* confesses in a moment of guilt 'I did not go to church a-Sunday' (chapter 52). In *Two on a Tower* things have slipped and it is said that there has been no Confirmation in the village church for twenty years before Bishop Helmsdale's visit because no bishop would 'take the trouble to come to such an out-of-the-way parish as ours' (chapter 23).

Nor is it a desire for religious worship that draws church attendance, even in *Under the Greenwood Tree*, though the narrative does revolve around the village church. But the focus of interest for attenders is the rivalry between the established choir and its musicians; the vicar who wishes to improve the music by replacing them with an organ played by Fancy Day, a schoolmistress. The connection between the choir's desire to continue their music and Christian worship is accidental. When not busy playing or singing (badly), they use the gallery as a vantage point to observe and comment on the doings of those below:

Such topics as that the clerk was always chewing tobacco except at the moment of crying Amen; . . . that during the sermon certain young daughters of the village had left off caring to study anything so mild as the marriage service for some years, and now regularly studied the one which chronologically follows it; that a pair of lovers touched fingers through a knot-hole between their pews . . . that Mrs Ledlow, the farmer's wife, counted her money and reckoned her week's marketing expenses during the first lesson; all news to those below, were stale subjects here. (part 1, chapter 6)

Similarly it is human interest which animates the Confirmation scene in *Two on a Tower*. The young girls waiting to be confirmed are 'gaily bedecked' for the ceremony. They walk about beforehand showing off their finery and preening themselves on their appearance. The main adult attenders are preoccupied with the relationship between Viviette and Swithin to whom she is secretly married. Viviette gazes fondly at her 'beloved youth' as she sees 'the great episcopal ring glistening in the sun among Swithin's brown curls' (chapter 24). Her brother observes closely both his sister and the man he fears she is recklessly infatuated with. Swithin himself suffers deep humiliation at being treated as an underling and being unable to approach in public the woman who is in reality his wife.

The rustics are dimly aware of the distinctions between varieties of Christianity so well known to Jude (and Hardy). They recognize a difference between the Church of England and Dissenters and some have vaguely heard of High or Low groupings within Anglicanism. These are the variations illustrated by the Reverend Clare and his two sons in *Tess*. News of them reaches Bathsheba's farmworkers in *Far from the Madding Crowd* through the traveller's tales of Cainy Ball after his historic visit to the city of Bath. Like some explorer back from darkest Africa, he tells how he went to 'grand churches and chapels' at the rate of two a day. He informs his listeners that 'There's two religions going on in the nation—now High Church and High Chapel. And thinks I, I'll play fair: so I went to High Church in the morning, and High Chapel in the afternoon.' He explains the difference between them fairly well: 'At High Church they pray singing and worship all the colours of the rainbow: and at High Chapel they pray preaching and worship drab and whitewash only' (chapter 33).

A fuller discussion takes place later in the same novel when Poorgrass, driving Fanny Robin's body to the church, pauses to join the drinkers at the Buck's Head. Feeling guilty about what he is doing, Poorgrass starts to lament his faults: 'I've been drinky once this month . . . I dropped a curse or two yesterday, so I don't want to go too far for my safety' (chapter 42). This unwelcome reminder of serious issues leads a listener to accuse him of Puritanism—'I believe ye to be a chapel-member, Joseph. That I do.' This is the moral equivalent of preferring 'drab and whitewash' to 'all the colours of the rainbow'. Another tipsy listener, Coggan, joins in to assert his own staunch adherence to the Church of England: 'I've stuck like a plaster to the old faith I was born in.' He explains his reasons which seem to him in his drunken state to be sound: 'there's this to be said for the church, a man can belong to the church and bide in his cheerful old inn, and never worry his mind about doctrines at all.' Chapel-goers or Dissenters are seen as kill-joys who are too serious about their beliefs. As Coggan views it, their seriousness is not altogether to be condemned for it has its penalties and fair rewards: 'to be a meetinger, ye must go to chapel in all winds and all weathers, and make yerself as frantic as a skit. Not but that chapel-members be clever chaps enough in their own way. They can lift up beautiful prayers out of their own heads, all about their families and ship-wracks in the newspaper.' Churchgoers, on the other hand, rely on the letter of the Christian word and 'must have it all printed afore-hand, or, . . . we should no more know what to say to a great gaffer like the Lord than babes unborn' (chapter 42). This in a comic form suggests some grasp of the difference between the established Church and Dissenters which is treated in a more sophisticated way in *A Laodicean*. Further, it shows the irrelevance of doctrine to this group: allegiance to Anglicanism is largely a matter of loyalty to what is familiar or traditional. As Coggan puts it, 'I hate a feller who'll change his old ancient doctrines for the sake of getting to heaven. I'd as soon turn King's-evidence for the few pounds you get . . . I'll stick to my side, and if we be in the wrong, so be it: I'll fall with the fallen' (chapter 42).

The nucleus of the rustics' 'doctrines' parallels Jude's. It consists of a belief in an interventionist Being or Lord (or occasionally 'gaf-fer') and a superstitious reliance on the words of the Bible which matches Jude's fascination with the sacred texts. In the early days at Christminster, Jude sees God as intervening to keep him on the straight and narrow; the workfolk are less clear about the objectives of the Providence they assume to exist. They simply feel that there is someone, as they put it, 'up there' controlling things. Poorgrass in *Far from the Madding Crowd* complains of his bad memory but is gratified that 'providence ordered that it should be no worse' (chap-ter 15). At the Buck's Head drinking session he expresses a pious hope that 'Providence won't be in a way with me for my doings', i.e. his drinking (chapter 42). Sycophantically he thanks heaven for mak-ing Gabriel Oak a clever and virtuous man 'for twould have been just as easy for God to have make the shepherd a loose low man—a man of iniquity, so to speak it—as what he is' (chapter 8). Cainy Ball recognizes the kindness of Providence in providing the citizens of Bath with 'water springs up out of the earth ready boiled for use'. But he sees it as a blot that 'God didn't provide 'em with victuals as well as drink' (chapter 33).

As well as controlling events, Providence is assumed to be keeping a balance-sheet of individual conduct. But in spite of the ten commandments, the rules for debit and credit are unclear to the workfolk. Chapel goers are known by Poorgrass to be 'more hand-in-glove with them above' than Anglicans. Coggan agrees: 'I baint such a fool as to pretend that we who stick to the church have the same chance as they' (chapter 42). Details are confused, however. When swearing is discussed at the Malthouse there is some feeling that it is 'a great relief to a merry soul'. The Maltster himself insists that 'Nature requires her swearing at the regular times, or she's not herself; and unholy exclamations is a necessity of life' (chapter 8). Poorgrass, by contrast, confesses his dropping a curse or two as a sin. In the same way he takes being 'drinky' as the object of Providence's disapproval; a companion, Mark Clark, sees the gift of enjoying 'a wet' as 'a talent the Lord has bestowed upon us, and we ought not to neglect it' (chapter 42). Poorgrass in a less guilty moment accepts this: 'victuals and drink is a cheerful thing . . . — 'tis the gospel of the body, without which we perish, so to speak it' (chapter 32). Behind these *ad hoc* statements lies a certain fatalism. Henery Fray in the same novel feels 'your lot is your lot'—and scripture is nothing (chapter 15). In *The Return of the Native* Christian Cantle, the man no woman will marry, feels ''Twas to be if twas, I suppose' (book 1, chapter 3). With the signal exceptions of fornication and murder, sin is not a concept that is unmistakeably identifiable.

A deeper belief among the workpeople is seen repeatedly in relation to what can only be called the preternatural, or white magic. They accept the existence of some non-natural, non-supernatural force which works according to arbitrary but known rules. The source of this power is not considered, nor is it a matter of interest. It simply exists for the rustics and other lower levels of society. In *Far from the Madding Crowd*, Bathsheba's maid Liddy persuades her to 'find out' who she is going to marry by placing a key on a certain page of the Bible and turning the volume to point to a particular part of the text. Susan Nunsuch makes a wax image of Eustacia in *The Return of the Native* and thrusts fifty or more pins into it to bring about Eustacia's death. In *The Mayor of Casterbridge*, Henchard consults the weather prophet, Wide-Oh, to predict the future by finding out what the weather is to be at harvest time and so plan his trade in corn. In *The Woodlanders*, at midnight on Midsummer-Eve, Grace Melbury and the other village girls, in order to discover who they are going to marry, engage in the practice of going into the wood and sowing hemp seed. They then expect to see their future husbands. The outcome of these practices is in most cases in accord with expectations: Eustacia dies, the weather is as disastrous as Wide-Oh predicts, the harvest is ruined as predicted, Grace meets and marries Fitzpiers. But with the exception of *The Woodlanders* where Fitzpiers manages to make sure he is the first man that Grace sees, it is left open as to what is the connection between waxen images and death, prophecy and catastrophic weather. Certainly for the country believers in the novels, events validate their belief in these practices.

The authority that is felt to reside in the Bible is seamlessly incorporated into some of these activities with no sense of incongruity. The words themselves can be used as magical incantations. Susan Nunsuch, as she melts the mutilated wax image of Eustacia in a fire, recites the Lord's Prayer backwards three times—Eustacia shortly after dies by drowning, the appropriate fate for a witch. Similarly, Poorgrass in *Far from the Madding Crowd*, lost and panicking in a wood at night, finds he cannot open a gate. 'Knowing there was a devil's hand in it', he kneels and rattles off all the sacred words he can remember: the Lord's Prayer, 'the Belief', the Ten Commandments, and 'Dearly Beloved Brethren'. As he recalls, when he reached 'Saying After Me' and thinks 'this makes four, and 'tis all I know out of a book', he rises to his feet and finds the gate opens (chapter 8).

With this sense that the very words of the Bible are powerful, the rustics use biblical references or snatches of prayers as a way of adding weight to their assertions almost at random. They show a good deal of familiarity with the words, phrases, and even rhythm of the Bible but little understanding of its substance. Even facts are confused: Cain Ball, for instance, is so called because his mother took Cain to be the name of the virtuous man who was killed by his brother in Genesis and so named him after the murderer, not the victim. His friends soften his murderous name to Cainy. Poorgrass tries to add respectability to his drink-induced double vision by claiming it as a mark of sanctity: 'Yes, I see two of every sort, as if I were some holy man living in the times of King Noah and entering into the ark.' Had he 'lived in Genesis', he would not have been called a drunkard any more than Noah was (chapter 42). Cainy Ball, 'the illustrious traveller' to Bath, adds to his kudos by informing his audience that 'the new style of pa'sons wear moustarchers and long beards . . . and look like Moses and Aaron complete, and makes we fokes in the congregation feel all over like the children of Israel' (chapter 33). Solomon Longways in *The Mayor of Casterbridge* lends emphasis to his description of Henchard's intolerance of drunken employees by asserting that 'if any of his men be so little overtook by a drop, he's down upon 'em as stern as the Lord on the jovial Jews' (chapter 5).

Like Hardy, the workpeople have integrated biblical language into their own. Poorgrass in particular, in *Far from the Madding Crowd*, is capable of producing a pastiche of even its rhythms whenever he feels like a 'man in the bible', issuing a dire warning. On the subject of whited sepulchres he warns 'evil do thrive so in these times that ye may be as much deceived in the clanest shaved and whitest shirted man as in the raggedest tramp upon the turnpike' (chapter 8). Later, to impress Cainy Ball with the seriousness of taking an oath, he tells him ''Tis a horrible testament, mind ye, which you say and seal with your bloodstone, and the prophet Matthew tells us that on whomsoever it shall fall it will grind him to powder' (chapter 33). All this does not take away from the comic effect of the use, misuse, and abuse of the Bible but underlying it all is the satirical point that this is what has been described by one historian as religion declining into magic.

Questions that Follow the Loss of Belief

When, in *Jude*, Hardy records the erosion of religion not by doctrinal doubts but by a series of what seem like uncontrollable and cruel misfortunes experienced by an individual, questions remain for him. These are repeatedly addressed in the late novels, passionately but never definitively. The only constant is the insistence that such cruelty does pose a question. In fact there is no reason from a scientific point of view to be baffled by human suffering. In general terms Darwin's account of the struggle for existence and the survival and production of progeny by those best adapted to their environment explains the history of animals as well as other life. On this view, in the words of a comment that appears copied into one of Hardy's notebooks, 'In the eyes of science man is not "higher" than the other animals'.[2]

Hardy overtly accepted the equality between human beings and other animals in the horror he expresses at the sufferings inflicted on the latter. His early reaction to the noises of the slaughterhouse in London is echoed by his later concern over the sufferings of animals. Tess, in the midst of her privations, is moved to pity by the game-birds left wounded by hunters. 'With the impulse of a soul who could feel for kindred sufferers', she breaks their necks 'tenderly' (chapter 41). Jude has a similar reaction to Arabella's wish to let the pig he has to kill die slowly so that the meat will be 'well bled'. Unable to bear the sound of its 'cry of despair; long-drawn, slow and hopeless' (part 1, chapter 10), he plunges the knife deep into its neck. The same sensitivity to the sufferings of the horses used to drag gun carriages during wartime is revealed in Hardy's poems, alongside his feelings for those of the soldiers. In 'Horses Aboard':

> They are horses of war,
> And are going to where there is fighting afar;
> But they gaze through their eye-holes unwitting they are,
> And that in some wilderness, gaunt and ghast,
> Their bones will bleach ere a year has passed,
> And the item be as 'war-waste' classed.
>
> (*Poems*, iii. 105)

At one point in a letter written during the Boer War he even suggests that the horses suffer more than the soldiers. He is speaking of a group trapped by hostile forces in a river bed: '& the mangled animals too, who must have terror superadded to their physical sufferings' (*Letters*, ii. 248). But obviously an explanation is available to account for the suffering of such animals: human beings create the pain and misery as the side-effect of actions which they see as necessary for their own survival.

If he were consistent, human suffering ought not to represent a problem for Hardy. Logically, if a human being such as Tess is the equivalent in the scheme of things to a fly on a billiard table, her sufferings are simply part of the universal struggle for existence which necessarily involves pain and destruction for some. Two assumptions are needed in order to conceive of human anguish as requiring an explanation. Yet that is Hardy's position. The two assumptions are that humanity is that part of the world which is more significant than any others and that human beings deserve to be treated justly by whatever controls creation, although there is no firm belief in a controller. Both of these beliefs are needed to account for the bitterness and resentment with which the afflictions of Tess and Jude are treated. Presumably the longing for justice is left over from the Christian belief in a Day of Judgement when all human beings will receive their just deserts. Hardy, although agnostic, seems to have retained an emotional and imaginative hankering for something to reconcile him to what could still appear malignly inspired. The rustics, thanks to their lowly position in society, are not shown to expect the ultimate justice that Christianity promises. They merely feel that someone else is in charge of their lives and future— presumably a familiar feeling in relation to their masters. Only a sophisticated creature like Jude expects justice and consequently is unable to accept its absence, even in a world he comes to believe is entirely godless.

The Significance of Human Beings and the Bible

This is one of the two major assumptions that Hardy makes recurrently: that humanity is the point of creation. In doing so, he produces not an argument but an enactment of the idea that human beings are by far the most significant creatures in the world, a belief in line with the Christian view. What he offers is an imaginative representation of them. The rustics allude to the Bible to add authority to their generalizations about life and conduct. Hardy deploys a similar technique to lend stature and significance to some central characters. By this means he creates a perception of humanity as the centre of and sum of the universe. Early in *The Mayor of Casterbridge* Henchard describes his state after selling his wife: 'I sank into one of those gloomy fits I sometimes suffer from, on account o' the loneliness of my domestic life, when the world seems to have the blackness of hell, and, like Job, I could curse the day that gave me birth' (chapter 12). This picture of Henchard as the archetype of human affliction in the Old Testament is repeated later in the narratorial commentary. It occurs when Henchard has tried in vain to make Farfrae return to Casterbridge where Lucetta is dangerously ill: 'He cursed himself like a less scrupulous Job, as a vehement man will do when he loses self-respect, the last mental prop under poverty' (chapter 40). The action of warning Farfrae is seen as the work of a 'repentant sinner' over whom 'there was to be no joy in heaven', an ironic reference to the statement in Luke 15: 7 that there is more rejoicing over one repentant sinner than over ninety-nine persons who have nothing to repent.

Similar biblical comparisons are made in *Tess* at crucial moments in the narrative with the same ironic force. At the point of the rape/seduction scene, the narrator asks where Tess's guardian angel was when this horror was allowed to happen. He answers his own question bitterly: 'Perhaps, like that other god of whom the ironical Tishbite spoke, he was talking, or he was pursuing, or he was in a journey, or he was sleeping and was not to be awaked' (chapter 11). This refers to Elijah's mockery of those who sacrificed a bullock to Baal and whose prayers were not answered (1 Kings, 18: 18). The reasons Elijah taunts them with are echoed by the last five clauses of Hardy's passage. Similarly ironic is the following use of God's threat (Exodus 20: 5) to visit 'the sins of the fathers upon the children'. This, says the narrator scornfully, 'may be a morality good enough for divinities' but 'it is scorned by average human nature; and it therefore does not mend the matter' (chapter 11).

After her marriage to Angel, Tess is in an ecstatic state for a brief time: 'she felt glorified by an irradiation not her own, like the Angel whom St John saw in the sun' (chapter 33). This transfers to her a passage in Revelation 19: 17: 'And I saw an angel standing in the sun; and he cried with a loud voice, saying to all the fowls that fly in the midst of heaven, Come and gather yourselves together unto the supper of the great God.' But Tess's joyous feelings last no longer than the sound of the wedding bells. The later misery at Flintcomb-Ash, after Clare has left her, becomes hellish with the arrival of the threshing machine and its soot-coated engineman like 'a creature from Tophet' (chapter 47), the valley of fire near Jerusalem where the idolatrous Jews burnt their children (Jeremiah 7: 31). When the born-again Alec meets Tess he sees her as the 'Witch' or Whore of Babylon, a symbol of universal harlotry (Revelation 17: 5). When she urges Angel Clare to marry her sister Liza-Lu after her death, she claims that 'if she were to become yours it would almost seem as if death had not divided us' (chapter 48). This recalls the lengthy lament of David for Saul and his son Jonathan beginning 'The beauty of Israel is slain upon thy high places: How are the mighty fallen.' It includes the verse 'Saul and Jonathan were lovely and pleasant in their lives, And in their deaths they were not divided' (2 Samuel, 1: 20–7).

In addition to the role of Job which Jude takes on, he is also repeatedly compared with the crucified Christ. Both Jude and Sue, though the former more than the latter, are seen as incarnations of this ultimate symbol of human suffering. Sue sees herself and Jude, when driven from Kennetbridge to Christminster after his dismissal for immorality, as Christ sent from one merciless judge, Caiaphas, to another, Pilate (part 6, chapter 1). Jude is associated, in the episode involving the model of Jerusalem, with Calvary, the site of the crucifixion (part 2, chapter 5). When Sue refuses at first to become his mistress, he tells her bitterly 'Crucify me if you will!' (part 4, chapter 5). Finally, when she decides to return to Phillotson he tears a pillow from their bed and cries 'Then let the veil of our temple be rent in two from this hour!' (part 6, chapter 3). This recalls the biblical description of the tearing of the curtain which concealed the innermost sanctuary of the temple at the time of Christ's death.

As is already evident, Hardy twists many of the Christian allusions to an ironically secular use but he relies on their imaginative power in doing so. This gives them a double force which mirrors the two visual perspectives that his narrators take on individuals: the close-up which enlarges them and the panoramic view which diminishes them. The biblical references work in the same way to enhance the stature of those Hardy associates them with; and simultaneously reduces them by the contrast they make with the figures in the Bible. Jude for instance is a Christ and, as he says himself, 'a poor Christ' (part 2, chapter 7). He is both profoundly significant and at the same time profoundly insignificant—a view which echoes the double visual perspective on human beings in Hardy's late novels.

Life's Injustice and Destiny

Looking at human existence through the spectacles of the Bible, Hardy was able temporarily to appropriate the significance naturally attaching to human beings in a narrative which represented them as God's consummate handiwork endowed with souls. This was so even though as an agnostic he did not accept the doctrinal framework of Christianity. In the same way he makes imaginative use of other forms of literature to create pathetic grandeur for humanity.

The rustics' acceptance of a Somebody, a Gaffer, a Master, is neutralized by them as Providence. Providence is a figure which has much in common with the more romantic notion of Destiny, a mysterious force which determines all events in human life in advance. The literary associations that had accrued to this concept of Destiny serve in place of logic for Hardy. In *The Mayor of Casterbridge* both Henchard's life and Elizabeth-Jane's provoke comments from the narrator. It is said of Elizabeth-Jane that 'her experience had consisted less in a series of pure disappointments than in a series of substitutions. Continually it had happened that what she had desired had not been granted her and that what had been granted her she had not desired' (chapter 25). This comment is made shortly after Farfrae, unknown to her, has transferred his affection from her to Lucetta. At that point also the narrator commiserates: 'Poor Elizabeth-Jane, little thinking what her malignant star had done to blast the budding attentions she had won from Donald Farfrae, was glad to hear Lucetta's word about remaining' (chapter 24). Her stepfather has similar experiences. On learning the news that Elizabeth-Jane is not his daughter, he suppresses his reaction: 'His usual habit was not to consider whether destiny were hard upon him or not—the shape of his ideas in cases of affliction being simply a moody "I am to suffer then I perceive"' (chapter 19).

Already in these comments destiny is extended to mean not only that the things which happen to these two are fixed in advance but that their experiences make a pattern: an inescapable repetition of disappointment or failure. Misfortune is not, however, a necessary corollary to fate: Farfrae takes his good fortune in being chosen, somewhat to his surprise, as Mayor of Casterbridge for something predestined: 'See now how it's ourselves that are ruled by the powers above us. We plan this, but we do that' (chapter 34). However, from the earliest introduction of the term *destiny* into English it became associated with the idea of malign experiences. A powerful influence was exerted by its occurrence in the many translations of Boethius' *De Consolatione Philosophiae*, *Concerning the Consolations of Philosophy*. This work was translated by, amongst others, Alfred the Great, Chaucer, and Queen Elizabeth I. In it Boethius, when he is unjustly imprisoned, questions Philosophy as to why injustice triumphs in this way and victimizes a man of integrity. Although in answering this Philosophy integrates destiny into Christianity by arguing for free will and final justice, the term even in Boethius has a pagan sense which overhangs the text. The pagan associations which continued to attach to destiny or fate involve the idea of an inexorably controlling force or the results of that force as embodied in an individual's life. The term retains persistently the tone of the Greek and Roman uses of equivalent terms and concepts. This is true even when it is said that Henchard on rare occasions feels himself to be in 'Somebody's hand' (chapter 41). This soon fades into a recognition that this somebody is not on his side. For most of the time both Tess and Jude share the narrator's belief that there are recurrent patterns of misfortune for certain people: this is the dominant discourse, though not the only one.

'Proof' that certain figures are doomed to misery and failure is provided by coincidental events in the narrative which work to bring about personal disaster. This lends force to an otherwise illogical account. It also introduces the idea of chance as operative in these lives in a strange way. Chance is essentially a name for an 'undesigned occurrence' and yet in Hardy's novels it works to produce a repetitive pattern of trouble to bring about what is destined. In *The Mayor of Casterbridge* Henchard's employment of Donald Farfrae leads to his loss of Lucetta, his business failure, and his replacement as mayor by the young Scotsman with whom he was originally so charmed. In the same way the reappearance of the furmity woman, after twenty years, in the very court where Henchard is presiding as magistrate, allows her to reveal that he once sold his wife for five guineas. This brings about his social shaming and downfall. The same pattern is discernible in the lives of Tess and Jude. Tess experiences the well-known sequence of coincidences which bring about her rape/seduction, her return to Alec, and his murder. Jude repeatedly finds his efforts frustrated by chance events and coincidences such as that which finds him on his first night with Sue in the very hotel where he has recently spent the night with Arabella. This results in Sue's discovery of what he has done.

The account of how destiny works in particular lives leads to a general application of such ideas to humanity as a whole. When, late in *The Mayor*, Henchard, after reverting to his old trade of haytrussing, returns to Casterbridge, there is nothing externally to hinder him from making a new start. He is not an old man and might regain a standing equal to that he formerly held. But, the narrator explains,

'Our immortals. "Ah, Mr Hardy, Mr Hardy, if you only knew all the circumstances."'

(by Will Dyson 1880–1938)

'the ingenious machinery contrived by the gods for reducing human possibilities of amelioration to a minimum—which arranges that wisdom to do shall come *pari passu* with the departure of zest for doing—stood in the way of all that' (chapter 44).

The same implication that chance works against the grain of individual character and circumstance is repeated in *Tess* apropos her unfortunate seeking out of Alec d'Urberville. The narrator raises a question:

Thus the thing began. Had she perceived this meeting's import she might have asked why she was doomed to be seen and coveted that day by the wrong man, and not by some other man, the right and desired one in all respects.

The answer to Tess's putative questioning is then supplied:

In the ill-judged execution of the well-judged plan of things the call seldom produces the comer, the man to love rarely coincides with the hour for loving. Nature does not often say 'See!' to her poor creature at a time when seeing can lead to happy doing; or reply 'Here' to a body's cry of 'Where?' till the hide-and-seek has become an irksome outworn game. (chapter 5)

The boy Jude learns from the tattered Latin grammar Phillotson sends him that the key to a foreign language cannot be provided as a code with a cipher which once known would allow him to change all the words of his native tongue into those of the foreign one. He faces a 'labour like that of Israel in Egypt' and regards his task as hopeless. This elicits a comment: 'Somebody might have come along that way who would have asked him his trouble, and might have cheered him by saying that his notions were further advanced than those of his grammarian'. This is a very particular point but the generalization that it evokes is framed in the true-at-all-times present tense: 'But nobody did come, because nobody does' (part 1, chapter 4). It has the same authority as the more familiar statement 'Man is moral'. What coincidence usually does in Hardy's novels is to frustrate the wished-for trajectories of individual lives by creating an actual, unwished-for trajectory such as Henchard, Tess, and Jude experience. The volitions of the characters become what Gillian Beer calls 'ghost' plots which contrast with real or actual plots.[3] In Hardy's world, because of the enigmatic force called Destiny, to wish for is to lose.

The connection forged in this way between unhappy lives and an inexorable force does not diminish those who endure such lives. The very invincibility of their opponent raises the stakes. However pointless it may be in practical terms, confronting such a force creates an impression of moral stoicism. It is a struggle that is bound to be lost: Destiny always wins in the end but resistance is shown to have its own powerful value.

Life's Injustice and Greek Tragedy

An alternative vision of Destiny is provided by other traditions beside Christianity and superstition. Hardy throughout his life shows a familiarity with the works of the Greek tragic dramatists, Aeschylus, Euripides, and Sophocles, whom he began to study at the time of his friendship with Horace Moule. In his *Life* he makes casually familiar reference to them: to argue that not all poets are alike but infinitely varied (p. 414); to claim that what appears true in poetry is not actuality but consummate artistry (p. 77); and to illustrate that when a married woman with a lover kills a husband it is not that she really wishes to kill the husband but to kill the situation. He also knew some of these plays in performance: in 1912 he saw *Oedipus* at Covent Garden and the Balliol Players came to Max Gate to perform 'The Curse of the House of Atreus' (*Agamemnon*) (1924), *Hippolytus* (1926), and *Iphigenia in Aulis* (1927). Greek tragedy was for him an aesthetically satisfying way of theorizing the cruelties and injustice of life not among kings and generals but among the poor. Describing the isolated hamlet of Little Hintock in *The Woodlanders* (which might serve as his representative setting), he writes:

It was one of those sequestered spots outside the gates of the world where may be usually found more meditation than action, and more listlessness than meditation: where reasoning proceeds on narrow premisses, and results in inferences wildly imaginative; yet where, from time to time, no less than in other places, dramas of a grandeur and unity truly Sophoclean are enacted in the real. (chapter 1)

Critics have seen an Oedipus figure in the blinded Clym Yeobright who feels himself responsible for the death of his mother. Though in traditional accounts Oedipus blinds himself and his mother hangs herself, the parallel between these two men in their disasters is obvious enough. More explicit is the final half-serious, wholly ironic suggestion at the end of *Tess* after her death by hanging that this is the story of a Greek tragedy: ' "Justice" was done, and the President of the Immortals (in Aeschylean phrase) had ended his sport with Tess' (chapter 49). What lies behind the allusion to 'the President of the Immortals' is Aeschylus' view of life as the slow but certain working out of divine justice which teaches humanity that whatever happens is the will of the father of the gods, Zeus. The placing of this allusion invites the reader retrospectively to read this story as possibly a Greek tragedy. The Aeschylean account, says the narrator, is one which fits well the events just described. The only way of dealing with them on this view is to accept them as the inevitable will of the gods.

It is similarly suggested that Jude can be read as an Aeschylean tragedy (amongst other options). Here the tragedy in question is that of the house of Atreus. In the Greek account, the father of Atreus was cursed by a dying enemy who called down disaster upon his descendants. After Atreus' uncle, Thyestes, seduced Atreus' wife he was banished from the kingdom. Later Atreus feigned reconciliation and summoned Thyestes back only to feed him at a banquet with the flesh of his own children. Thyestes later fathered Aegisthus who became a further agent of the curse on this family. In *Jude* before there is a mention of Atreus, Mrs Edlin warns him against marriage because the family has a history of what appear to be disastrous marriages. She tells how Jude's parents came to hate each other and separated. The marriage of Sue's parents followed a similar course. Her mother ran away from her father, taking with her a child who later died. The husband broke into his wife's house to steal the coffin, was arrested for burglary and hanged and gibbeted. After his death, his wife went mad. Jude's great-aunt regards marriage as a mistake for their doomed house. Later, just before Jude and Sue's intended marriage, Sue, alluding to the old woman's account, relates it to the House of Atreus: 'I suppose we must go on. How horrid that story was last night! . . . It makes me feel as if a tragic doom over-hung our family, as it did the house of Atreus' (part 5, chapter 4). Though Sue and Jude co-habit rather than marrying after all, they do not avoid disaster. After the deaths of the children, Sue asks hopelessly 'What ought to be done?'—remembering the cursed house of Atreus and the murder of Thyestes' children. In reply Jude quotes from one of the choruses in the *Agamemnon* which captures

Aeschylus' view of human life: 'Nothing can be done . . . Things are as they are and will be brought to their destined issue' (part 6, chapter 2). Neither Sue nor Jude finally accept this reading of events. Sue seeks refuge in an oppressive form of Christianity; Jude abandons himself to his vices and commits a protracted suicide. After Sue's return to Phillotson he uses of himself the words that Antigone uses when walled up alive as a punishment for carrying out funeral rites contrary to Creon's command: 'As Antigone said, I am neither a dweller among men nor ghosts' (part 6, chapter 9). This is a speech which Hardy had marked in his translation of *Antigone*. Like the biblical allusions, the Greek references serve to create an imaginative significance for human beings which scientific logic cannot allow them.

Life's Injustice and Schopenhauer

The enactment of a grand significance of human beings, albeit by imaginative means, facilitates the idea that life's cruelty is unjust. Hardy is certainly troubled by such a belief, especially since, as he represents it, misfortune is more likely to fall on the noble individual rather than on the pragmatist or the corrupt. Whether his felt need for justice derived from Christianity which offered justice and resulted from his abandoning that prospect, it was strong and permanent in Hardy. As well as giving Henchard, Tess, and Jude heroic stature, he also attempts to present a more logical explanation for life's cruelty. In doing this he used among other things the philosophical theories of Arthur Schopenhauer (1788–1860) and Eduard von Hartman as he had used the Bible and Greek tragedies to provide an alternative way of possibly looking at tragic events. There is no final commitment to any of these ideas.

At the end of *The Mayor of Casterbridge*, the narrator's comment on Elizabeth-Jane's state of mind transforms the perception of individual injustice into a universal one: though happily married to the prosperous Farfrae, she is not grateful for her lot in life:

Her experience had been of a kind to teach her, rightly or wrongly, that the doubtful honour of a brief transit through a sorry world hardly called for effusiveness, even when the path was suddenly irradiated at some half-way point by daybeams rich as hers. But her strong sense that neither she

nor any human being deserved less than was given, did not blind her to the
fact that there were others receiving less who had deserved much more.
(chapter 45)

What is here recognized as 'the fact' is occasionally spelt out in
other passages like this. In *The Woodlanders* there is a reference to
'the Unfulfilled Intention, which makes life what it is' (chapter 7),
a phrase that may be an allusion to the force behind human existence as a 'blind incessant impulse' related to Schopenhauer's central ideas. A differently phrased description in *Tess* may refer to
the same concept when the narrator speaks of the 'ill-judged execution of the well-judged plan of things' (chapter 5). Significantly
both of these descriptions suggest that justice was intended but
thwarted. So in spite of Hardy's overt scepticism there is an
implication that justice was somehow a possibility which has been
crushed.

The 'fact' of injustice alluded to in these accounts is also demonstrated by the events in the narratives themselves. It is inherent in
the bitter irony of Henchard's intermittent belief that he is in
'Somebody's' hands when what awaits him is rejection, loneliness,
and death. This is matched by the contrast between the disasters in
Tess Durbeyfield's life and the comment after she has been hanged
that '"Justice" was done'. This is literally true in the sense that the
judgement of the law has been executed. In Hardy's terms, however,
it is the worst injustice that has ended Tess's life in this way. This is
the pattern of the late novels: a contrast between the most admirable
characters and their wretched fates.

In the poems such conclusions are applied to humanity at large
and in vehement terms. In 'Unkept Good Fridays', for instance, the
speaker compares the annual remembrance of the suffering of Christ
at the Crucifixion with the sufferings of countless virtuous human
beings which go uncommemorated:

> These nameless Christs' Good Fridays,
>   Whose virtues wrought their end,
> Bore days of bonds and burning,
>   With no man to their friend,
> Of mockeries, and spurning;
>   Yet they are all unpenned.
>   (*Poems*, iii. 175)

This is because, in spite of his agnosticism, Hardy cannot leave Christianity alone. He evidently agreed with Frederic Harrison's remark which is recorded, presumably with approval, in one of his notebooks: 'The evil legacy of Theology has been to bequeath to those who surrender Revelation a craving for Absolute objects of belief'.[4] Yet paradoxically he writes sometimes in a way expressing precisely such a 'nostalgie de l'Absolue'. In 'The Impercipient: At a Cathedral Service', the speaker regrets that he cannot be one of the 'bright believing band' taking part as he longs to: 'Why thus my soul should be consigned | To infelicity ... Abides a mystery' (*Poems*, i. 87–8). Similarly 'A Drizzling Easter Morning' begins by quoting from the service: 'And he is risen? Well be it so . . . ' It goes on to contrast the joy of Christians on Easter Day, devoted to commemorating Christ's Resurrection with the dreariness and pain of toilers in the world who 'ache' 'For endless rest—though risen is he' (*Poems*, ii. 437). This is a violent reversal of the orthodox Christian view that the Crucifixion symbolizes a divine sharing in humanity's suffering.

Aside from this residual nostalgia many poems, as well as novels, revert to the question of what brings about the random and unjust cruelty that human beings endure. To this Hardy, as he always insists, has no conclusive answer. Instead, he offers a series of what he calls in his Preface to *Late Lyrics and Earlier* (1922) 'obstinate questionings' and 'blank misgivings' (*Poems*, ii. 318). He is well aware of his own lack of what he calls pointless mathematical consistency in his accounts of what makes life as it is. In the 1892 Preface to *Tess* he writes 'Let me repeat that a novel is an impression not an argument'. He is a 'mere tale-teller, who writes down how the things of the world strike him'. Even more explicitly he says of *Jude* in the Preface to the first edition:

Like former productions of this pen, *Jude the Obscure* is simply an endeavour to give shape and coherence to a series of seemings, or personal impressions, the question of their consistency or their discordance, of their permanence or their transitoriness, being regarded as not of the first moment. (pp. xxxv–xxxvi)

His approach is increasingly exploratory and, as these comments indicate, he recognizes that even in a single novel he is adopting more than one stance. The novels in question reveal a variety of responses to what for him is the central question of life's injustice. He tries them out for a time like someone swept by fluctuating moods.

In verse the approach may or may not be consistent within a single poem but there are several poems which focus on one way of raising the question of life's injustice. Hardy cannot leave God alone any more than he can leave Christianity alone. Following Milton, he stages arguments with God in 'Doom and She' (*Poems*, i. 152), 'A Plaint to Man' (*Poems*, ii. 332), 'Nature's Questioning' (*Poems*, i. 86), 'A Dream Question' (*Poems*, i. 316), 'The Absolute Explains' (*Poems*, iii. 68), and 'A Philosophical Fantasy' (*Poems*, iii. 234). Each addresses the same issue: if there is a God, why is he malign? This is perhaps another way of approaching that ambiguous word 'destiny' in Hardy's novels. Such a reading is suggested by equations of God with 'crass casualty', a 'blind doomster', or a 'vast imbecility'. But these pejoratives are not offered as definitive. The poems explore a variety of alternatives. In 'By the Earth's Corpse' the creating force explains that it was unaware that Time would devastate its creation, turning it to pain and misery. Now 'That I made earth, and life, and man | It still repenteth me!', God explains, that 'my too oft unconscious hand | Let enter undesigned' the destruction of the earth and those in it (*Poems*, i. 161–2).

This question of intention is raised again by the debater in the argument with God of 'A Philosophical Fantasy':

> 'Tis this *unfulfilled intention*,
> O Causer, I would mention:—
> Will you, in condescension
> This evening, ere we've parted,
> Say why you felt fainthearted,
> And let your aim be thwarted,
> Its glory be diminished,
> Its concept stand unfinished?
> (*Poems*, iii. 235)

He or It, as the debater has now been given permission to call him, adds 'I've no sense of ever | Or of ethical endeavour, | Or of justice to Earth's creatures, | Or how Right from Wrong to sever' (iii. 237). It claims its creation was the result of 'purposeless propension'.

In 'Doom and She' It claims to be without the capacity to feel emotion and therefore unable to understand humanity's troublesome questions: 'But since nor joy nor pain | It lies in me to recognize, |

Thy questionings are in vain' (*Poems*, i. 153). All these theories indicate an It with power but less than human capacities. This is made even more obvious in 'Fragment' where the dead in a catacomb or burial chamber tell how they are waiting for 'one called God', though by some called 'the Will or Force, or Laws', to realize how badly things have gone on earth. Ironically they add:

> By some still close-cowled mystery
> We have reached feeling faster than he.
> But he will overtake us anon,
>   If the world goes on.
>   (*Poems*, ii. 261)

So a malign force is represented as possibly without purpose, not in control of its own creation, incapable of feeling, and in too primitive a state to know of what is happening on earth. Instead of the all-powerful destiny of Greek tragedy, there is a vision of a dinosaur-like power: strong but defective. The philosophical ideas that Hardy uses relate to this blundering power. He uses them just as he uses the Bible and Aeschylus to embody alternative views of existence. Biblical, literary, and philosophical texts are all part of the same medium for him. He deploys them as Eliot deploys such material in 'The Waste Land'. In this respect philosophical writing deserves the same treatment as any other text. Uses of it are part of the web of allusion that permeates Hardy's writing and is used to create imaginative power. Using allusion in this way also allows Hardy to remain at arm's length from the view he is propounding. All allusions are theoretically preceded by 'as the Bible/Aeschylus/Novalis/ Schopenhauer might put it'.

Schopenhauer's views were black in the extreme. He was a nihilist who gave a name to what was for Hardy a force without a name. For Schopenhauer this was the Will or the Immanent Will. The Will constitutes the Ultimate reality which is not free and has no purpose. It is all-consuming, pointless, and negative. It is expressions of this last idea that Hardy recorded in a notebook from the translation of Schopenhauer that he used: 'Every state of welfare, every feeling of satisfaction, is negative in its character . . . [and] consists in freedom from pain'; and 'Life presents itself chiefly as a task'.[5] Individuals are not free and individuality is a delusion. All work under the compulsions of the Will. The only peace for humanity lies in acquiescence and death. This does not mean suicide which is an attempt to assert one's own delusory will.

Hardy had by the 1890s done a fair amount of reading in Schopenhauer's work in all its blackness. When writing *Tess* and *Jude* he used some of these ideas. Mary Ann Kelly, in a much-cited chapter 'Schopenhauer's Influence on Hardy's *Jude the Obscure*',[6] attempts to detail Hardy's use of the philosopher's ideas in *Jude*. The main ones she distinguishes are: the recognition that individuality and personal ambition are illusions; the claim that the Will is a sleepwalker or somnambulist; that human actions are not freely chosen but compulsions determined by the will; the conclusion that as a result of all this, death is the ultimate form of acquiescence in the Will. A yearning for death is therefore natural.

Certainly the language of *Jude* fits this account. The aspirations of Jude to become a student at Christminster are based on illusions. Some of these are visual: his first view of what he believes to be Christminster may be only the city 'miraged in the peculiar atmosphere' (part 1, chapter 3) which he sees with the eye of faith. He hears and accepts unreliable accounts from vague witnesses. His last view before setting out leaves him only sure that the city had seemed to be there. Once there, he peoples it with imaginary figures of great men who once studied there. He believes it to be intellectually 'a city of light', rich in scholarship and religion. After his rejection by the colleges, he learns that his city of light is an impregnable fortress and his own ambition is social, not intellectual and religious, 'mundane ambition masquerading in a surplice'. Like Tess after her return to Alec, he too after the loss of Sue sinks into passivity and abandons his individual will. The regression of Sue after the children's death is said by the narrator to show that 'the First Cause worked automatically like a somnambulist and not reflectively like a sage' (part 6, chapter 3). Jude, having abandoned will and individuality, succumbs to a protracted acquiescence in death.

Schopenhauer's ideas colour *Jude* but not in the form of dogma nor in their entirety and they co-exist with the idea of humanity as sometimes profoundly significant as well as with the Greek idea of destiny under which human beings are helpless but may be heroic. All contribute, along with a residue left from Christianity, to a continual search for some permanent view of life as it is. Instead, Hardy produces a volatile and shifting vision unified only by vehemence.

CHAPTER 8

HARDY RECONTEXTUALIZED

BY the twentieth century a Hardy myth flourished which film-makers confronted when in the 1910s they decided to base films on his work. By that time Hardy (now graced with the Order of Merit and critical acclaim) was lionized as the grand old man of literature, a truly 'great' writer. The adulation manifested itself in the pilgrimage of the Prince of Wales as one more admiring visitor to Max Gate, as well as in the consort of famous writers who carried Hardy's coffin (minus his heart) into Westminster Abbey in 1928. Hardy by now was popularly constructed as the poet of the distinctively English landscape of Wessex and, as a great writer, necessarily the recorder of timeless truths about human nature, giving his works relevance to all periods. When his narratives were bleak they were seen to be major tragedies set against a timeless backdrop, rather like King Lear on the blasted heath.

This construction of a simplified as well as a timeless Hardy was already emerging towards the end of his career as a novelist. One contemporary critic wrote: 'As long as he can find passions to paint and characters to draw and dramas to unfold as profoundly moving as he continues to find in Wessex, we have no desire to see him go elsewhere in search of subjects.'[1]

Meantime, back in the real world, 'Wessex' began to take on a reality that confirmed and enhanced the tradition of Hardy as poet and tragedian of the mythical place. He himself soon recognized the value of 'Wessex' as a logo and wrote to his publisher accordingly:

Could you, whenever advertising my books, use the words 'Wessex novels', at the head of the list? I mean, instead of 'By T.H.', 'T.H.'s Wessex novels' or something of that sort? I find that the name *Wessex*, wh. I was the first to use in fiction, is getting to be taken up everywhere: & it would be a pity for us to lose the right to it for want of asserting it. It might also be used on the paper covers of the novels. (*Letters*, i. 171)

In 1895 he called the first collected edition of his novels the 'Wessex

Novels' and the more luxurious 1912–13 collected edition the 'Wessex Edition'. By now Wessex was his property. Like some explorer planting the Union flag on newly discovered territory, Hardy himself provided a map in 1895 for 'The Wessex of the Novels', distinguishing real and fictitious names by different markings. But in spite of his collusion with the now fairly lucrative symbol of Wessex, he wrote on his map a careful disclaimer: 'It is to be understood that this is an imaginative Wessex only, & that the places described under the names here given are not portraits of any real places, but visionary places which may approximate to the real places more or less' (*Biography*, p. 250).

But by now Wessex was unstoppable and the industry it had created flourished. In 1901 began a series of guide books to the 'real' Wessex with B. C. A. Windle's *The Wessex of Thomas Hardy*. This was followed by the work of a professional topographer, C. G. Harper's book *The Hardy Country* (1904) and Hermann Lea's *Handbook to the Wessex Country of Thomas Hardy's Novels and Poems* (1904). The blurring of the nature of Wessex continued well into the twentieth century. In 1948 Clive Holland writes in *Thomas Hardy's Wessex Scene*, 'As I write it is spring in Wessex'.[2] He goes on to tell how Dorset has become a place of pilgrimages for Wessex worshippers from around the world. Artists too joined in vigorously and produced pictures of scenes and places from the novels or illustrations for postcards. At the end of the twentieth century and later, tours are still advertised in the *Thomas Hardy Journal* which offer visits to 'the birthplace' and Max Gate as well as 'a wide range of alternative accommodation throughout Wessex'. Ironically, in the 1990s yet more substance was given to the region by the royal creation of one of the Queen's sons and his wife as the Earl and Countess of that mythical region.

This persistent cult of Wessex combined with the old insistence on Hardy as 'a pundit of the human heart' and his legacy as a profound revealer of human nature which offset his unfortunate gloom and pessimism. Nearly halfway through the twentieth century, William Rutland summarizes the prevailing view that Hardy's 'instinctive' knowledge that 'the thoughts and emotions of the human heart were to that heart itself the most important and possibly the only real things in that universe'. Rutland expands in familiar terms which stress the unchanging nature of these truths, independent of any context, with Wessex itself no more than stage scenery:

In this, also, is to be found the central theme of all his greatest writings. By whatever names they are called, two elements are always present in his art; and in the dramatic and emotional juxtaposition of them lies its essence. One of these elements is the human heart. The other is the unchanging, impassive and indifferent surroundings in which that heart finds itself.[3]

During this period of adulation and myth-making in the early twentieth century, the search for such 'greatness' in writers was the focus of academic criticism. The critics' aim was to distinguish good from bad, great from inferior, by their personal standards. Novels, plays, and poems were seen as aesthetically pleasing or displeasing artefacts, comparable with statues, paintings. They were supposed to be as free of their backgrounds, as (in the title of one critical work) 'The Well-wrought Urn'. The role of the critic was assumed to be that of an art expert authenticating a painting as genuine (or not), deciding on its aesthetic quality and informing non-experts how to appreciate it. The natural result of this was to suggest hierarchies of artistic merit. The constant practice of ranking in this way naturalized the process—made it seem the natural thing for a critic to do.

The taste of one critic might be questioned by another. Some critics believed that *Far from the Madding Crowd* epitomized Hardy's best work; others were convinced that late works like *Tess* and *Jude* were supreme. In such discussions of Hardy, supporters of the early novels saw the coincidences in the later narratives as flaws and weaknesses. The opposing view was that these novels, by the use of such devices, said something significant about fate. Seeing these things as flaws or merits were two sides of the same coin. Both descriptions strengthened the practice of ranking: of awarding plus or minus points as though the writer were a candidate in a competitive examination. The practice of ranking led to what came later to be called 'the canon', a term used earlier for the authentic books of the Bible but now sometimes used derisively. The word was applied for instance to F. R. Leavis's account in *The Great Tradition* (1948) of the 'great' novelists in English literature. He named these unhesitatingly as Jane Austen, George Eliot, Henry James, and Joseph Conrad. Thackeray was excluded because he 'has nothing (apart from some social history) to offer the reader'.[4] Hardy too is rejected, though no social history is discerned in his works: 'On Hardy (who owes enormously to George Eliot) the appropriately sympathetic note is struck by Henry James: "The good little Thomas Hardy has scored a great success with *Tess of the d'Urbervilles*, which is chock-full of faults and falsity, and yet has a singular charm".'[5]

Such an approach among academic critics gave way in the course of the mid- to late twentieth century to a variety of new and disparate approaches which generated many interpretations. Though these may sometimes seem contradictory, they share a common basis in two ways. First, all require a critic presenting a reading of a text to provide a rationale for their approach and not to pluck 'standards' out of the air as Leavis does. Secondly, the rationale itself must take account of the fact established by linguists in the period from 1900 to 1920 that language, wherever it was used, was already necessarily charged with values, assumptions, and ideas belonging to the society that used it. Recognizing that language is not a transparent but a highly complex medium meant accepting that this applied to all kinds of writing. Hence literature was seen to be on a par in this respect with scientific, historical, or other kinds of writing. Gillian Beer's work on Darwin's language in *The Origin of Species*, for instance, makes clear that he too grappled with a medium which made it difficult to describe a blind process of evolution without implying an intending agent (or God). Since the values encoded in language were social, political, and religious, the fact has relevance to Hardy's preoccupations with social class and with the nature and position of women. These issues matched the interests of twentieth-century Marxist and feminist critics whose readings focused on them to produce many of the late-twentieth-century political and gender-based readings of Hardy's novels, since, as has been shown, issues of class, gender, and race are written into his texts. It is to this group of context-oriented reading that interpretations in earlier chapters above belong.

At the time when Hardy wrote, some reviewers had also registered the fact that he challenged contemporary views about social class, gender, and religion in a way that was subversive of their society. Some few approved but most regarded the treatment of these subjects as unsavoury defects in his novels. This began with his first published novel *Desperate Remedies*, with its story of a middle-class and wealthy woman who has had an illegitimate child in her youth and yet managed to sustain the illusion of respectability. Worse still, by the time of his late novels he had idealized a girl who allowed herself to be seduced or at least only half-raped and who then committed murder. Finally, he wrote a work attacking those central pillars of the state—the Church and the universities. Consequently he revealed himself as someone bent on destroying the very fabric of society. Reviewers of this kind castigated his works in damning reviews, treating them as not only discreditable to the author but as the literary and intellectual equivalent of bomb-throwing.

The argument by contemporaries used against some features of Hardy's work is usually that they distort reality—they are untrue to the facts. One critic wrote of *Tess* in 1892: 'it is very difficult to read, because in almost every page the mind rebels against the steady assumptions of the author, and shrinks form the untrue picture of a universe so blank and godless'.[6] Another contemporary wrote of *Jude*, as Edmund Blunden reports, 'When a doctor in the story was made to say that child murderers and suicides were becoming common, owing to "the universal wish not to live" it was "too much . . . We all knew perfectly well that baby Schopenhauers are not coming into the world in shoals"'.[7] The case was even made by A. J. Butler, writing of *Jude* in 1896, that its perversely dangerous nature is the product of a writer who disregards the truth when he sees it:

But when a man possessing Mr. Hardy's power of observation and knowledge of human nature, conscious as he must be that upon the validity of the axiom, the authority of the formula, the whole fabric of society depends, when such a man gets caught by the fashion of the period, he turns upon society as if it were the creator of axiom and formula instead of, in a sense, their creature, and rates it.

These critics assume, as Butler puts it, 'Fiction has no more to do with "problems" than *Paradise Lost* has to do with demonstrations'.[8] Their hostility is the measure of reviewers' accurate recognition of the attack in Hardy's late novels on contemporary society and its institutions, including the universities and the established Church and legal system. These issues were rendered invisible, as time elapsed, by the Hardy myth already described, as well as by the social and cultural changes which foregrounded other issues and debates. What this chapter will show is that, though many films repeat and confirm visually the myth of a strictly dehistoricized Hardy, some later productions rediscover the lost first context in the light of their own contemporary concerns.

Hardy and Early Films

When film-makers decided to create films from Hardy's novels they were alert only to the myth that tradition had constructed and not to the social and cultural context from which he wrote. That was lost sight of. In addition they were handling a medium that required certain choices to be made which could radically affect the interpretation of the narratives. Significantly, some of the choices to be made (and to which others were added later) were the same as those which faced the first visual interpreters of the text—the illustrators of the serialized and censored versions of them. Often the artist, like the film-maker later, had had a free hand in choosing who and what to illustrate.

It seems to have been Hubert von Herkomer and three of his pupils, who provided the illustrations for the *Graphic* version of *Tess*, who also chose the scenes to be drawn. This was the heavily censored serial in which the rape/seduction was replaced by a mock marriage which Angel later fears might be legal. Yet unexpectedly the artist chose to depict and so to highlight several scenes of violence and scenes implying sexual desire. They include the death of the horse Prince, pierced by a shaft; Tess with the pheasants severely wounded by the hunters; Alec forcing the strawberry between Tess's lips; and the scene between her and Angel in the overgrown garden; and Angel passionately embracing Tess while she is milking.[9]

When, as in the rare case of *The Return of the Native*, Hardy briefed the illustrator, Arthur Hopkins, he focused on physical details of appearance and more particularly on the question of what to select for illustration. He gives a precise account of 'The order of importance of the characters': '1 Clym Yeobright 2 Eustacia 3 Thomasin & the reddleman 4 Wildeve 5 Mrs Yeobright' (*Letters*, i. 53). This is a warning to Hopkins not to give too many drawings of a character other than Clym. As Hardy sees it, this would alter the meaning of his text, since visual prominence was naturally equatable with narrative significance. Ironically, over a century later it was precisely this charge that some critics in 1994 levelled at the film of this same novel, directed by Jack Gold. His *The Return of the Native* gave visual emphasis to the actress Catherine Zeta Jones whose centrality was figured by the camera's lingering luxuriously on her face and form. The effect of such selection by early directors was compounded by the fact that their films were of short duration, lasting minutes rather than hours. Since they were also silent, the camera alone supplied orientation.

The new medium provided the visual equivalent of the literary context described in Chapter 3 and it too involved particular choices to be made. The first of these depends on the fact that in a novel the problem is what to put in and in a film what to leave out. With Hardy films both choices have usually to be made: cuts to abbreviate and insertions to clarify things Hardy chooses to pass over. In *Tess*, for instance, he is carefully reticent: about the details of the letter which Tess writes to Angel before their wedding and which he does not find; and about exactly what words she uses when confessing on their wedding night to her affair with Alec. The captions of silent films scarcely allowed details of either of these. But a later version, LWT's 1998 *Tess*, spells out both of them in detail presumably thought to be necessary and so gave Tess a voice she lacks in the original. Sometimes cuts to abbreviate are somewhat hamfisted. In a projected (1950) film of *The Mayor of Casterbridge* the film-maker, Thorold Dickinson, decided to cut out Elizabeth-Jane's mother, Susan Henchard. This was because he thought her to have very little function in the plot and saw her as 'a pale, pathetic, dull figure who lingers too long in the text'. Consequently he arbitrarily decided to transfer her role to a newly invented character, Mayor Henchard's housekeeper, Mrs Trimlett, whose partly comic role 'came more and more into the foreground as our work progressed' (*Sight and Sound*, January 1951, 364).

With the introduction of talking pictures in 1928, a special problem offered a third choice to be made: how to handle the narrator's commentary on characters, events, and issues. Descriptions of place are readily translated into a visual medium but much else cannot be. A simple solution is to add a voice-over which comments; one Hardy-based film of *Tess* does so with unfortunate results which will be discussed later. There is also a fourth decision to be made in translating novels from an earlier period into film. Hardy's texts, when he wrote them, related to a vaguely recent past with appropriate references to contemporary matters such as divorce law or types of tenancy. Already by the early twentieth century the recent past of the novels was now distant. If issues handled were thought to have contemporary relevance to a film-maker's own time, then the question of updating arose. Presumably for this reason a silent version of *Tess* made by Marshall Neilan in 1924 went in for a crude modernizing. According to the *New York Times* it was 'brought up to date with modern telephones and automobiles and the fashions of both sexes' (*Literature/Film Quarterly*, 9/2, 1981). These were technical considerations necessarily brought to bear on the process of adapting Hardy's novels for the large and small screen. In brief, those who decided in the early twentieth century to make films of Hardy's novels faced a preconceived account of 'Hardy of Wessex' and these delicate choices to be made. They created visual versions of his narratives with the reverence and thought due to a man now treated as the greatest living writer.

Hardy's attitude to films, however, was irreverently commercial, unlike his contemporary Tolstoy (1828–1910). The latter took a more serious view of the effect of this new medium on literature: 'this little clicking contraption with the revolving handle will make a revolution in our life—in the life of writers . . . We shall have to adapt ourselves to the shadowy screen and to the cold machine'.[10] By contrast Hardy is quite ready to let his publishers negotiate freely for film rights, apparently with no anxiety about his work being mangled. He tells them hard-headedly in 1911 that his chief interest is in whether films 'would affect the book-sales' (*Letters*, iv. 143). In 1915 he acquiesces without prohibition in the transference of the film rights of *Far from the Madding Crowd* from Siegfried, the son of the illustrator of *Tess*, Hubert von Herkomer (*Letters*, v. 103). And in the same year he makes his feeling explicit to his publishers about 'the moving picture-rights' of some of his novels in the United States: 'Of course if anything is to be made out of such exhibitions it is just as well to make it in these hard times: & please (if anything comes of it) charge whatever percentage on results that you think proportionate' (*Letters*, v. 83). As a result of these negotiations and others by Macmillan, two versions of *Far from the Madding Crowd* were made in America, in 1909 and 1911, as well as one in England in 1915 directed by Larry Trimble. Two adaptations of *Tess* also appeared in 1913 and 1924, while a film of *The Mayor of Casterbridge* was shot in Dorset in 1921.

Hardy himself actually saw the last of these films being shot and wrote gleefully to Florence Henniker: 'The film-makers are here doing scenes for the Mayor of C. & they asked us to come & see the process. The result is that I have been talking to The Mayor, Mrs Henchard, Eliz. Jane, & the rest, in the flesh' (*Letters*, vi. 93). Earlier in 1913 he had been pressed to attend the current film of *Tess*, then showing at a cinema in Leicester Square. He describes it as a 'rehearsal or review of *Tess* in film pictures' and makes only a guarded comment: 'It was a curious production, & I was interested in it as a scientific toy; but I can say nothing as to its relation to, or rendering of, the story' (*Letters*, iv. 312).

The terms used by Hardy when referring to these films are significant of how he and others regarded them: as a natural progression from graphic illustration. The phrase 'a rehearsal or review . . . in film pictures' reflects the brevity of such a film which might well be described as a selection of scenes from *Tess*. The British Film Institute's *Silent Shakespeare* video reveals the early Shakespeare films to be a sequence of striking scenes from the plays. The absence of dialogue reduced the narrative to a few interposed captions still further predisposing the reviewer to see the film as the kind of 'in the flesh' materialization that Hardy saw being produced in Dorchester.

The reviews of these early films used the same kind of language as Hardy. After seeing the American version of *Tess* made by the Famous Players Film Company, which Hardy saw, a reviewer in the *Bioscope* writes:

We have always held that the cinematograph has one of its finest opportunities in the visualization of novels. The novel as an art form is nearer, perhaps, than anything to the picture-play, and the latter is often seen in one of its happiest aspects when materializing the former in a series of living illustrations. (13 Oct. 1913, p. 391)

The wording of the passage captures well the sense of a series of scenes loosely linked by verbal captions such as silent films offered. The captions give only the barest account of narrative connections: it is the materializing into what looks like reality which is seen as the point. The films are evidently captivating in that they link photographic realism to imagined people and events: a technique anticipated by photographers like Julia Margaret Cameron who delighted in dressing her sitters as mythical or heroic figures.

Even this simplified reaction involves a recognition of the two traditional features to which the 'picture play' must be faithful: Wessex and human tragedy. Of the two, the former is given more attention by far in the *Bioscope* review itself, presumably reflecting its importance in the film. It is simply identified with Dorset and used interchangeably with that term:

One's natural regret that the various scenes have not been played in Dorsetshire amidst the original surroundings of which Hardy's wonderful (and frequently minute) descriptions have become famous, is lessened by the extraordinary skill with which the Wessex countryside has been matched by the producer. (p. 391)

Apart from one or two references to Tess as 'one of the greatest tragic figures in literature', full of 'tenderness and poignant beauty', the whole piece of some 1,000 words is devoted to visual effects and to Wessex.

The same emphasis appears in the review of an early film based on *Far from the Madding Crowd*:

In all Mr. Hardy's stories, the topographical interest is paramount. The countryside of North, South, Upper, Lower, Outer and Mid Wessex . . . is something more than a mere stage for his characters to enact their dramas upon. In every case, it is at least as important a part of the story as the human protagonists. (*Bioscope*, 15 Nov. 1915)

The reviewer objects to the lack of fidelity to the detail of Dorset, even though he knows that Hardy described Wessex as a 'partly real, partly dream country'. Many landmarks, he says, have disappeared but 'On the other hand, several of them still exist, including, surely, the Dorchester Corn Exchange'. As a result 'the essential atmosphere' of the novel 'that makes it a great work' is lacking. The filmmaker has provided 'a few fairly typical Dorset landscapes and numerous pastoral scenes' but he has failed to strike 'the distinctive note of Hardy's mid-Victorian Wessex'. Even the costumes are not exact but 'a compromise'.

The dramas enacted upon this setting are dismissed in a few clichéd lines as 'an entertainment leaving little to be desired':

The buffetings by Fate of poor Bathsheba, the faithful love of stout Gabriel Oak, the heartless gallantries of the volatile Sergeant Troy, the ill-starred courtship of quick-passioned Farmer Boldwood and the tragic romance of ill-used Fanny—all these matters, cunningly interwoven, make up as excellent a plot as one could wish for. (*Bioscope*, 15 Nov. 1915, p. 954).

Later Film Versions of Hardy's Novels

The early films set a pattern which is followed by many later adaptations in its insistence on a dehistoricized Hardy, the tragedian of Wessex. After the coming of sound, the use of Hardy's novels as sources was at first sparing: the first 'talkie' was *Under the Greenwood Tree* in 1929, followed by a BBC version of *Tess* in 1952 and another one in 1960. Interest revived in the late 1960s with John Schlesinger's *Far from the Madding Crowd* (1967) in which Julie Christie played Bathsheba. Then in 1970 came a BBC *The Woodlanders*; in 1971 a BBC *Jude*; in 1978 a lengthy BBC adaptation of *The Mayor of Casterbridge* scripted by Dennis Potter; and in 1979 the more well-known *Tess* directed by Roman Polanski. But the real flood of Hardy films occurred in the 1990s: an American version of *The Return of the Native* with Catherine Zeta Jones as Eustacia (1994), a British *Jude* (1996); *The Woodlanders* (1997) directed by Phil Agland; LWT television *Tess* (1998); a Granada *Far from the Madding Crowd* (1998); and LWT *The Mayor of Casterbridge* (2000), and in the same year *The Claim*, also based on that novel. In the middle of all this *The Times* reported (14 May 1996) that 'Claudia Shaffer, who runs the rights department of Curtis Brown, the literary agents, said she had been inundated over the past few months with requests for Hardy's novels from film, theatre and dance companies. "They are selling like hot cakes. I am getting phone calls every day".' The account also reports curious ideas for such things as bouncing sheep in *Far from the Madding Crowd—the Musical*.

The earlier films of the silent period showed clearly that the decisions to be made about the deployment of the medium of film depend on what the adaptors see as the core meaning of a novel. In the silent films this was Wessex and its tragedies but film-makers from other cultures can perceive a very different essence. This is sharply illustrated by an Indian adaptation of *Tess* shot in Bombay in 1996 by the three Kapoor brothers and called *Prem Granth* ('Love Story'). They read the novel in the light of a Hindu culture based on a rigid caste system in which rape brings ineradicable dishonour to the victim. For them the episode in the Chase is unambiguously rape and constitutes the central event of the narrative around which meaning accrues. Hardy's class system is equated with the Hindu caste system. In this context Tess's place in society becomes that of the low-caste Kajri, and Angel Clare's that of the high-caste Brahmin, Somen, who falls in love across the social divide. Like Tess, Kajri becomes pregnant but in her case as the result of what is unarguably a brutal rape. When this happens and the baby dies, the high-caste priests refuse to carry out the last rights at the crematorium. Somen, like Angel, rejects Kajri without discovering how her pregnancy came about. It is the interplay of social and religious beliefs against a more western notion of romantic love that drives the story. When Somen discovers the truth about the rape, he overthrows convention by defending Kajri against the priests. Finally, the rapist is killed by Kajri and burnt by the authorities. The film retains in a bizarre form aspects of meaning central to Hardy's novel; criticism of a rigidly hierarchical society and of religion seen as a dead hand. It transforms them in terms of its own culture and amalgamates them with a view of women vastly different from Hardy's liberalism.

A similar process of recontextualizing in terms of a society far removed from Hardy's is found in the American film *The Claim* (2000). This is based on *The Mayor of Casterbridge* and earlier was called *The Mayor of Kingdom Come*, then *Kingdom Come*, and finally *The Claim*. The film critic, Philip French, once observed on the subject of transferring Hardy's novels from text to screen: 'Some years ago the film historian, Charles Barr, wrote that all good Westerns begin like Hardy novels by establishing their characters in a landscape. It may well be that the best way to film Hardy would be to turn the tales into Westerns' (*Observer*, 8 Feb. 1998). This is precisely what the makers of *The Claim* (directed by Michael Winterbottom) do. According to the producer, Andrew Eaton, they wished to make a film set in the 1849 Goldrush in 'the Wild West'. They looked for a story that would work in that context. The attraction of *The Mayor of Casterbridge*—in relation to a setting where conditions were primitive, greed was all-consuming, and sexual transactions frequently commercial—is the wife-selling episode. This both conforms to the mores of the time and place and has a symbolic significance. Henchard becomes an impoverished goldminer, Dillon, who

A twenty-first century version of *The Mayor of Casterbridge* (*The Claim*, 2000).

Jodhi May as Marty South in *The Woodlanders* (Phil Agland, 1997).

sells his wife and daughter at the outset in 1849 to another miner. The two women return later in 1867 at a time when Dillon has made a huge fortune. Elizabeth-Jane becomes Hope; her mother Elena; Farfrae Dalgleish is now a railroad constructor; and Lucetta is Lucia, a brothel-keeper and Dillon's mistress. The final title of the film plays on the meaning of a 'claim' as the legal ownership of a piece of ground in which to mine for gold and the emotional claim that his wife and daughter embarrassingly represent for Dillon. The social fabric of Casterbridge, with its economic dependency upon the weather for the harvest, is swept away and replaced by a very different community but one still dependent upon the land for gold-mining and the lucrative results of routing a railway through a particular area. The bones of the story are still there but their significance is transformed by the dynamics of the society in which they are found.

These two films are exceptions in that they discard Wessex and all it stands for as well as the customs and legalities which govern it. This entails radically different settings and behaviour from those in the novels. All the other films listed as based on Hardy's novels remain located in Wessex and offer a relative faithfulness to the time and place described in the texts. Even within these limits, however, they sometimes make references which are evidently particular to the date of filming and to a very limited context. Schlesinger's *Far from the Madding Crowd* was made in the mid-1960s. Peter Widdowson points out in his *Hardy in History* (1989) that 'despite its "period effects" the film looks modern'. He quotes a contemporary reviewer, Alexander Walker, who captures the impression given by the film of a '1960s pastoral' when he asks ironically 'What's a swinging 1967 girl doing in Hardy's Dorset . . . she sings radiantly, pays her tenants radiantly, even milks cows radiantly. But no amount of inner radiance can lift the curse of looking and sounding like a 1960s girl.'[11] Julie Christie, who plays Bathsheba Everdene, unwittingly confirms that this is the effect she tried to create of an exuberant 1960s free spirit, hippy, or flower-person: 'I see her as instinctive rather than intellectual, spirited but never petulant' (*ABC Film Review*, July-Oct. 1967). Paradoxically this is a film which strove for pictorial accuracy to the extent of hand-picking extras from among inhabitants of Dorset.

Similarly there are other films throughout the century which

A swinging sixties Bathsheba (Julie Christie) in *Far From the Madding Crowd* (John Schlesinger, 1967).

Sergeant Troy (Terence Stamp) at his most seductive in the same film.

point to a specific time of production. At least two film adaptations of Hardy's novels can be identified as of this type. The first is Thorold Dickinson's projected *The Mayor of Casterbridge* (1949–50). As has already been indicated, he allowed himself a free hand with the plot, though at the same time he looked for authenticity in the setting. Having disposed of Mrs Henchard early on and replaced her with a housekeeper, Mrs Trimlett, and a comic companion, Mr Bulge, he eliminates Henchard's bankruptcy and death. Dickinson feels that Hardy lays on the blows of fate too thickly and so adjusts Henchard's life to remedy this. Seeing Henchard as 'a rugged, impulsive character', he believes 'It is unthinkable that any but a robust Englishman should play it'. He also decides that Farfrae and Lucetta 'should provoke the comedy' and that 'everything that Henchard does should be done, too, with a sense of humour' (*Sight and Sound*, Jan. 1951, p. 371). Since it is difficult to see where the comedy lies in the text, these comments require an explanation. The answer to why a film-maker, having chosen a novel as dark as this, should then decide to liven it up lies in the date. This was 1950, the year before the Festival of Britain. Though the war had ended six years earlier, rationing and privation had continued until this time. The Festival was a government attempt to cheer up and energize the nation or 'To commemorate the centenary of the Great Exhibition and to offset the austerity of previous years' as a government statement put it. The government planned a national display 'illustrating the British contribution to civilization, past, present and future, in the arts, in science and in industrial design'. A theatre and a concert hall were built on the South Bank in London, together with a Skylon—a steel and aluminium needle 200 feet high, pointing skywards. Elsewhere in the country events and exhibitions were created to spread the effect. The Festival worked its celebratory magic as intended in a way the Millennium Dome dismally failed to do fifty years later. It encouraged both cheerfulness and nationalism, the two qualities with which Dickinson wished to endow his version of *The Mayor of Casterbridge* which was being planned at the same time as the Festival. How this might have worked had Dickinson produced his film is not clear but his plan is an obvious attempt to produce a commodity that would suit the mood of the moment.

Dickinson's planned film makes an interesting contrast to Dennis

Potter's script based on the same novel, written for the BBC serialization in 1978. The serial met with warm approval despite the fact that, unlike Dickinson's, Potter's script left no misery undisplayed. The reason would appear to be in part the result of the making and screening of the film at a time of rising inflation and severe industrial unrest culminating in 'the winter of discontent' at the end of the year. Famously at that time there were repeated and extended strikes and power cuts, rubbish lay uncollected in the streets and the dead were left unburied. The film carries Potter's hallmark gloom as well as Hardy's. It is shot almost entirely indoors in dark-panelled rooms with low lighting. Even Farfrae's successful party is a sedate affair, set not under canopied trees but indoors in a gloomy granary. In outdoor scenes, daylight and such colours as exist are tinged with grey. Potter even went so far as to borrow Jude's characteristic exclamation from the Book of Job for Henchard to murmur in his distress, 'Let the day perish wherein I was born'.

In these ways the film fitted the gloom and lack of hope which at the time afflicted the country which was suffering privations that had been more willingly endured in wartime. The *Daily Telegraph* critic (6 March 1978) confesses to having 'tears . . . streaming down my face' while watching it. He says that Potter rightly sees as its 'key phrase' 'the persistence of the unforeseen' and praises its realism. The *Daily Mail* (21 Jan. 1978) feels, understandably, given the social conditions prevailing, that the film is putting into words 'things we all feel, taken to an extreme'. Potter himself is quoted in the review as pointing to a contemporary application:

I think that's what makes Hardy very relevant . . . *Under our present tensions and traumas* we very rarely have the sense of the shape of our lives . . . There is very little of that sense that everything you do has significance and that something you have done has reverberations that go on and on and on . . . Hardy reminds us that the act of living is very much concerned with what you have been, what you are and what you will be and that you can't escape the consequences of it. (my emphasis)

What stands out here, and is perhaps an assumption behind Dickinson's plan, is the usual conviction that Hardy's standing as 'a great author' must mean that the core meanings of his novels are pertinent to all times and places. The film-makers see their role as revealing this relevance. Certainly that is how twenty years later Phil Agland regarded his film of *The Woodlanders* in which he rewrites Hardy's novel in modern terms. Agland had previously been known as a documentary film-maker whose reputation had been built on *Baka— the People of the Rainforest*. Whilst making this documentary Agland had lived for two years with a pygmy community in Cameroon, Central Africa. In a 'Production Story' (held by the British Film Institute), Agland describes how he came to make a film of *The Woodlanders*:

The way in which the pygmies embrace their environment is similar to the way woodland people did in rural England a century ago. The Victorian woodlanders were a very poor, close-knit group of people who worked with and fed off the land where they lived. Against this back-drop Hardy deals with compelling themes of human emotion. (p. 11)

The compelling themes for this late twentieth-century version turned out to be, as Agland sees it, 'love, the family, trust and the environment'. The two salient terms here are 'the family' and 'the environment'. The latter is not used in the neutral sense of 'habitat' familiar from Darwin. Instead, it has the newly developed meaning that has turned it into what some would describe as a buzz-word: meaning a harmonious natural world threatened by the destructiveness of an industrialized society and all its polluting works. This specifically modern meaning is now so familiar that it is taken for granted in the name of a government Department of the Environment. Agland's account of his film is reflected in reviews such as that of the *Independent* (13 Feb. 1998) which sees the film as 'a portrait of changing seasons, rural poverty encroached on by the new technology and changing social mores of the industrial age'. *The Times* (5 Feb. 1998) happily accepts this late twentieth-century view of Wessex:

There is another key character—the woodland itself—and the director Phil Agland treats the landscape with the close scrutiny you would expect from a renowned maker of TV documentaries about China and Africa's rainforests . . . to him, Hardy's Wessex was a similar enclosed community, threatened by the outside world.

Certainly Agland took pains to produce the effect of changing seasons by splitting the filming schedule into two periods: one in the spring and one in the autumn. He also shot the film in the New

Forest so that he was able to create the impression of an utterly remote community moving slowly along woodland tracks with barely a road in sight. As one critic puts it succinctly: 'The forest is the novel's overarching personality under whose rustling roof the characters get on with mucking up their lives' (*Independent Eye*, 6 Feb. 1998). Despite what the *Independent*'s critic says, there is no sign of new technology; the disruptive factor, as Agland himself says, is the outside world. This comes into conflict with the lives of those who are seen as living in harmony with nature—in particular Giles Winterborne and Marty South. The other cause of disruption is the control that Melbury exercises over his daughter or, as Agland calls it, 'the family'. Particularly since Margaret Thatcher announced that there is no such thing as society, the true/ideal/appropriate meaning of the word *family* has been in dispute. In this film the relationship between Grace and her father works to entirely negative ends, for this is the family as a kind of prison. In focusing on this issue, Agland allows himself a free hand to cut away what one critic calls 'dead wood'. Grace's stepmother is written out, leaving the father–daughter relationship the only family tie. Much of Hardy's precise social detail is omitted such as the death of Marty South's father and the effect of an unrenewed life-tenancy upon Giles's prospects since he merely overlooks the need to renew his tenancy.

In this surgery on the plot, the interest of Grace Melbury as a woman with unconventional reactions to her husband's adultery is lost. There is no longer a scene where she ironically allows her husband's two distraught mistresses to visit what they think is his sick-bed; there is no sudden surge of pity for them. The stress on her strange lack of sexual jealousy disappears. Instead Grace is shown as the site of a contest between her enduring love for Giles and the superficial social ambitions that her father fostered in her. As she gradually sloughs off these ambitions in the film, her accent changes to a more rustic one as an indication that she is returning to her roots. As a result of this shift in emphasis and the consequent simplification, the final sequence in which Fitzpiers slowly woos her back to him, leaving him in possession of a rich wife and a new life, is erased. Grace, now the country girl for ever, shakes off the outsider with absolute resolution. In this way, the film overrides the significance of the subject of the treatment endured by Grace and her reaction to it. Along with this loss goes the loss of the prediction that Grace's reconciliation with her unfaithful husband will lead to repetitions of his infidelity and her accommodation to them. She becomes a liberated woman of the nineties. A *Sunday Telegraph* (8 Feb. 1998) critic, however, sees the film as sticking 'faithfully to the events of the book, give or take a reconciliation or two'.

Perhaps the most well-known film based on a Hardy novel is Roman Polanski's *Tess*, filmed in 1979, which also assumes a timeless relevance. Polanski, who made the film in Europe while in flight from a court sentence for a sexual offence in the United States, dedicated it to his murdered pregnant wife, Sharon Tate. This history and his previous work led to an expectation of something shocking, probably in terms of explicit sex and violence. Some critics seem to have been disappointed by what did emerge when the film was released: 'if you are a Polanski fan in the tradition of *Chinatown* and *Rosemary's Baby* you might be lulled into a stupor by the wondrous—and wonderful—lack of violence and sex in *Tess*' (*Cineaste*, 1980–1, p. 37). The director was also noted for his attention to detail and in this instance the care was directed towards authenticity of visual and verbal detail. He too accepted the Wessex myth. The film was shot in rural France where a landscape could be found closer to nineteenth-century Dorset than the industrialized farming areas of Britain. Similarly, having chosen a young German actress, Nastassia Kinski, to play the part of Tess, Polanski sent her to England for four and a half months to be coached by an expert in the Dorset accent.

The success of this care is evidenced by some writers. One wrote 'The director has applied his usual painstaking attention to detail in recreating Hardy's Wessex' (*Screen International*, 24 Feb. 1979). An academic review by William V. Costanzo is even more emphatic (although he has reservations):

Capturing the visible realities of life is, of course, what films do very well. Photographically, *Tess* is an exceptionally beautiful film; it glows with brilliant 'optical effects'. The Chase scene is an imaginative study of moonlight, dark foliage, and forest mists. Flintcomb-Ash, that 'starve-acre place' where Tess is forced to seek employment after Angel's desertion, is a forbiddingly desolate terrain, frost-bitten and barren, where bent figures of peasants hack at row upon row of gristly turnips. (*Literature/Film Quarterly*, 9/2, 1981)

Hardy's chosen Tess: Gertrude Bugler in a 1924 dramatization.

Roman Polanski's Tess (Nastassia Kinski) in 1979.

But superficial fidelity to details of this kind is as far as Polanski goes. He harks back to the traditional interpretations of Hardy's novels in which Wessex is a backcloth to a universal tragedy. Wessex has lost its layers of history, including the richly ambiguous significance of Tess's d'Urberville blood and the passions suggested by the legend of the d'Urberville coach. Polanski in effect persists in dehistoricizing the novel, ignoring what academic critics had now been pointing out for decades about its relation to the Victorian social and cultural context. Consequently the lingering close-ups of Tess are not strongly offset by diminishing long-shots. For Polanski its core meaning is still the traditional one of the Hindu *Prem Granth*, that 'Tess is above all a great love story . . . a very romantic and topical love story'. He takes a twentieth-century male view of the episode in the Chase. When asked by an interviewer 'Was she raped or was she seduced? Was it consent or coercion?', he replies 'It's half and half. It happens by insistence, and by using physical strength in certain ways. But physical strength was almost inevitable in those days; it was part of Victorian courtship. Even on her wedding night a woman might be expected to resist' (*American Film*, Oct. 1979, p. 64). This appears to interpret the scene as seduction with an unavoidable element of violence, given that Tess is a virgin. Alec, the seducer, is shown as an amiable second string to Tess's romantic bow. In scenes following her first sexual encounter she is shown, fetchingly dressed, trying on an expensive-looking bonnet—a present from Alec. As critics noted, Alec d'Urberville is certainly seen as truly attached to Tess in the film. He is a rotter but a polite, generous, and likeable one. The romantic nature of his affair with Tess is indicated by a picture of the lovers in an idyllic boating scene with the two floating luxuriously on a lake or river. They present a scene reminiscent of an Impressionist painting. It is not until the episode at Sandbourne, immediately before the murder, that Alec is shown as a cynical and indifferent bully. In accordance with what is taken for an essentially romantic story, the murder, as in the text, is revealed by the blood which stains the ceiling of the room below the bedroom in which Alec dies.

In making cuts and changes to the text, Polanski too believes that he is stripping away Victorian redundancies to reach an essential meaning. The scene indicating that Tess is hanged—when Clare and Liza-Lu see the black flag flying—is omitted. Polanski claims that

'Even in Hardy the hanging is almost an epilogue. I don't think it's essential. The story is clear enough and sad enough without it. You know Tess is doomed.' He omits Alec's 'belated and improbable conversion to Christianity' on the grounds that it is 'so typically Victorian' (*American Film*, Oct. 1979, p. 64). He wishes to keep only the core that he has identified. The way in which he characterizes the universal applicability of the novel has an authentically twentieth-century and perhaps personal note:

She broke Victorian moral codes but she responded to natural law, to nature, her nature. That's what the whole book is about. The film is an accusation of the hypocrisy and injustice of that rigid society and by extension of any rigid and repressive society. (*American Film*, Oct. 1979, p. 66).

A decade passed after the Polanski film without any further adaptations of Hardy's novels for the screen. Then in the 1990s, as the millennium approached, and some thought because the arrival of the year 2000 was for the superstitious an ominous year, Hardy's darker novels (with all their sex and violence) were chosen for adaptation. The by now canonical *Tess* and *The Mayor of Casterbridge* appear in new versions. To these were added the first film version of *The Return of the Native* and *Jude* (which had had one previous serial version on television in 1971). One reviewer claims that in adaptations of 'classic novels' for the screen film-makers chose most readily those which had a woman's name in the title. Though this is not literally true of versions of Hardy novels, it does point to a new recognition of the centrality of women in his work which may have contributed to their selection for filming. The topic of gender, and in particular the status of women, has been a continuous preoccupation since the late 1960s and Hardy's concerns resonated with the contemporary debate. Consequently, as Hardy films appeared in the 1990s, a discussion on the subject of femininity and its nature was provoked in the reviews. A ready catalyst for this was the fact that a series of films based on Jane Austen's novels was now succeeded by a preoccupation with Hardy. *Jude*, with the contrasting figures of Arabella and Sue, concentrated the discussion. There were both traditionalists and feminists amongst the critics.

One pro-Austen writer in the *Daily Telegraph* (15 May 1996) insisted that 'The least authentic thing about them [Hardy's novels] is the heroines. There can be few famous novelists as uninterested in believable female character as was Hardy.' Though this reviewer, John Casey, claims to be discussing plausibility, he is in fact alluding to a traditional view of 'woman' or the feminine. This becomes clear when he condemns the coarseness of the fleshly Arabella as unfeminine and contrasts it with the 'realism' of Jane Austen's Emma Woodhouse who 'in the end determines to marry the one man who had the courage and authority to rebuke her. In its artfully reticent way the novel makes this an unforgettable picture of a woman surrendering fully to a man.' Ironically in his very condemnation of Hardy's women, Casey is recognizing that *Jude* anticipates a later twentieth-century approach to gender which he finds unpalatable. He dislikes it in the film and so calls it unrealistic— women are not like that. But he cannot deny its presence in Hardy's text and in Winterbottom's film.

On the other side of the debate were several reviewers who also saw the modern relevance of Hardy's treatment of gender and approved it. Naturally they too thought it realistic. As one writes in the *Evening Standard* (29 Dec. 1995), 'Hardy is also honest about sex'. He contrasts comments on women from Austen and Hardy and, in doing so, he quotes Bathsheba's strikingly untraditional comment 'It is hard for a woman to define her feelings in language which is chiefly made by men to express theirs'. Adam Mars-Jones in the *Independent* (3 Oct. 1996) writes of Winterbottom's *Jude*: 'It's tragic, raw and brutal. As it should be.' He praises particularly the scene where 'Sue offers herself sexually to Jude' after Arabella's reappearance. He sees its explicitness as a translation for his own time of what Hardy's treatment referred to in its own historical context:

Full frontal nakedness is not normally a requirement, or even a defensible option in adaptations of Victorian novels, but here it is emotionally convincing. Sue is defenceless more than desirous, and she trusts Jude in a way that is poignant for us because we know he is hardly expert in the business on which they are embarking. They live in a society where you can be a moral outcast and still a virtual stranger to your flesh.

Other critics such as Philip Goodhew, a film director, echo the ideas that Mars-Jones expresses. Goodhew regards the film as historically realistic in 'its stark brutality' (*Sight and Sound*, July 1997) and its treatment of women. For along with the rehistoricizing of gender issues in this version of *Jude* goes a reconstruction of Hardy's views on social and religious issues. As Mars-Jones points out in his *Independent* review, the film makes these clear: 'Jude and Sue are rejected by institutions, he by the university he would dearly love to join, she by a teacher-training school that likes pupils and teachers alike to ask no awkward questions.'

Of course, alongside this new recognition that Hardy's novels interlocked with contemporary issues, the traditional view of their content persisted. A text is commodified even further by the 1994 American *Return of the Native* in which the novel becomes merely a vehicle for a rising Hollywood star, Catherine Zeta Jones. The film is aimed at a mass public who are assumed to want a certain formula showing tragic love in an attractive rural setting. The Egdon Heath scenes were shot on Exmoor, which is very different in appearance from the location on which it was based. As Lucy Ellman wrote in the *Independent* (7 Jan. 1996), 'Hardy's Egdon Heath was obscenely wild, guilt-ridden and forlorn: this version, aimed at the tourist trade, made Exmoor seem wholly placid and picturesque'. Egdon Heath in the film is merely a scenic backdrop and the focus is on the *femme fatale*, Eustacia Vye.

This effect is captured in what is almost the only favourable British review with its headline 'Catherine returns as a woman of mystery' (*Daily Mail*, 16 Nov. 1994). The critic here describes Eustacia/Catherine as an 'alluring and mysterious woman . . . torn between love and her West Country roots'. This surprising description of Eustacia's attachment to her home is necessary to produce the sought-for triangle in which Clym Yeobright represents the West Country roots and Damon Wildeve equals tragic love. Zeta Jones's sexual allure is in fact the focus of the film and Eustacia's character lacks complexity. Hardy may have wished Clym to dominate but here the film becomes a vehicle for the actress. The general consensus of critical opinion was that the overall effect was to trivialize Hardy's novel. Reviewers compared it derisively to the radio soap opera, *The Archers*, which is set in a fictional rural area called Borsetshire, or they saw Yeobright as 'a classical clean-cut American hero' and Wildeve as 'a stock rep rake' (*Daily Mail*, 1 Jan. 1995).

Interestingly, similar criticism was launched against the 1998 *Tess* produced for LWT, even though it more obviously attempts to be faithful to Hardy's text. The film was cast in the familiar romantic and sentimental mode as a timeless account of the life of a tragic heroine. The *Sun* newspaper responded to it exactly as the director must have wished when their reviewer praised it as a genuine Wessex tragedy of a hopeless 'doomed love triangle'. The justification for seeing Alec as the third member of this triangle is found in the film itself. Crucially the episode in the Chase is presented as seduction not rape, for there are clear signs of Tess's positive response. The confirmation of this comes when, after her confession, Angel Clare asks Tess whether she found Alec attractive and whether he was entirely to blame. She agrees that she was attracted and denies that the blame was solely his. The 'love triangle' is given further prominence by the deletion of Clare's clerical family from the visual scene and with them the anti-religious sentiments of the narrator. So too are Tess's feelings of relief and the fact that in the novel she feels no guilt for the killing of Alec. Instead she is filled with dutifully feminine feelings of guilt and shame as she thinks of herself as a murderer.

The fatal mistake in this version, however, for most reviewers, and presumably other viewers, lies in the voice-over. The presence of a narrating voice is exceptional in Hardy films and this one is marked also by a West Country accent. Unfortunately the film-makers had not foreseen the effect of such a voice in a film on commercial television which was itself interspersed with advertisements using voice-overs. As one critic commented, 'One second Tess buries a breakfast knife in Alec's torso. The very next moment we are being advised of the virtues of Always Flexitowel' (*Independent on Sunday*, 15 March 1998). The immediate association was made with advertising commercials and, because of the accent, with one in particular. The West Country voice was identified in at least five newspapers and magazines with 'the man who sells Mr Kipling's cakes' (*Independent*, 10 March 1998). Only the *Sun* found Wessex as portrayed here idyllic; the rest identified the rural scenes with an advertising pastiche of country life. The *Guardian* (9 March 1998) referred ironically to 'idyllic sun-lit fields and exquisite colour co-ordinated costumes'. The *Sunday Telegraph* (15 March 1998) described how the use of the voice-over early in the film affected the way subsequent Wessex scenes were viewed:

Tess of the D'Urbervilles . . . opened with a narration that suggested Mr Hardy had handed over control to Mr Kipling—not Rudyard, but he of the exceedingly good cakes—before swelling into full-colour Hovis vision. So much use had been made of yellow camera-filters that at times the sky turned bright green.

The film was generally recognized as the commodity it was—designed to persuade viewers to buy into the traditional idea of the Wessex idyll. Paul Hoggart in *The Times* (28 March 1998) indicates the 'specularly gorgeous' visual effects which recall 'Corot paintings, or one of those English Victorians addicted to thatched cottages nestling in thickets of milk maids'. But he also points out that such effects result from the fact that 'Tess has become a national icon, like Heathcliff, a melodramatic archetype ... who has taken on a life independent of the original novel'. This view recognizes the dehistoricized nature of many Hardy films which have tended to see little beyond Tess or Henchard as interesting and heroic figures. Another recognition follows from this: that the historical context to which the novels strongly relate has been overlooked or discarded. Details to do with social class and religion are seen as peripheral enough to be disregarded; the plums in the pie are the heroes and the rest is thrown away.

By contrast, the *Guardian* critic, writing of this film of Tess (9 March 1998), complains of the lack of social history to be gleaned from it while the *New Statesman* (13 March 1998) draws attention to the alteration to the final narratorial comment now made by the Mr Kipling voice-over:

My only real question of Ted Whitehead is why, having taken so much dialogue from the book, he messed with the famous punchline. 'Justice was done, and the president of the Immortals, in Aeschylean phrase, had ended his sport with Tess' became 'Justice was done. Mankind in the honoured way had finished its sport with Tess'.

The significance removed by this change, as the reviewer perceives, is profound. The reference to the President of the Immortals is the last desperate resort of a narrator who has tried every other explanation of what happens to Tess. Now ironically he offers a translation of a line from Aeschylus' *Prometheus* which is a pointed alteration made by Hardy from an earlier version—'Time, the Arch-satirist'. The *New Statesman* reviewer describes the effect of the change in the film in terms which point out the modernity of such an alteration of the original: 'The change not only robbed a generation of viewers of familiarity with one of the bitterest cries of atheism in literature but turned Hardy into a woolly liberal bleating that we are all to blame.' Such criticism makes it clear that the ideas of late twentieth-century academic critics of the novels which reinstate their contexts as part of their significance has by now reached some film critics. It is all a far cry from Polanski in 1979 stripping away outdated Victorian values from 'his' beloved *Tess*.

NOTES

CHAPTER 1. The Life of Thomas Hardy

1. H. Orel (ed.), *Thomas Hardy's Personal Writings* (London: Macmillan, 1967), 220.
2. Ibid. 192.
3. Ibid. 194–5.
4. Ibid. 227.
5. H. L. Voss, 'Motoring with Thomas Hardy', in Monograph no. 7 (Beaminster: Toucan Press, 1963).
6. W. M. Parker, 'A Visit to Thomas Hardy', in Monograph no. 24 (Beaminster: Toucan Press, 1966).
7. F. A. Hedgcock, *Essai de Critique: Thomas Hardy, penseur et artiste* (Paris: Librairie Hachette, 1911), 6.
8. *Select Poems of William Barnes*, ed. Thomas Hardy (Oxford: Oxford University Press, 1908), pp. vii–viii.
9. M. Millgate, *Thomas Hardy: His Career as a Novelist* (London, Sydney, Toronto: Bodley Head, 1971), 401–2.
10. T. Hardy, 'Laws the Cause of Misery', *Nash's Magazine*, 6 (March 1912), 683.

CHAPTER 2. The Fabric of Society

1. H. L. Voss, 'Motoring with Thomas Hardy', in Monograph no. 7 (Beaminster: Toucan Press, 1963).
2. Quoted in J. M. Golby, *Culture and Society in Britain 1850–1890* (Oxford: Oxford University Press, 1988), 5.
3. D. Read, *England 1868–1914* (London and New York: Longman, 1979), 65.
4. Golby, *Culture and Society in Britain*, 287.
5. J. Burnett, *Plenty and Want: A Social History of Food in England from 1815 to the Present Day* (London: Routledge, 1989), 133–4.
6. Ibid. 147.
7. Ibid. 143.
8. Golby, *Culture and Society in Britain*, 41.
9. S. Smiles, *Self-Help* (1859; London: John Murray, 1906), 1.
10. *Memorials of Alfred Marshall*, ed. A. C. Pigou (London: Macmillan, 1925), 102.
11. Ibid. 102–3, 105–7.
12. F. B. Smith, *The Making of the Second Reform Bill* (Cambridge: Cambridge University Press, 1966), 86–7.
13. M. Arnold, *Culture and Anarchy*, ed. S. Lipman (New Haven and London: Yale University Press, 1994), 70.

14. H. G. Wells, *An Experiment in Autobiography* (New York: Macmillan & Co., 1934), 68.

15. J. P. C. Roach, 'Victorian Universities and the National Intelligentsia', *Victorian Studies*, 3 (1959), 131–50, at pp. 131, 147.

16. J. S. Mill, *Principles of Political Economy*, Books IV and V, ed. D. Winch (Harmondsworth: Penguin, 1985), 119.

17. *Oxford University Extension Gazette* (Oxford: Oxford University Press, 1893), 34.

18. *University Extension Congress Report* (Oxford: Oxford University Press, 1894), 56.

19. G. Romanes, 'Mental Differences between Men and Women', *Nineteenth Century*, 21 (1887), 654–72, at p. 656.

20. Quoted in E. K. Helsinger *et al.* (eds.), *The Woman Question*, 3 vols. (Manchester: Manchester University Press, 1983), ii. 138.

21. Quoted in D. Spender (ed.), *The Education Papers: Women's Quest for Equality in Britain 1850–1912* (New York and London: Routledge and Kegan Paul, 1987), 203.

22. Ibid. 236.

23. Ibid. 58–9.

24. Ibid. 62.

25. Quoted in M. Poovey, *Uneven Developments: The Ideological Work of Gender in Mid-Victorian England* (London: Virago Press, 1989), 173.

26. K. D. M. Snell, *Annals of the Labouring Poor: Social Change and Agrarian England 1660–1900* (Cambridge: Cambridge University Press, 1997), 63–4.

27. J. R. Walkowitz, *Prostitution and Victorian Society: Women, Class and the State* (Cambridge: Cambridge University Press, 1988), 15.

28. Ibid. 35.

29. A. H. Manchester, *A Modern Legal History of England and Wales 1750–1950* (London: Butterworths, 1980), 393.

30. Quoted ibid. 368–9.

31. J. Eeklaar and S. Katz, *The Resolution of Family Conflict* (Toronto: Butterworths, 1984), 42.

32. R. D. Altick, *The English Common Reader: A Social History of the Mass Reading Public 1800–1900* (Chicago and London: University of Chicago Press, 1957), 220.

33. F. Engels, *The Condition of the Working Class in England*, ed. V. Kiernan (Harmondsworth: Penguin, 1987), 151.

34. C. Lyell, *Principles of Geology*, ed. J. A. Secord (Harmondsworth: Penguin, 1997), p. xi.

35. Ibid. 437.

36. Ibid. 356.

37. C. Darwin, *The Origin of Species*, ed. G. Beer (Oxford and New York: Oxford University Press, 1996), 6.

38. Ibid. 396.

39. Ibid. 70.

40. G. Beer, *Darwin's Plots: Evolutionary Narrative in Darwin, George Eliot and Nineteenth Century Fiction* (London: Ark, 1983), 9.

41. Ibid. 10.

42. Quoted in D. R. Dean, ' "Through Science to Despair": Geology and the Victorians', in J. Paradis and T. Postlethwait (eds.), *Victorian Science and Victorian Values* (New Brunswick, NJ: Rutgers University Press, 1985), 111–36, at p. 123.

CHAPTER 3. The Literary Context

1. P. Dalziel and M. Millgate (eds.), *Thomas Hardy's Studies, Specimens &c. Notebook* (Oxford: Clarendon Press, 1994), pp. xv–xvi.

2. Ibid., p. xvi.

3. K. Flint, *The Woman Reader 1837–1914* (Oxford: Clarendon Press, 1993), 78.

4. G. A. Mantell, *The Wonders of Geology or a Fundamental Exposition of Geological Phenomena* (London: Relfe and Fletcher, 1838), 4.

5. Ibid. 6.

6. G. Beer, *Darwin's Plots: Evolutionary Narrative in Darwin, George Eliot and Nineteenth Century Fiction* (London: Ark, 1983), 53.

7. C. Darwin, *The Origin of Species*, ed. G. Beer (Oxford and New York: Oxford University Press, 1996), 69 (my emphases).

8. Ibid. 53.

9. Ibid. 396.

10. G. L. Griest, *Mudie's Circulating Library and the Victorian Novel* (Indiana: Indiana University Press, 1970), 86.

11. Quoted ibid. 71.

12. C. E. Mudie, 'Mr Mudie's Library', *Athenaeum*, 1716 (6 Oct. 1860), 451.

13. A. Trollope, 'On English Prose Fiction as a Rational Amusement' (1870), in *Four Lectures by Anthony Trollope*, ed. M. I. Parrish (London: Constable and Co. Ltd., 1938), 110.

14. E. K. Helsinger *et al.* (eds.), *The Woman Question*, 3 vols. (Manchester: Manchester University Press, 1983), ii. 25.

15. L. Stone, *The Road to Divorce: England 1530–1987* (Oxford and New York: Oxford University Press, 1992), 371.

16. Helsinger *et al.*, *The Woman Question*, ii. 163.

17. R. G. Cox (ed.), *Thomas Hardy: The Critical Heritage* (New York: Barnes and Noble, 1970), 1, 5.

18. *Desperate Remedies*, ed. M. Rimmer (Harmondsworth: Penguin, 1998), 451.

19. Cox (ed.), *Hardy: The Critical Heritage*, 11.

20. R. L. Purdy, *Thomas Hardy: A Bibliographical Study* (Oxford: Clarendon Press, 1968), 336.

21. Ibid. 16.

22. Ibid. 338.

23. Ibid. 27.

24. S. Gatrell, *Hardy the Creator: A Textual Biography* (Oxford: Clarendon Press, 1988), 36–7.
25. Purdy, *Thomas Hardy*, 32–3.
26. Ibid. 55–6.
27. T. Hardy, *Tess of the d'Urbervilles*, ed. J. Grindle and S. Gatrell (Oxford: Clarendon Press, 1983), 8–9.
28. Ibid. 3.
29. Helsinger *et al.*, *The Woman Question*, iii. 124.
30. Ibid. 131.
31. Ibid. 129.
32. V. Jones, *James the Critic* (London and Basingstoke: Macmillan, 1985), 110.
33. G. Moore, 'Literature at Nurse or Circulating Morals', ed. P. Coustillas (Hassocks: Harvester, 1976), 18–19.
34. *Thomas Hardy's Personal Writings*, ed. H. Orel (London: Macmillan, 1967), 127–8, 131–2.
35. Cox (ed.), *Hardy: The Critical Heritage*, 257.
36. *Thomas Hardy's Personal Writings*, 134.
37. Ibid. 135.
38. Ibid. 137.
39. *The Literary Notes of Thomas Hardy*, ed. L. A. Björk, 2 vols., Gothenburg Studies in English, 28 (Gothenburg: University of Gothenburg, 1974), ii. 144–5.
40. Ibid., ii. 16–17.
41. Cox (ed.), *Hardy: The Critical Heritage*, 11.
42. *Tess of the d'Urbervilles*, ed. Grindle and Gatrell, 7.
43. D. Kramer (ed.), *The Cambridge Companion to Thomas Hardy* (Cambridge: Cambridge University Press, 1999), 30.

CHAPTER 4. Social Issues: Class in Hardy's Novels

1. R. G. Cox (ed.), *Thomas Hardy: The Critical Heritage* (New York: Barnes and Noble, 1970), 30.
2. K. D. M. Snell, *Annals of the Labouring Poor: Social Change and Agrarian England 1660–1900* (Cambridge: Cambridge University Press, 1997), 399, 395.
3. *Thomas Hardy's Personal Writings*, ed. H. Orel (London: Macmillan, 1967), 46.
4. C. J. Weber, 'Chronology in Hardy's Novels', *PMLA* 53 (1838), 100.
5. M. Millgate, *Thomas Hardy: His Career as a Novelist* (London, Sydney, and Toronto: Bodley Head, 1971), 215.
6. Snell, *Annals of the Labouring Poor*, 395.
7. *Thomas Hardy's Personal Writings*, 91.
8. *Tess of the d'Urbervilles*, ed. J. Grindle and S. Gatrell (Oxford: Clarendon Press, 1983), 48.
9. S. Ledger, *The New Woman: Fiction and Feminism at the Fin de Siècle* (Manchester: Manchester University Press, 1997), 35.

10. E. Showalter, 'The Unmanning of the Mayor of Casterbridge', in D. Kramer (ed.), *Critical Approaches to the Fiction of Thomas Hardy* (London and Basingstoke: Macmillan, 1979), 102.
11. S. Smiles, *Self-Help* (1859; London: John Murray, 1906), 6–7.
12. Cox (ed.), *Hardy: The Critical Heritage*, 292, 298.

CHAPTER 5. Social Issues: Women and Society

1. 'George Egerton', *Keynotes*, ed. M. Vicinus (London: Virago, 1983), 22–3.
2. *Thomas Hardy's Personal Writings*, ed. H. Orel (London: Macmillan, 1967), 128.
3. E. L. Linton, 'The Wild Women as Social Insurgents', *Nineteenth Century*, 30 (1891), 596–605, at p. 596.
4. 'The Apple and the Ego of Woman', *Westminster Review*, 131 (1889), 374–82, at p. 382.
5. T. Hardy, *Tess of the d'Urbervilles*, ed. T. Dolin and M. Higonnet (Harmondsworth: Penguin, 1998), 409.
6. R. G. Cox (ed.), *Thomas Hardy: The Critical Heritage* (New York: Barnes and Noble, 1970), 189.
7. Ibid. 258.
8. Ibid. 251.
9. P. Boumelha, *Thomas Hardy and Women: Sexual Ideology and Narrative Form* (Brighton: Harvester Press, 1982), 143.

CHAPTER 6. Hardy and Science

1. C. Darwin, *The Origin of Species*, ed. G. Beer (Oxford and New York: Oxford University Press, 1996), 6.
2. Ibid. 13.
3. C. Darwin, *The Descent of Man, and Selections in Relation to Sex* (New York: Hurst and Co., 1874), 633.
4. G. A. Mantell, *The Wonders of Geology or a Fundamental Exposition of Geological Phenomena* (London: Relfe and Fletcher, 1838), 447–8.
5. *Origin of Species*, ed. Beer, p. xxi.
6. *Descent of Man*, 125.
7. R. G. Cox (ed.), *Thomas Hardy: The Critical Heritage* (New York: Barnes and Noble, 1970), 143–4.
8. *Descent of Man*, 242.
9. Ibid. 609.
10. *The Literary Notes of Thomas Hardy*, ed. L. A. Björk, 2 vols., Gothenburg Studies in English, 28 (Gothenburg: University of Gothenburg, 1974), ii. 122.
11. *Origin of Species*, ed. Beer, p. 342.
12. Cox (ed.), *Hardy: The Critical Heritage*, 218, 220.
13. G. Beer, *Darwin's Plots: Evolutionary Narrative in Darwin, George Eliot and Nineteenth Century Fiction* (London: Ark, 1983), 139.
14. *Origin of Species*, ed. Beer, p. 396.

15. *Descent of Man*, 643–4.
16. G. Beer, *Open Fields: Science in Cultural Encounter* (Oxford: Clarendon Press, 1996), 231.
17. C. Belsey, *Critical Practice* (London and New York: Methuen, 1980), 75.

CHAPTER 7. Religious Issues

1. *Jude the Obscure*, ed. P. Ingham (Oxford: Oxford University Press, 1985), 450.
2. *The Literary Notes of Thomas Hardy*, ed. L. A. Björk, 2 vols., Gothenburg Studies in English, 28 (Gothenburg: University of Gothenburg, 1974), ii. 416.
3. See G. Beer, *Darwin's Plots: Evolutionary Narrative in Darwin, George Eliot and Nineteenth Century Fiction* (London: Ark, 1983).
4. *Literary Notes of Thomas Hardy*, ii. 3.
5. Ibid. 28, 29.
6. In E. Von der Luft (ed.), *Schopenhauer: New Essays in Honour of his 200th Birthday*, Studies in German Thought and History, 10 (Lewiston, Queenston, and Lampeter: Edwin Mellen Press, 1988), 232–48.

CHAPTER 8. Hardy Recontextualized

1. R. G. Cox (ed.), *Thomas Hardy: The Critical Heritage* (New York: Barnes and Noble, 1970), 177.
2. (Dorchester: Longmans, 1948), 66.
3. W. R. Rutland, *Thomas Hardy* (London and Glasgow: Blackie and Son, 1938), 74–5.
4. F. R. Leavis, *The Great Tradition: George Eliot, Henry James, Joseph Conrad* (Harmondsworth: Penguin, 1948), 31.
5. Ibid. 33.
6. Cox (ed.), *Hardy: The Critical Heritage*, 194.
7. E. Blunden, *Thomas Hardy* (1942; repr. London, Melbourne, and Toronto: Macmillan, 1967), 88.
8. Cox (ed.), *Hardy: The Critical Heritage*, 288.
9. *Tess of the d'Urbervilles*, ed. T. Dolin and M. Higonnet (Harmondsworth: Penguin, 1998), 479.
10. D. Cartmell and I. Whelehan (eds.), *Adaptations: From Text to Screen, Screen to Text* (London and New York: Routledge, 1999), 5.
11. Quoted in P. Widdowson, *Hardy in History: A Study in Literary Sociology* (London and New York: Routledge, 1989), 109.

FURTHER READING

1. CONTEXTUAL MATERIAL

(a) Social Class

Cornfield, P. J. (ed.), *Language, History and Class* (Oxford: Basil Blackwell, 1991).

Joyce, P., *Visions of the People: Industrial England and the Question of Class 1848–1914* (Cambridge: Cambridge University Press, 1991).

Reader, W. J., *Professional Men: The Rise of the Professional Classes in Nineteenth-Century England* (London: Weidenfeld and Nicolson, 1966).

Thompson, F. M. L., *The Rise of Respectable Society: A Social History of Victorian Britain 1830–1900* (London: Fontana, 1988).

Vincent, D., *Literacy and Popular Culture: England 1750–1914* (Cambridge: Cambridge University Press, 1989).

(b) Gender and marriage

Caine, B., *English Feminism 1780–1980* (Oxford: Oxford University Press, 1997).

Hall, Lesley A., *Sex, Gender and Social Change in Britain since 1880* (Basingstoke: Macmillan, 2000).

Hammerton, A. J., *Cruelty and Companionship: Conflict in Nineteenth-Century Married Life* (London: Routledge, 1992).

Helsinger, E. K. *et al.*, *The Woman Question: Society and Literature in Britain and America, 1837–1883* (Manchester: Manchester University Press, 1983).

Lewis, J. (ed.), *Labour and Love: Women's Experience of Home and Family 1850–1940* (Oxford: Blackwell, 1986).

McHugh, P., *Prostitution and Victorian Social Reform* (London: Croom Helm, 1980).

Mason, M., *The Making of Victorian Sexual Attitudes* (Oxford: Oxford University Press, 1994).

Shanley, M. L., *Feminism, Marriage, and the Law in Victorian England, 1850–1895* (London: Tauris, 1989).

Small, H., *Love's Madness: Medicine, the Novel and Female Insanity 1800–1865* (Oxford: Clarendon Press, 1996).

Vicinus, M. (ed.), *A Widening Sphere* (Bloomington: Indiana University Press, 1975).

(c) Science

In addition to Gillian Beer's edition of Charles Darwin's *The Origin of Species* (Oxford, 1996); and J. A. Secord's edition of Charles Lyell's *Principles of Geology* (Penguin, 1997), the following secondary works are useful:

Bowler, P. J., *Evolution: The History of an Idea* (Berkeley, Los Angeles, and London: University of California Press, 1984).

Christie, J., and Shuttleworth, S. (eds.), *Nature Transfigured: Science and Literature, 1700–1900* (Manchester: Manchester University Press, 1989).

Jones, Greta, *Social Darwinism and English Thought: The Interaction between Biological and Social Theory* (Brighton: Harvester, 1980).

Levine, G., *Darwin and the Novelists: Patterns of Science in Victorian Fiction* (Cambridge, Mass., and London: Harvard University Press, 1988).

Morton, P., *The Vital Science: Biology and the Literary Imagination, 1860–1900* (London: Allen and Unwin, 1984).

Szreter, S., *Fertility, Class and Gender in Britain, 1860–1940* (Cambridge: Cambridge University Press, 1996).

Wickens, G. G., 'Literature and Science: Hardy's Response to Mill, Huxley and Darwin', *Mosaic*, 14/3 (1981), 63–79.

2. CRITICISM

(a) Articles or chapters on individual Hardy novels or specific areas

Ball, D., 'Tragic Contradiction in Hardy's *The Woodlanders*', *Ariel*, 18 (1987), 17–25.

Barloon, J., 'Star Crossed Love: The Gravity of Science in Hardy's *Two on a Tower*', *Victorian Newsletter*, 94 (Fall 1998), 27–32.

Beech, M., 'Thomas Hardy: Far From the Royal Observatory', *Thomas Hardy Journal*, 8/2 (May 1992), 74–78.

Boumelha, P., 'A Complicated Position for a Woman: *The Hand of Ethelberta*', in M. R. Higonnet (ed.), *A Sense of Sex* (Urbana: University of Illinois Press, 1993), 242–59.

Bullen, J. B., 'Hardy's *The Well-Beloved*, Sex, and Theories of Germ Plasm', in P. V. Mallett and R. P. Draper (eds.), *A Spacious Vision: Essays on Hardy* (Newmill, Cornwall: Patten Press, 1994), 77–89.

Dalziel, P., 'Anxieties of Representation: The Serial Illustrations to Hardy's *The Return of the Native*', *Nineteenth Century Literature*, 51/1 (1996), 84–111.

Davies, S., '*The Hand of Ethelberta*: De-Mythologizing "Woman"', *Critical Survey*, 5/2 (1993), 123–30.

Dellamora, R., 'Male Relations in Thomas Hardy's *Jude the Obscure*', *Papers on Language and Literature*, 27 (1991), 453–72.

Devereux, J., 'Thomas Hardy's *A Pair of Blue Eyes*: The Heroine as Text', *Victorian Newsletter*, 81 (1992), 20–3.

Ebbatson, R., 'The Plutonic Master: Hardy and the Steam Threshing Machine', *Critical Survey*, 2/1 (1990), 63–9.

Edwards, D. D., '*The Mayor of Casterbridge* as Aeschylean Tragedy', *Studies in the Novel*, 4 (1972), 608–18.

Giordano, F. R., 'The Martyrdom of Giles Winterborne', *Thomas Hardy Annual*, 2 (1984), 61–78.

Goode, J., 'Sue Bridehead and the New Woman', in Mary Jacobus (ed.), *Women Writing and Writing about Women* (London: Croom Helm, 1979).

Green, L., 'Strange (in)difference of Sex: Thomas Hardy, the Victorian Man of Letters, and the Temptations of Androgyny', *Victorian Studies*, 38 (1995): 523–49.

Greenslade, W., 'The Lure of Pedigree in *Tess of the D'Urbervilles*', *Thomas Hardy Journal*, 7/3 (1991), 103–15.

Harris, M., 'Thomas Hardy's *Tess of the d'Urbervilles*: Faithfully Presented by Roman Polanski', *Sydney Studies in English*, 7 (1981–2), 115–22.

Higonnet, M. R., 'Woman's Story: Tess and the Problem of Voice', in *The Sense of Sex: Feminist Perspectives on Hardy* (Urbana: University of Illinois Press, 1993), 14–31.

Hochstadt, P. R., 'Hardy's Romantic Diptych: A Reading of *A Laodicean* and *Two on a Tower*', *English Literature in Transition*, 26/1 (1983), 23–34.

Hunter Brown, S., '"Tess" and *Tess*: An Experiment in Genre', *Modern Fiction Studies*, 28/1 (1982), 25–44.

Ingham, P., 'Jude the Obscure', in *The Language of Gender and Class: Transformation in the Victorian Novel* (London and New York: Routledge, 1996), 160–82.

—— 'Provisional Narratives: Hardy's Final Trilogy', in L. St J. Butler (ed.), *Alternative Hardy* (London: Harvester Wheatsheaf, 1989), 49–73. (*Jude* and *The Well-Beloved*.)

Irvin, G., 'High Passion and High Church in *Two on a Tower*', *English Literature in Transition*, 3 (1985), 121–9.

Jacobus, M., 'Sue the Obscure', *Essays in Criticism*, 25 (1975), 304–28.

—— 'Tess's Purity', *Essays in Criticism*, 26 (1976), 318–38.

Jones, L., '*Under the Greenwood Tree* and the Victorian Pastoral', in Colin

Gibson (ed.), *Art and Society in the Victorian Novel* (London: Macmillan, 1989).

Kiely, R., 'The Menace of Solitude: The Politics and Aesthetic of Exclusion in *The Woodlanders*', in M. R. Higonnet (ed.), *The Sense of Sex: Feminist Perspectives on Hardy* (Urbana: University of Illinois Press, 1993), 188–202.

Levine, G., 'Shaping Hardy's Art: Vision, Class and Sex', in J. Richetti (ed.), *The Columbia History of the British Novel* (New York: Columbia University Press, 1994), 533–59.

Miller, J. Hillis, *Fiction and Repetition: Seven English Novels* (Oxford: Basil Blackwell, 1982). (*Tess of the d'Urbervilles*.)

—— 'Topography in *The Return of the Native*', *Essays in Literature*, 8/2 (1989), 119–34.

Morrison, R. D., 'Love and Evolution in Thomas Hardy's *The Woodlanders*', *Kentucky Philological Review*, 6 (1991), 32–7.

O'Hara, P., 'Narrating the Native: Victorian Anthropology and *The Return of the Native*', *Nineteenth Century Contexts*, 20/2 (1997), 147–63.

Peck, J., '*The Woodlanders*: The Too Transparent Web', *English Literature in Transition*, 24/3 (1981), 147–54.

Pykett, L., 'Ruinous Bodies: Women and Sexuality in Hardy's Late Fiction', *Critical Survey*, 5 (1993), 158–65.

Pyle, F., 'Demands of History: Narrative Crisis in *Jude the Obscure*', *New Literary History*, 26 (1995), 359–78.

Quéré, H., and Sénéchal, J., 'Hardy's Alternatives in *The Woodlanders*, Chapter 39', in L. St J. Butler (ed.), *Alternative Hardy* (London: Macmillan, 1989).

Rimmer, M., 'Club Laws: Chess and the Constitution of Gender in *A Pair of Blue Eyes*', in M. R. Higonnet (ed.), *The Sense of Sex: Feminist Perspectives on Hardy* (Urbana: University of Illinois Press, 1993), 203–20.

Schweik, R., 'Theme, Character and Perspective in Hardy's *The Return of the Native*', *Philological Quarterly*, 41 (1962), 554–7.

Shires, L. M., 'Narrative, Gender and Power in *Far From the Madding Crowd*', in M. R. Higonnet (ed.), *The Sense of Sex: Feminist Perspectives on Hardy* (Urbana: University of Illinois Press, 1993), 49–65.

Showalter, E., 'The Unmanning of *The Mayor of Casterbridge*', in Dale Kramer (ed.), *Critical Approaches to the Fiction of Thomas Hardy* (London and Basingstoke: Macmillan, 1979), 99–115.

Thompson, C., 'Language and the Shape of Reality in *Tess of the D'Urbervilles*', *English Literary History*, 50/4 (Winter 1983), 729–62.

Timko, M., 'Edinburgh, Oxford, Christminster: Self and Society in Victorian England', *Victorian Institute Journal*, 19 (1991), 25–40.

Waldman, N. K., 'All That She Is: Hardy's Tess and Polanski's', *Queen's Quarterly*, 88/3 (Autumn 1981), 429–36.

Wright, T., 'Space, Time and Paradox: The Sense of History in Hardy's Last Novels', *Essays and Studies*, 44 (1991), 41–52.

(b) Books on Hardy

Boumelha, P., *Thomas Hardy and Women: Sexual Ideology and Narrative Form* (Brighton, Sussex: Harvester Press, 1982).

Bullen, J. B., *The Expressive Eye: Fiction and Perception in the Work of Thomas Hardy* (Oxford: Clarendon Press, 1986).

Garson, M., *Hardy's Fables of Integrity: Women, Body, Text* (Oxford: Clarendon Press, 1991).

Goode, J., *Thomas Hardy: The Offensive Truth* (Oxford: Basil Blackwell, 1988).

Gregor, I., *The Great Web: The Form of Hardy's Major Fiction* (London: Faber and Faber, 1974).

Higonnet, M. R. (ed.), *The Sense of Sex: Feminist Perspectives on Hardy* (Urbana: University of Illinois Press, 1993).

Ingham, P., *Thomas Hardy: A Feminist Reading* (London: Harvester Wheatsheaf, 1989).

Kramer, D. (ed.), *The Cambridge Companion to Thomas Hardy* (Cambridge: Cambridge University Press, 1999). (A range of critical essays by M. Millgate and others.)

Miller, J. Hillis, *Thomas Hardy: Distance and Desire* (Oxford: Oxford University Press, 1970).

Page, N. (ed.), *Oxford Reader's Companion to Hardy* (Oxford: Oxford University Press, 2000). (A useful alphabetized collection of detailed information on Hardy and his work.)

Springer, M., *Hardy and the Art of Allusion* (Basingstoke and London: Macmillan, 1983).

WEBSITES

http://yale.edu/hardysoc   Thomas Hardy Assocation.

http://webuser.com/hardy   Includes complete texts of eight Hardy novels, articles, and links.

http://lang.nagoya-u.ac.jp/~matsuoka/victorian.html   The most comprehensive guide to websites dealing with contextual material from the nineteenth century. Everything from the Great Exhibition to Jack the Ripper and much more.

http://landow.stg.brown.edu/victorian/victov.html   Victorian web overview, leading to material on authors, economics, politics, philosophy, visual arts, technology.

VERSIONS OF HARDY'S NOVELS FOR CINEMA AND TELEVISION

Under the Greenwood Tree (GB; director Henry Lachman, 1929)

Far from the Madding Crowd (US; Edison, 1909)
Far from the Madding Crowd (US; Edison, 1911)
Far from the Madding Crowd (GB; director Larry Trimble, 1915)
Far from the Madding Crowd (GB; director John Schlesinger, 1967)
Far from the Madding Crowd (Granada TV, 1998)

The Mayor of Casterbridge (GB; 1921; filming watched by Hardy)
The Mayor of Casterbridge (projected by Thorold Dickinson 1949–50 but abandoned)
The Mayor of Casterbridge (BBC TV, 1978; adapted by Dennis Potter, starring Alan Bates)
The Mayor of Casterbridge (LWT TV, 2000; adapted by Ted Whitehead)
The Claim (based on *The Mayor of Casterbridge*; GB/Canada/France; director Michael Winterbottom, 2000)

The Woodlanders (BBC TV, 1970)
The Woodlanders (Channel 4 TV, 1995)
The Woodlanders (GB; director Phil Agland, 1997)

The Return of the Native (US TV; director Jack Gold, 1994; with Catherine Zeta Jones as Eustacia)

Tess of the d'Urbervilles (US; Famous Players' Company, 1913)
Tess of the d'Urbervilles (US; director Marshall Neilan, 1924)
Tess of the d'Urbervilles (BBC TV, 1952)
Tess of the d'Urbervilles (ITV, 1960)
Dulhanek raat ki ('Bride for a Single Night') (Indian film version of *Tess of the d'Urbervilles*; director Dharm Dev Kashyap, 1967)
Tess (France/GB; director Roman Polanski, 1979)
Prem Granth ('Love Story') (Indian film version of *Tess of the d'Urbervilles*, director Rajiv Kapoor, 1996)
Tess of the d'Urbervilles (ITV, 1998)

Jude the Obscure (BBC TV, 1971)
Jude (GB; director Michael Winterbottom, 1996)

FILMED VERSIONS OF HARDY SHORT STORIES

The Secret Cave (GB film version of 'Our Exploits at West Poley'; director John Durst, 1953)

The Distracted Preacher (BBC TV, 1969)

Wessex Tales (BBC TV, 1973; six short stories: 'The Withered Arm', 'Fellow-Townsmen', 'A Tragedy of Two Ambitions', 'An Imaginative Woman', 'The Melancholy Hussar', 'Barbara of the House of Grebe')

Our Exploits at West Poley (UK film version directed by Diamiurd Lawrence for Children's Film and Television Foundation, 1985)

The Day after the Fair (BBC TV version of 'On the Western Circuit', 1986)

The Scarlet Tunic (GB film of 'The Melancholy Hussar', director Stuart St Paul, 1997)

INDEX

Hardy, Thomas: life (*cont.*)
21–3; death of Emma 23–6; first marriage, to Emma 10–11, 31; formal education 3, 47; funeral in Westminster Abbey 1–2, 31, 213; ill-health 12; infatuations 17–18, 27; lionized 213; London literary circle 11–12, 13, 73; Order of Merit 72, 213; permanent return to Dorset 12; relationships with upper-class women 18–21, 42; second marriage, to Florence 24, 26; self-education 6, 7, 9–10, 62, 69–70

opinions: anti-censorship 94; anti-war 30, 33; on children in his 70s 26–7; on consistency 72; films 220–1; marriage and divorce laws 148–9; religion 28–31, 59, 68, 181, 197–8, 209; women's role in society 23, 31, 59, 104, 112

WORKS: essays and articles 7–8, 14, 23, 148; 'Dorset in London' 6; on naturalistic 'realism' 96–7

novels: biblical references 198–200; critics and 215–18; dates represented by 105–7; dialect forms in 114–15; editorial interference 87–9; evolution 159–67; female characterization 129–52; film adaptations 218–40; French naturalistic influence 95–7; Greek tragedy 205–6; heredity 167–76; life's injustice 200–12; panoramic/microscopic perspectives in 155–9; religion 181–96; science in 73, 76, 153–67; serialization and three-decker format 77, 80, 87–91; social realism 105–14; use of epigraphs 70–1; view of the future in 176–80; Wessex location 98–103; *see also individual novels in bold*

poetry 13, 18, 20, 22; 'A Broken Appointment' 20, 21; 'A Dream Question' 210; 'A Drizzling Easter Morning' 209; 'A Philosophical Fantasy' 210; 'A Plaint to Man' 210; 'A Thunderstorm in Town' 20; 'Afterwards' 3; 'By the Earth's Corpse' 210; 'Doom and She' 210–11; *Famous Tragedy of the Queen of Cornwall* 27; 'Fragment' 211; 'Heredity' 169–70; 'Horses Aboard' 197; *Human Shows, Far Phantasies, Songs and Trifles* 27; *Late Lyrics and Earlier* 27, 209; *Moments of Vision* 27; 'Nature's

Questioning' 210; '1967' 178–9; 'Poems of 1912–13' 24–6, 31; *Poems of the Past and the Present* 27; *Satires of Circumstance* 27; 'The Absolute Explains' 210; 'The Aërolite' 166; 'The Convergence of the Twain' 171–2; 'The Impercipient: At a Cathedral Service' 209; 'The Pedigree' 170; 'The Strange House' 179; 'The Unborn' 178; *Time's Laughingstocks* 27; 'To an Unborn Pauper Child' 178; 'Unkept Good Fridays' 208; *Wessex Poems* 22; *Winter Words* 27

Hardy, Thomas (father) 1, 9, 17, 22
Harper, C. G. 214
Harper's New Monthly Magazine 91
Harrison, Frederic 209
Hartman, Eduard von 207
harvest failures 36–7, 194–5
Hatfield, Hertfordshire 2
Hedgcock, Frank 7, 14–15
Hellenism 185, 187
Hemans, Felicia 75
Henniker, Florence 19, 20–1, 30, 130, 221
heredity 159–60, 167–76
Herkomer, Hubert von 218
Herkomer, Siegfried von 220
Herschel, William 64, 67, 153
Hicks, John 4, 6, 28, 98
history 156, 157–8
Hoare, Lady (Alda) 26
Hoggart, Paul 239
Holland, Clive 214
Hopkins, Arthur 218
housing 37, 41, 46
Housman, A. E. 1
humanism 185, 187
humanity: and the Bible 198–200; evolution and 160–5; injustice 200–12
hunting 14, 61
Huxley, Thomas Henry 12, 68, 177–8

illegitimacy 56–7, 81, 136, 146, 151
Illustrated London News 33, 77
illustrations 77
imperialism 33
impressionists 102
incest 45, 59
Indiscretion in the Life of an Heiress, An (Hardy) 8, 117, 119, 120
individualism 177
industrialization 32, 34, 36, 39

A SELECTION OF **OXFORD WORLD'S CLASSICS**

JANE AUSTEN	**Emma**
	Persuasion
	Pride and Prejudice
	Sense and Sensibility
MRS BEETON	**Book of Household Management**
ANNE BRONTË	**The Tenant of Wildfell Hall**
CHARLOTTE BRONTË	**Jane Eyre**
EMILY BRONTË	**Wuthering Heights**
WILKIE COLLINS	**The Moonstone**
	The Woman in White
JOSEPH CONRAD	**Heart of Darkness and Other Tales**
	Nostromo
CHARLES DARWIN	**The Origin of Species**
CHARLES DICKENS	**Bleak House**
	David Copperfield
	Great Expectations
	Hard Times
GEORGE ELIOT	**Middlemarch**
	The Mill on the Floss
ELIZABETH GASKELL	**Cranford**
THOMAS HARDY	**Jude the Obscure**
	Tess of the d'Urbervilles
WALTER SCOTT	**Ivanhoe**
MARY SHELLEY	**Frankenstein**
ROBERT LOUIS STEVENSON	**Treasure Island**
BRAM STOKER	**Dracula**
WILLIAM MAKEPEACE THACKERAY	**Vanity Fair**
OSCAR WILDE	**The Picture of Dorian Gray**

MORE ABOUT   **OXFORD WORLD'S CLASSICS**

The Oxford World's Classics Website

www.worldsclassics.co.uk

- Information about new titles
- Explore the full range of Oxford World's Classics
- Links to other literary sites and the main OUP webpage
- Imaginative competitions, with bookish prizes
- Peruse the Oxford World's Classics Magazine
- Articles by editors
- Extracts from Introductions
- A forum for discussion and feedback on the series
- Special information for teachers and lecturers

www.worldsclassics.co.uk